A-Level
Chemistry

Exam Board: AQA

A-Level Chemistry exams coming up? We don't envy you... but that's mainly because we've been too busy making this brilliant Exam Practice Workbook. It'll help you with your exam prep no end.

Inside, you'll be greeted by page after page of realistic exam-style questions covering both years of the AQA course — perfect for making sure you've mastered it all.

And if that's not enough to bring a smile to your face, the fully worked answers and top exam tips should do the trick.   There's no better way to prepare for the real exams!

A-Level revision? It has to be CGP!

Published by CGP

Editors:
Alex Billings, Katie Burton, Mary Falkner, Paul Jordin, Caroline Purvis.

Contributors:
Sarah Binns, Mike Dagless, David Paterson, Megan Pollard, Andy Rankin, Sarah Rich, Louise Watkins.

IR spectrum on page 113 — Source: NIST Chemistry WebBook (http://webbook.nist.gov/chemistry).

ISBN: 978 1 78294 913 8

With thanks to Jamie Sinclair and Barrie Crowther for the proofreading.
With thanks to Ana Pungartnik for the copyright research.

Printed by Elanders Ltd, Newcastle upon Tyne

Based on the classic CGP style created by Richard Parsons.

Contents

☑ Use the tick boxes to check off the topics you've completed.

Exam Advice

To pick up every mark you can you'll need tip-top exam technique as well as your knowledge of chemistry.

Get Familiar with the **Exam Structure**

If you're sitting the AS-Level in Chemistry rather than the A-Level, you'll be sitting a different set of exams to the ones described here.

For **A-Level Chemistry**, you'll be sitting **three papers**.

Paper 1 — this will test you on **Units 1** and **2** of this book. 2 hours **105** marks **35%** of your A-Level	**Short** and **long** answer questions.
Paper 2 — this will test you on **Units 1** and **3** of this book. 2 hours **105** marks **35%** of your A-Level	**Short** and **long** answer questions.
Paper 3 — this will test you on **Units 1-3** of this book. 2 hours **90** marks **30%** of your A-Level	**40 marks** of **practical techniques** and **data analysis** questions. **20 marks** of **general** questions. **30 marks** of **multiple choice** questions.

1) All three papers will test you on the **facts** that you need to know and on whether you can **apply your knowledge** to unfamiliar contexts.

2) They'll also test you on **practical skills**, and at least **20%** of the marks will require **maths skills**.

3) Each paper will usually contain at least one **extended response question,** which requires a **written English** answer or an **extended calculation**. These questions are marked on the **quality** of your responses as well as their chemistry **content**. Your answers should be **coherent**, **fully explained**, and have a **logical structure**.

Manage Your Time Sensibly

1) Use the **number of marks** available to help you decide **how long** to spend on a question.

2) Some questions will require **lots of work** for only a **few** marks but other questions may be much quicker. **Don't** spend ages struggling with questions that are only worth a couple of marks — move on. You can always **come back** to them later when you've bagged loads of marks elsewhere.

3) **Multiple choice** questions can be quite **time-consuming,** but they're still only worth **one mark** each. So if you're pressed for time, you might want to focus on the **written answer** questions, where there are **more marks** available.

If you're really stuck on a multiple choice question, making an educated guess is better than leaving it blank.

Be Careful Drawing **Diagrams**

1) Draw all your diagrams nice and big, so you can clearly show all the **detail** you need to get the marks.

2) Make sure your answer includes **everything** the question **asks** for. For example, if the question asks you to show **lone pairs** and **dipoles** in a diagram, don't forget to add them, and make sure it's **clear** what they are.

3) When you're drawing **mechanisms**, remember to pay close attention to your **curly arrows**. They need to be clearly coming from a **lone pair** or **bond** for you to get the marks.

4) If you're asked to draw a **formula**, make sure you give your answer in the format asked for. For example, if you're asked for a **displayed** formula **don't** draw a **skeletal** formula instead. If the question doesn't specify and just asks for a structure, or you're drawing a mechanism, **either** displayed or skeletal formulae are fine.

Remember to Use the **Exam Data Sheet**

1) In your exams, you'll be given a **data sheet**. It'll contain lots of **useful information**, such as:
   - the characteristic **infrared absorptions** of some bonds in organic molecules;
   - ^{13}C **NMR** and ^1H **NMR chemical shifts** of some common functional groups;
   - the **structures** of some important biological molecules, such as the DNA bases, some amino acids, common phosphates and sugars and haem B;
   - a copy of the **periodic table**.

You'll find a data sheet containing this information on p.192-194 of this book.

2) Unless you're told otherwise in the question, you should **always** use the values given on the data sheet.

Atomic Structure — 1

Ideas about atomic structure have changed a lot over the past 200 years, and yes, you do need to know how. The Bohr model's the one to really concentrate on though — that still gets used all the time today.

For each of questions 1-5, give your answer by ticking the appropriate box.

1   Which of the following shows the correct relative mass and relative charge for an electron?

	Relative mass	Relative charge	
A	$\frac{1}{2000}$	+1	☐
B	1	−1	☐
C	$\frac{1}{2000}$	−1	☐
D	$\frac{1}{2000}$	0	☐

(1 mark)

2   How many neutrons would you find in the nucleus of a copper-64 atom?

A   34   ☐   **B**   32   ☐

C   35   ☐   **D**   37   ☐

(1 mark)

3   What is the electron configuration of chromium?

A $1s^2\ 2s^2\ 2p^6\ 3s^2\ 3p^6\ 3d^4\ 4s^2$ ☐

B $1s^2\ 2s^2\ 2p^6\ 3s^2\ 3p^6\ 3d^6 4s^2$ ☐

C $1s^2\ 2s^2\ 2p^6\ 3s^2\ 3p^6\ 3d^5\ 4s^1$ ☐

D $1s^2\ 2s^2\ 2p^6\ 3s^2\ 3p^6\ 3d^4\ 4s^1$ ☐

(1 mark)

4   A sample of neon has a relative atomic mass of 20.187. The relative abundances of all the isotopes present in the sample are given in **Table 1**. Which isotope of neon is isotope **X**?

Table 1

Isotope	Neon-21	Neon-20	X
Relative abundance / %	0.3	90.5	9.2

A   Neon-19   ☐   **B**   Neon-22   ☐

C   Neon-24   ☐   **D**   Neon-23   ☐

(1 mark)

5   Which **one** of the following elements has exactly three unpaired electrons in its electronic structure?

A   Fluorine   ☐

B   Oxygen   ☐

C   Phosphorus   ☐

D   Scandium   ☐

(1 mark)

4

6   **Figure 1** shows an oxygen atom.

Figure 1

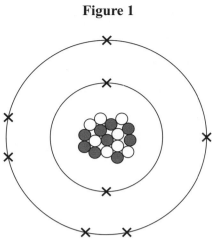

6.1   State the meaning of the term isotope.

       ....

       ....
       (1 mark)

6.2   Write the nuclear symbol for the isotope of oxygen shown in **Figure 1**.
       Include both the mass number and the atomic number of the isotope in your answer.

       ....
       (1 mark)

6.3   Explain why the three stable isotopes of oxygen, oxygen-16, oxygen-17 and oxygen-18,
       travel at different speeds in a time of flight (TOF) mass spectrometer.

       ....

       ....
       (2 marks)

6.4   State the full electron configuration of oxygen.

       ....
       (1 mark)

6.5   Samples must be ionised before they can be accelerated in a TOF mass spectrometer.
       Use the electron configuration of oxygen that you gave in question **6.4** to explain why the first ionisation
       energy of oxygen is lower than that of nitrogen, despite oxygen having a greater nuclear charge.

       ....

       ....

       ....
       (2 marks)

6.6   **Figure 1** is based on a model of the atom that is widely used today.
       Suggest why this model is still used by scientists when more accurate models have since been developed.

       ....

       ....

       ....
       (2 marks)

7 Calcium is found in Group 2 of the Periodic Table.

7.1 State the full electron configuration of calcium.

....

(1 mark)

7.2 Calcium usually forms ions with a charge of +2.
Give the name of the noble gas which has the same electronic configuration as a Ca^{2+} ion.

....

(1 mark)

Figure 2 shows the first 11 successive ionisation energies of calcium.

Figure 2

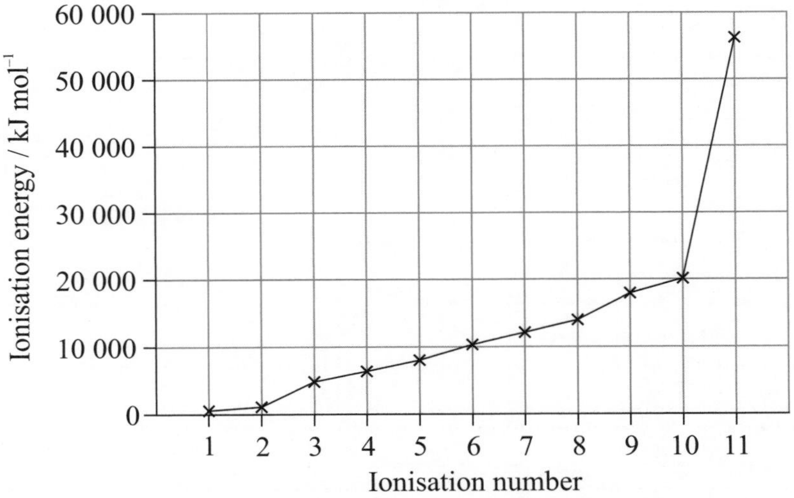

7.3 Explain why the second ionisation energy of calcium is greater than the first ionisation energy.

....

....

....

(2 marks)

7.4 Explain how **Figure 2** provides evidence of the structure of a calcium atom.

....

....

....

....

....

....

....

(4 marks)

EXAM TIP

It's really easy to slip up and put too many electrons in your electron configurations. Make a note of how many you should have before you start writing (you'll need to think about how many electrons have been added or taken away from the atomic number for ions), then add them all up at the end and check they match. Another good check (for atoms) is to see if the number of electrons the outermost shell matches the Group number of the element.

Score

22

Atomic Structure — 2

1   Time of flight (TOF) mass spectrometry is a technique used by scientists to help identify elements and compounds.

1.1   Explain how a TOF mass spectrometer works and how it can be used to accurately measure the relative abundances of different isotopes present in a sample of an element.

....

....

....

....

....

....

....

....

....

....

....

(6 marks)

Figure 1 shows the mass spectrum of a sample of an element, **J**.

Figure 1

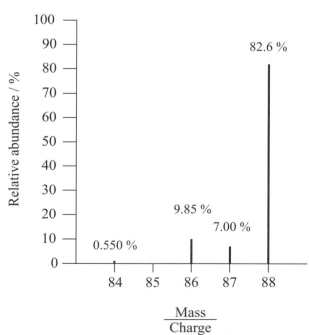

1.2 Use the information in **Figure 1** to calculate the relative atomic mass of element **J**.
Give your answer to an appropriate number of significant figures.

A_r of element **J** = ...
(3 marks)

1.3 Use your answer to question **1.2** and the Periodic Table to identify element **J**.

....
(1 mark)

1.4 During the analysis of element **J**, a single particle with mass/charge = 88 and 2.000×10^{-16} J of kinetic energy was found to take 1.338×10^{-5} s to travel a distance of 0.7000 m inside the mass spectrometer.
Use this information and the equation given below to calculate the mass, in kg, of the particle.
Give your answer to an appropriate number of significant figures.

$$t = d\sqrt{\frac{m}{2KE}}$$

(t = time / s, d = distance travelled / m, m = mass / kg and KE = kinetic energy / J)

Mass = ... kg
(3 marks)

1.5 Compounds can also be analysed using a TOF mass spectrometer.
Outline how the M_r of a sample of a compound may be determined from its mass spectrum.

....

....
(2 marks)

2 **Table 1** shows the successive ionisation energies of an element, **X**, in Period 3 (Na to Ar) in the Periodic Table.

Table 1

Ionisation energies / kJ mol^{-1}							
1st	2nd	3rd	4th	5th	6th	7th	8th
1012	1907	2914	4964	6274	21 267	29 872	35 905

2.1 Suggest why the difference between the 5th and 6th ionisation energies shown in **Table 1** is so much larger than that between the 4th and 5th ionisation energies. Explain your answer.

....

....

....

....
(3 marks)

2.2 Write an equation to represent the 6th ionisation energy of element **X**.
Use **X** as the chemical symbol for the element and include state symbols.

....

(1 mark)

2.3 Use your answer to question **2.1** to help you identify element **X**.

....

(1 mark)

3 Elements in the same Groups or Periods of the Periodic Table display patterns in their ionisation energies.

3.1 State the meaning of the term first ionisation energy.

....

....

(1 mark)

Figure 2 shows the first ionisation energies of the elements in Period 3.

Figure 2

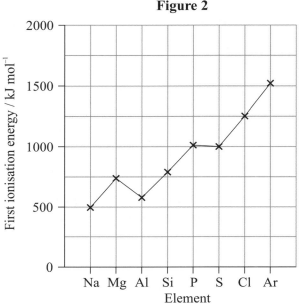

3.2 Suggest how a graph of the first ionisation energies of the Period 2 elements drawn on the same scale would be similar to **Figure 2** and how it would be different. Explain your answer.

....

....

....

....

....

....

(4 marks)

When using atomic structure to describe some pattern in the Periodic Table, you just need to think carefully about how each of three things change moving from element to element: the nuclear charge acting on the electrons, the distance of the outermost electrons from the nucleus, and the amount of shielding experienced by those outermost electrons. That's it — smashing.

Score

25

Amount of Substance — 1

What's that speck on the horizon? Is it a bird? A plane? A bird disguised as a plane? A plane disguised as a bird? I've no idea — I can't even see the horizon from where I'm sitting. All I know is that it's time for more questions.

For each of questions 1-4, give your answer by ticking the appropriate box.

1 How many chlorine atoms are present in one mole of PCl_5? (Avogadro constant $= 6.02 \times 10^{23}$)

  A 6.02×10^{23} ☐

  B 3.01×10^{24} ☐

  C 6.02×10^{24} ☐

  D 3.01×10^{23} ☐

  (1 mark)

2 Which of the following shows the balanced equation for the complete combustion of ethanol?

  A $C_2H_5OH + 3O_2 \rightarrow 2CO_2 + 2H_2O$ ☐

  B $C_2H_5OH + 3O_2 \rightarrow 2CO_2 + 3H_2O$ ☐

  C $2C_2H_5OH + 5O_2 \rightarrow 4CO_2 + 5H_2O$ ☐

  D $C_2H_5OH + 3.5O_2 \rightarrow 2CO_2 + 2H_2O$ ☐

  (1 mark)

3 Excess barium chloride reacts with copper sulfate solution to form a precipitate of barium sulfate.

  The equation for the reaction is: $BaCl_{2(aq)} + CuSO_{4(aq)} \rightarrow CuCl_{2(aq)} + BaSO_{4(s)}$. What volume of 0.650 mol dm^{-3} copper sulfate solution is needed to form 3.16 g of barium sulfate ($M_r = 233.4$)?

  A 87.8 cm^3 ☐

  B 0.0208 cm^3 ☐

  C 20.8 cm^3 ☐

  D 8.80 cm^3 ☐

  (1 mark)

4 A scientist burned 1.86 g of phosphorus in oxygen. 4.26 g of an oxide of phosphorus was produced. What is the empirical formula of this oxide?

  A PO_2 ☐

  B P_2O_4 ☐

  C P_2O_5 ☐

  D P_4O_{10} ☐

  (1 mark)

8 A student is preparing 250 cm³ of a standard solution of sodium hydrogencarbonate ($NaHCO_3$).

She uses the following method:

1. Weigh out the required mass of sodium hydrogencarbonate into a weighing boat.
2. Tip the solid into a 250 cm³ volumetric flask.
3. Add distilled water to the flask until the bottom of the meniscus touches the line.
4. Stopper the flask and turn it upside down a few times to mix the contents.

8.1 State **two** ways in which the student's method could be improved.

1. ....

....

2. ....

....

(2 marks)

The student fixes the mistakes in her method and repeats the procedure.
She makes a standard solution with a concentration of 0.30 mol dm⁻³.

8.2 Calculate the mass of sodium hydrogencarbonate that would be required to make a
250 cm³ solution with a concentration of 0.30 mol dm⁻³.

mass = ... g

(2 marks)

8.3 The student pours 100 cm³ of the solution into a beaker containing 150 cm³ of distilled water.
Calculate the concentration of the solution in the beaker.

concentration = ... mol dm⁻³

(2 marks)

The student then carries out a titration of a standard solution of sodium hydroxide against 25 cm³ of
hydrochloric acid. She adds the hydrochloric acid and indicator to a conical flask. The standard solution
of sodium hydroxide is then slowly added from a burette.

The student makes the following errors when preparing the standard solution of sodium hydroxide:

1. She didn't notice that the mass balance was showing a negative reading before the solid sodium
    hydroxide was weighed out.
2. Some of the sodium hydroxide was spilt on the bench when the student transferred it from the
    weighing boat to the volumetric flask.

8.4 For each of the errors the student made, deduce how the mean titre volume would be affected.

Error 1 ....

Error 2 ....

(2 marks)

Holey moley, this section involves quite a lot of maths. But all the hard work you're putting
in here will be worth it when it comes to the exams — at least 20% of the marks in the exams
will require you to use some sort of maths skill. Maths skills include things like rearranging
equations, calculating uncertainties, converting between units and calculating means.

Score

34

Amount of Substance — 2

1   Metals such as lead and titanium are extracted from their ores using a series of chemical reactions.

Galena (PbS) is a common ore of lead. The extraction of lead from galena is a two step process.

Step 1: $2PbS + 3O_2 \rightarrow 2PbO + 2SO_2$ **Step 2:** $2PbO + C \rightarrow 2Pb + CO_2$

1.1   Calculate the mass of oxygen needed to react with 4.50 tonnes of PbS in Step 1.
(1 tonne = 1000 kg)

mass = ... kg
(3 marks)

1.2   Calculate the mass of lead that can be produced from 4.50 tonnes of PbS.

mass = ... kg
(2 marks)

Iron can also be extracted from a sulfur-containing ore, pyrite (FeS_2).
The first step involves burning pyrite in oxygen to form iron oxide (Fe_2O_3) and sulfur dioxide.

1.3   Construct a balanced equation for the reaction of pyrite with oxygen.

....
(1 mark)

The Kroll process is use to extract titanium from its ore. The final step in the Kroll process involves the reaction of titanium (IV) chloride, $TiCl_4$, with a more reactive metal, usually magnesium or sodium.

1.4   Calculate the atom economies of reactions **A** and **B** shown below.

Reaction A: $TiCl_4 + 2Mg \rightarrow Ti + 2MgCl_2$ **Reaction B:** $TiCl_4 + 4Na \rightarrow Ti + 4NaCl$

atom economy of reaction A = ... %

atom economy of reaction B = ... %
(2 marks)

2 A scientist reacts 0.0784 g of an unknown metal, X, with an excess of hydrochloric acid to form 29.4 cm³ of hydrogen gas at 298 K and 101 kPa.

The equation for the reaction is: $X + 2HCl \rightarrow XCl_2 + H_2$

Identify metal X. (The gas constant, $R = 8.31$ J K^{-1} mol^{-1})

metal X = ...
(4 marks)

3 Ammonia (NH_3) is produced in the Haber Process.
Gaseous ammonia reacts with water to form ammonium hydroxide.

3.1 A scientist is analysing a sample of ammonium hydroxide which contains 40.0% nitrogen and 14.3% hydrogen by mass. The rest of the mass is oxygen.

Use this data to show that the empirical formula of ammonium hydroxide is NH_5O.

(3 marks)

3.2 0.0820 moles of ammonia gas was trapped in a gas jar at a temperature of 298 K and pressure of 101 kPa. Calculate the volume of the gas jar used to trap the ammonia. (The gas constant, $R = 8.31$ J K^{-1} mol^{-1})

volume = ... dm³
(3 marks)

3.3 Calculate the number of ammonia molecules in this sample. (Avogadro constant = 6.02×10^{23})

....
(1 mark)

4   Limestone is an ore of calcium that contains a high proportion of calcium carbonate ($CaCO_3$).

Calcium carbonate reacts with hydrochloric acid (HCl) according to the equation:

$$CaCO_3 + 2HCl \rightarrow CaCl_2 + CO_2 + H_2O$$

A 1.75 g sample of limestone is added to a solution of excess hydrochloric acid at a pressure of 101 kPa. 280 cm^3 of carbon dioxide gas (CO_2) is formed at a temperature of 22.0 °C. It was assumed that all of the CO_2 gas produced was formed during the reaction between $CaCO_3$ and HCl.

4.1   Calculate the percentage of $CaCO_3$ in the limestone sample. (The gas constant, $R = 8.31$ J K^{-1} mol^{-1})

.... %

(5 marks)

A different ore contains copper carbonate, $CuCO_3$.
A pure sample of $CuCO_3$ decomposes on heating to form CuO and CO_2.

$$CuCO_3 \rightarrow CuO + CO_2$$

A sample of $CuCO_3$ is heated to form 3.60 g of CuO. The percentage yield for this reaction is 92.4%.

4.2   Calculate the mass of $CuCO_3$ that was heated.
Give your answer to an appropriate number of significant figures.

mass = ... g

(4 marks)

4.3   Determine the atom economy of this reaction.

atom economy = ... %

(1 mark)

4.4 Give **one** environmental and **one** economic reason why reactions with high atom economies are preferable to reactions with low atom economies.

Environmental reason: ....

....

Economic reason: ....

....

(2 marks)

5 Solutions of two different acids, sulfuric acid (H_2SO_4) and hydrochloric acid (HCl), are made up and put in unlabelled bottles. Both acids have the same unknown concentration.

Explain how the identity of each acid could be determined by titration using a standard solution of 0.1 mol dm^{-3} sodium hydroxide (NaOH). Include in your answer the procedures involved, equations for any reactions taking place and the expected results.

....

....

....

....

....

....

....

....

....

....

....

....

....

....

....

....

(6 marks)

In the exam you might be faced with a question about planning an experiment that involves unfamiliar chemicals or strange reactions. Don't panic, you should have covered all the chemistry you need to answer the question in class — it's just a case of applying your knowledge of chemistry to a situation that you've not come across before. Splendid.

Score

37

Bonding — 1

The name's bond, coval... Hmm, no, that's too predictable. As predictable as the properties of substances when you understand the way their structures are bonded. Which is just what this section is all about, handily.

For each of questions 1-5, give your answer by ticking the appropriate box.

1 Which of the following molecules contains a double covalent bond?

    A H_2O ☐

    B C_2H_4 ☐

    C CH_4 ☐

    D   HCN   ☐

(1 mark)

2 What is the formula of the ionic compound caesium selenide?

    A Cs_2Se ☐

    B   CsSe   ☐

    C $CsSe_2$ ☐

    D $CsSe_4$ ☐

(1 mark)

3 Which of these statements explains why metals have high melting points?

    A   The atoms are closely packed.   ☐

    B   There is a strong electrostatic attraction between the metal ions and the free electrons.   ☐

    C   The atoms have a regular arrangement.   ☐

    D   The positive metal ions repel each other.   ☐

(1 mark)

4 Which of these molecules is polar?

    A F_2 ☐

    B CBr_4 ☐

    C CO_2 ☐

    D PF_3 ☐

(1 mark)

5 Which of these molecules has a trigonal bipyramidal shape?

    A IF_5 ☐

    B ICl_3 ☐

    C PF_5 ☐

    D SF_4 ☐

(1 mark)

6   **Table 1** shows the names and formulas of some ionic compounds.

Table 1

Name	Formula	Formulas of ions present	
Iron(III) sulfate	$Fe_2(SO_4)_3$		
Aluminium nitrate	$Al(NO_3)_3$		
Chromium (III) hydroxide		Cr^{3+}	OH^-
Ammonium carbonate		NH_4^+	CO_3^{2-}

6.1   Use the information given to complete **Table 1**.

(4 marks)

6.2   Draw the displayed formula of the ammonium ion, NH_4^+, showing the coordinate bond.
       Define the term coordinate bond.

       Diagram

       Definition ....

       ....

(2 marks)

6.3   Draw a diagram showing the 3D shape of the ammonium ion.

(1 mark)

7   A chloride with the formula XCl_2 can be made by gently heating element X in chlorine gas.
       The chloride has a high melting point and dissolves readily in water.
       The chloride can conduct electricity when molten or in solution, but not when solid.

7.1   State the type of structure you would expect XCl_2 to have.

       ....

(1 mark)

7.2   Explain why XCl_2 has a high melting point.

       ....

       ....

(1 mark)

7.3   A student predicts that element X is a Group 2 metal.
       Explain how the formula of the chloride supports this prediction.

       ....

       ....

(2 marks)

7.4 Explain how melting or dissolving XCl_2 enables it to conduct electricity.

....

....

(1 mark)

8   Graphite and iodine are both solids at room temperature, but their crystals have different structures.

8.1 Describe the structure of graphite. Include a diagram to illustrate your answer.

Diagram

Description ....

....

....

(4 marks)

8.2 Name all the types of bonding and intermolecular forces present in an iodine crystal.

....

....

(1 mark)

8.3 Explain why graphite has a very high melting point.

....

....

(2 marks)

8.4 Describe and explain the electrical conductivities of graphite and iodine.

Graphite ....

....

Iodine ....

....

(2 marks)

EXAM TIP

You could be asked to use the structure of a material to explain why it has the properties that it does, so you'll need to understand the differences between the different types of structure. Electrical conductivity can be tricky — make sure you know exactly what particles are moving to allow a current to flow and any special conditions that are needed for conduction to happen.

Score

26

Bonding — 2

1   The apparatus shown in **Figure 1** was used in an experiment to determine the polarities of different liquids.

Figure 1

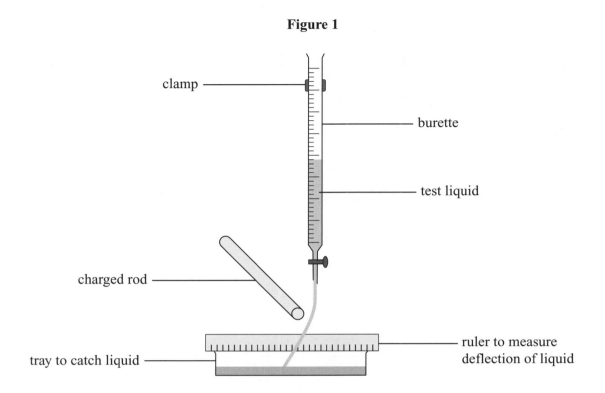

The test liquid was released from the burette and a charged plastic rod was held close to the liquid as it fell. Any deflection of the liquid from the vertical was measured as the liquid entered the tray.

Table 1 shows the results of the experiment.

Table 1

Liquid Formula	Deflection/cm	Polarity
H_2O	4	Polar
Br_2	0	
CCl_4	0	Non-polar
$CHCl_3$	3	

1.1   Complete **Table 1** to show the polarities of Br_2 and $CHCl_3$.

(1 mark)

1.2   List **three** variables which must be controlled to make this a valid experiment.

1 ....

2 ....

3 ....

(3 marks)

1.3 Explain why Br_2, CCl_4 and $CHCl_3$ showed the polarity observed.
You may include diagrams to illustrate your answer.

....

....

....

....

....

....

....

....

....

....

....

....

(6 marks)

2 **Figure 2** shows part of the structure of a silicon dioxide crystal.

Figure 2

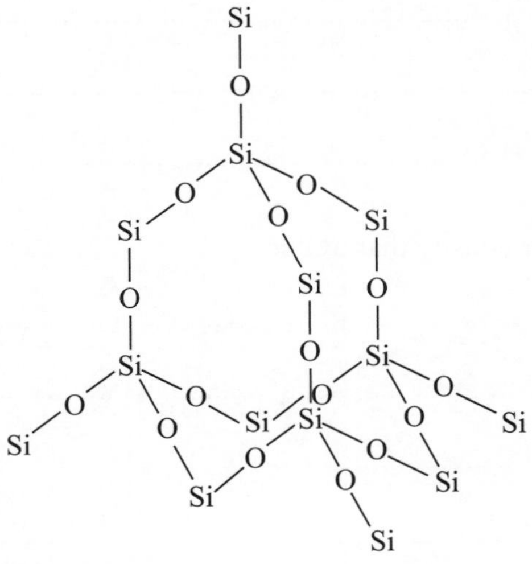

2.1 Silicon dioxide has a similar structure to diamond.
Name the shape that the oxygen atoms adopt around a central silicon atom in silicon dioxide.

....

(1 mark)

2.2 State the approximate bond angle for the oxygen atoms
around a central silicon atom in silicon dioxide.

....
(1 mark)

2.3 Ice is another crystalline substance, but it has a different structure to silicon dioxide.
State the structure of each compound.

Silicon dioxide ....

Ice ....
(2 marks)

2.4 Hydrogen bonding takes place in water and ice. **Figure 3** shows a water molecule. Complete **Figure 3**
to show how this molecule would form a hydrogen bond with another water molecule. You should use
a dashed line to represent the hydrogen bond and show any lone pairs and charges on the atoms.

Figure 3

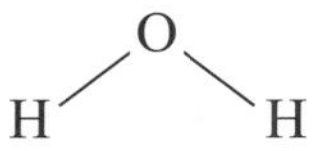

O

H   H

(2 marks)

2.5 The melting points of silicon dioxide and ice are 1883 K and 273 K, respectively.
Explain why the melting point of silicon dioxide is so much higher than that of ice.

....

....

....

....
(3 marks)

2.6 Describe and explain what happens to the molecules in ice when it is heated to its melting point.

....

....

....

....
(3 marks)

2.7 Explain why ice has a lower density than water.

....

....

....
(2 marks)

Score

24

Bonding — 3

1   SF$_2$ and SF$_6$ are the formulas of two sulfur fluorides.

1.1   Draw a diagram to show the shape of each molecule.
Include any lone pairs and indicate the values of the bond angles. Name the shapes you have drawn.

SF$_2$

Name of shape ....

SF$_6$

Name of shape ....

(4 marks)

1.2   Justify the shape for SF$_2$ that you gave in your answer to question **1.1**.

....

....

....

....

(3 marks)

1.3   The Pauling scale is a measure of electronegativity. On the Pauling scale, fluorine has an electronegativity of 4.0 and sulfur has an electronegativity of 2.6. Explain why SF$_6$ is non-polar, but SF$_2$ is polar.

....

....

....

....

....

....

(4 marks)

24

1.4 Explain why it is difficult to predict which of the two fluorides has the higher melting point.

....

....

....

....

(3 marks)

2 **Figure 1** shows the boiling points of some of the Group 5 hydrides.

Figure 1

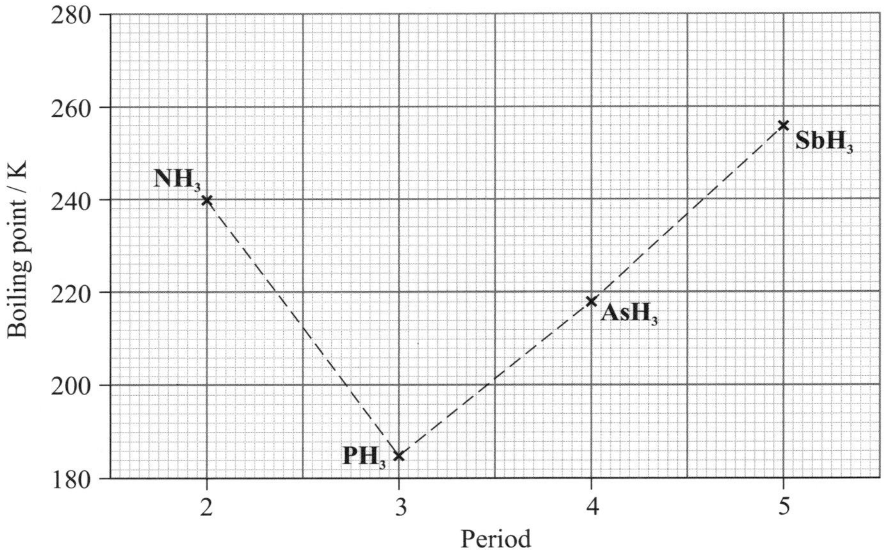

2.1 Describe and explain the trend in the boiling points of PH_3, AsH_3 and SbH_3.

....

....

....

(1 mark)

2.2 Explain why the boiling point of NH_3 does not fit this trend.

....

....

....

....

....

....

(4 marks)

EXAM TIP Melting and boiling point questions for simple covalent substances can be confusing. Before you start writing your answer, it might be worth drawing a sketch of the molecule and working out whether it forms hydrogen bonds, permanent dipoles, or just Van der Waals forces. Don't forget to think about how the size of the molecule might affect its intermolecular forces too.

Score

19

Energetics — 1

Energetics — not quite as lively as it sounds. In fact, it's mostly just maths, which may or may not fill you with joy. All it really takes is practice though, which is where these next few pages come in handy...

For each of questions 1-4, give your answer by ticking the appropriate box.

1 What does the symbol $\Delta_c H^\ominus$ represent?

A The energy given out when 1 g of a substance is burned under standard conditions. ☐

B The enthalpy change when 1 mole of a substance is completely burned under standard conditions. ☐

C The temperature change when 1 g of a fuel is burned. ☐

D The enthalpy change when 1 mole of a substance is formed from its elements under standard conditions. ☐

(1 mark)

2 Which of the following statements is correct?

A During exothermic reactions, energy is given out and ΔH is positive. ☐

B During exothermic reactions, energy is absorbed and ΔH is negative. ☐

C During endothermic reactions, energy is absorbed and ΔH is positive. ☐

D During endothermic reactions, energy is given out and ΔH is negative. ☐

(1 mark)

3 Chloroethane can be produced by the reaction of ethene with hydrogen chloride gas:

$$C_2H_{4(g)} + HCl_{(g)} \rightarrow C_2H_5Cl_{(g)}$$

Some bond enthalpy data for this reaction is shown in **Table 1**.

Table 1

Bond	C=C	C–H	H–Cl	C–C	C–Cl
Bond enthalpy / kJ mol⁻¹	612	413	432	347	346

What is the value of ΔH for the reaction?

A +85 kJ mol⁻¹ ☐   **B** –494 kJ mol⁻¹ ☐

C +351 kJ mol⁻¹ ☐   **D** –62 kJ mol⁻¹ ☐

(1 mark)

4 250 cm³ of 0.50 mol dm⁻³ sodium hydroxide solution was neutralised by an excess of hydrochloric acid. The total volume of the reaction mixture was 500 cm³. The maximum temperature change was +3.5 °C. Calculate the molar enthalpy change of the reaction with respect to sodium hydroxide. You should assume that $c = 4.18$ J K⁻¹g⁻¹.

A –29 kJ mol⁻¹ ☐   **B** –59 kJ mol⁻¹ ☐

C +29 kJ mol⁻¹ ☐   **D** +59 kJ mol⁻¹ ☐

(1 mark)

5 A student is investigating the energetics of the reaction shown in the following equation.
$$Cu^{2+}_{(aq)} + Mg_{(s)} \rightarrow Mg^{2+}_{(aq)} + Cu_{(s)}$$

5.1 The standard enthalpies of formation ($\Delta_f H^\ominus$) of the ions $Cu^{2+}_{(aq)}$ and $Mg^{2+}_{(aq)}$ are +64.8 kJ mol^{-1} and $-$467 kJ mol^{-1}, respectively.
Use this information to calculate the enthalpy change of the reaction under standard conditions.
Give your answer to an appropriate number of significant figures.

Enthalpy change of reaction = ...kJ mol^{-1}
(4 marks)

5.2 The student investigated the reaction experimentally by adding an excess of magnesium ribbon to 20 cm^3 of 0.50 mol dm^{-3} CuSO$_{4(aq)}$ in a beaker. They recorded the temperature at one minute intervals, beginning three minutes before adding the magnesium. They stirred the mixture regularly.
Their results are shown in **Table 2**.

Table 2

Time / min	0	1	2	3	4	5	6	7	8	9	10
Temperature / °C	19.0	19.0	19.0	(not taken)	72.0	70.0	67.5	66.0	64.0	61.5	59.5

On the grid below, draw a graph of the results in **Table 2**.
Use your graph to determine the maximum temperature change of the reaction.

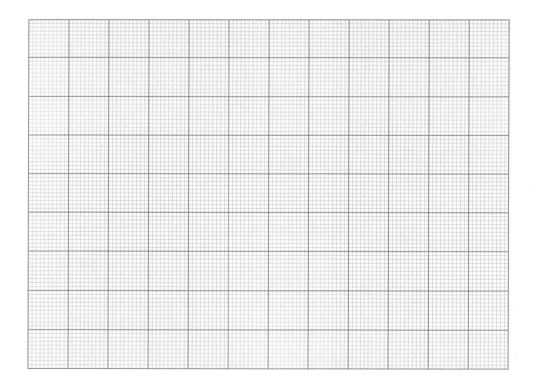

Maximum temperature change =.......................................°C
(5 marks)

5.3 Explain how the graph you drew in question **5.2** shows that the reaction was exothermic.

....

....

(2 marks)

5.4 Use your temperature change from question **5.2** to calculate a value for
the molar enthalpy change of the reaction with respect to $CuSO_{4(aq)}$.
Assume the specific heat capacity of the mixture is $4.18 \text{ J K}^{-1}\text{g}^{-1}$.
Give your answer to an appropriate number of significant figures. Give units in your answer.

Molar enthalpy change of reaction = ...

(4 marks)

5.5 The experimentally determined value for the enthalpy change of the reaction that you found in
question **5.4** is lower than the true value under these conditions. Explain why this is the case.
Suggest **one** change the student could make to the experiment to make their result more accurate.

Explanation ....

....

Change...

....

(2 marks)

5.6 Explain why the student stirred the reaction mixture regularly during their experiment.

....

....

(1 mark)

5.7 Copper sulfate solution is an irritant and is toxic to aquatic plants and animals.
The student wore safety glasses and a lab coat when carrying out the experiment.
Suggest **one** other precaution that the student should have taken to minimise the risk of using copper sulfate.

....

....

(1 mark)

Score

23

Energetics — 2

1   A student is studying the complete combustion of propane, C_3H_8.
The equation for this reaction is shown below.

$$C_3H_{8(g)} + 5O_{2(g)} \rightarrow 3CO_{2(g)} + 4H_2O_{(g)}$$

1.1   **Table 1** shows mean bond enthalpies for the bonds involved in this reaction.
Use the data in **Table 1** to calculate the enthalpy of complete combustion of propane.

Table 1

Bond	C–C	C–H	C=O	O–H	O=O
Bond enthalpy / kJ mol^{-1}	347	413	805	464	498

Enthalpy of complete combustion = ... kJ mol^{-1}

(3 marks)

1.2   **Table 2** shows the enthalpies of formation of the compounds involved in the reaction.
Use the data in **Table 2** to calculate the enthalpy of complete combustion of propane.

Table 2

Compound	$\Delta_f H$ / kJ mol^{-1}
$C_3H_{8(g)}$	−104.5
$CO_{2(g)}$	−393.5
$H_2O_{(l)}$	−241.8

Enthalpy of complete combustion = ... kJ mol^{-1}

(3 marks)

1.3 Explain why the value for the enthalpy of combustion of propane calculated using enthalpies of formation is not the same as the value calculated from mean bond enthalpies.

....

....

....

(2 marks)

1.4 Another student decides to use calorimetry to investigate the complete combustion of propan-2-ol. They burned propan-2-ol in a spirit burner and recorded the change in the mass of the burner and the change in temperature of the water in the calorimeter. Their results are shown in **Table 3**.

Table 3

Mass of burner before	75.2 g
Mass of burner after	74.8 g
Volume of water in calorimeter	50.0 cm^3
Initial temperature of water	21.5 °C
Final temperature of water	74.0 °C

Use these results to calculate the enthalpy of complete combustion of propan-2-ol in kJ mol^{-1}. The specific heat capacity of water is 4.18 J K^{-1} g^{-1}.

Enthalpy change of complete combustion = ... kJ mol^{-1}

(6 marks)

2 **Figure 1** shows a reaction between ethanol and ethanal which produces **Compound R**.

Figure 1

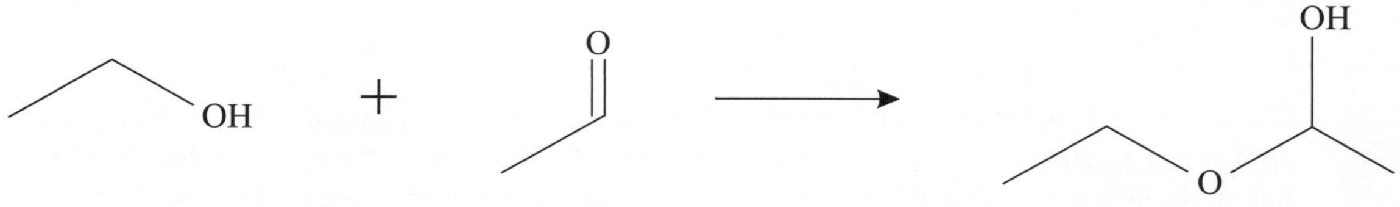

Compound R

2.1 The enthalpy change of this reaction is 20.00 kJ mol^{-1}. The enthalpies of formation of ethanol and ethanal are -277.1 kJ mol^{-1} and -191.5 kJ mol^{-1}, respectively. Use this information to calculate the enthalpy change of formation of **Compound R**.

Enthalpy of formation of **Compound R** = ... kJ mol^{-1}

(3 marks)

2.2 The average enthalpy of the C=O bond is 736 kJ mol^{-1}.
Use this value and the value for the enthalpy change of the reaction given in question **2.1** to determine the average enthalpy of the C–O bond in **Compound R**.

Average enthalpy of C–O bond = ... kJ mol^{-1}

(3 marks)

2.3 Explain why the value for the bond enthalpy of the C–O bond in **Compound R** is an average for this compound.

....

....

....

....

(2 marks)

Kinetics, Equilibria and Redox Reactions — 1

Hmm, "kinetics, equilibria and redox" sounds a bit like some fancy new exercise regime to me. It isn't though, it's just yet more good old chemistry fun. Well, more chemistry anyway...

For each of questions 1-4, give your answer by ticking the appropriate box.

1 Consider this reaction: $2SO_{2(g)} + O_{2(g)} \rightleftharpoons 2SO_{3(g)}$ $\quad \Delta H = -197$ kJ mol^{-1}
Which of the following would shift the equilibrium in favour of the product the most?

A Decreasing the temperature and increasing the pressure. ☐

B Decreasing the temperature and decreasing the pressure. ☐

C Increasing the temperature and decreasing the pressure. ☐

D Increasing the temperature and increasing the pressure. ☐

(1 mark)

2 Zinc carbonate reacts with nitric acid according to the equation below.
$$ZnCO_{3(s)} + 2HNO_{3(aq)} \rightarrow Zn(NO_3)_{2(aq)} + H_2O_{(l)} + CO_{2(g)}$$
In one experiment, the initial mass of the reaction mixture was measured as 10.47 g.
After 1 minute, the mass of the reaction mixture had decreased to 10.32 g.
What is the average rate of the reaction during the first minute?

A 4.2×10^{-3} g s^{-1} ☐

B 3.6×10^{-3} g s^{-1} ☐

C 1.5×10^{-3} g s^{-1} ☐

D 2.5×10^{-3} g s^{-1} ☐

(1 mark)

3 Which of the following statements about catalysts is true?

A Adding a catalyst will increase the yield from a reversible reaction. ☐

B Catalysts increase the rate of a reaction by offering an alternative reaction pathway with a higher energy. ☐

C A catalyst is chemically unchanged at the end of a reaction. ☐

D Adding a catalyst will decrease the value of K_c for a reversible reaction. ☐

(1 mark)

4 Vanadyl sulfate has the chemical formula $VOSO_4$.
What is the oxidation state of vanadium in vanadyl sulfate?

A +2 ☐

B +3 ☐

C +4 ☐

D +6 ☐

(1 mark)

5   When heated in air, potassium can react with oxygen to produce potassium peroxide, K_2O_2.
The overall equation for this reaction is:

$$2K_{(s)} + O_{2(g)} \rightarrow K_2O_{2(s)}$$

In this reaction, oxygen gas acts as an oxidising agent and potassium acts as a reducing agent.

5.1   Define the term reducing agent.

....

....

(1 mark)

5.2   Write a half-equation for the oxidation of potassium in this reaction.

....

(1 mark)

5.3   Give the oxidation state of oxygen in potassium peroxide.

....

(1 mark)

5.4   Predict the effect of increasing the pressure on the rate of this reaction.
Explain your prediction.

....

....

....

....

....

(4 marks)

5.5   **Figure 1** shows the Maxwell-Boltzmann distribution of the energies
of the oxygen molecules in the reaction mixture.

Shade in the area on **Figure 1** that corresponds to the number of
oxygen molecules that are able to react with the potassium.

Figure 1

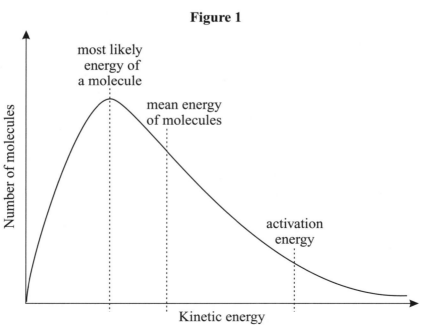

(1 mark)

5.6 State how adding a catalyst to the reaction mixture would change the number of oxygen molecules that are able to react. Explain your answer.

....

....

....

....

(3 marks)

6 Methanol (CH_3OH) has a number of important uses in the chemical industry.
It can be produced from carbon monoxide and hydrogen using the reaction shown below.

$$CO_{(g)} + 2H_{2(g)} \rightleftharpoons CH_3OH_{(g)} \qquad \Delta H = -90 \text{ kJ mol}^{-1}$$

This reaction is performed at high pressure and at a temperature of 250 °C.

6.1 This reaction can be described as a homogeneous reaction.
Explain what is meant by the term homogeneous reaction.

....

....

(1 mark)

6.2 Write the expression for the equilibrium constant, K_c, for this reaction.

....

....

(1 mark)

6.3 Use Le Chatelier's principle to explain why a high pressure is used for this reaction in industry.

....

....

....

....

(3 marks)

6.4 Give **one** disadvantage of using a high pressure for this reaction in industry.

....

....

(1 mark)

6.5 Increasing the temperature would increase the rate of the reaction.
Give **two** reasons why using a higher temperature would increase the rate of reaction.

1. ....

....

2. ....

....

(2 marks)

6.6 A catalyst is typically used for this reaction. This is so that the reaction can be carried out at a relatively low temperature, but will still proceed at a reasonable rate.

In terms of the effect on the equilibrium position, explain why using a catalyst is a better option than increasing the temperature to increase the rate of this reaction.

....

....

....

....

....

....

(4 marks)

6.7 State the effect that using a catalyst will have on the value of K_c.

....

(1 mark)

7 An excess of powdered copper is added to 20 cm³ of 0.5 mol dm⁻³ silver nitrate solution. A redox reaction occurs in which the copper acts as a reducing agent and the silver ions act as an oxidising agent. Copper(II) nitrate solution and silver are produced. Silver nitrate solution is colourless and copper(II) nitrate solution is blue, so a colour change is seen during the reaction.

7.1 Write a half equation for the reduction of silver ions, Ag^+, to silver.

....

(1 mark)

7.2 Write a half-equation for the oxidation of copper to copper(II) ions, Cu^{2+}.

....

(1 mark)

7.3 Write a redox equation for the reaction of copper with silver ions to form copper(II) ions and silver.

....

(1 mark)

7.4 Suggest how increasing the concentration of the silver nitrate solution used to 1 mol dm⁻³ would affect the time taken for the reaction mixture to change from colourless to blue. Explain your answer.

....

....

....

....

(4 marks)

You're probably sick of hearing it by now but OIL RIG — Oxidation Is Loss, Reduction Is Gain — is the most important thing to remember when you're thinking about redox reactions in terms of movement of electrons. If you know where the electrons are coming from, and where they're going to, you should hopefully be able to work everything else out from there...

Score

35

Kinetics, Equilibria and Redox Reactions — 2

1 Magnesium reacts with hydrochloric acid to give magnesium chloride and hydrogen as shown by the equation below.

$$Mg_{(s)} + 2HCl_{(aq)} \rightarrow MgCl_{2(aq)} + H_{2(g)}$$

Some students are investigating how the rate of the reaction changes with temperature. To do this, they add magnesium ribbon to 1 mol dm^{-3} hydrochloric acid and measure the volume of hydrogen produced by the reaction over time. Then they repeat this procedure at different temperatures.

1.1 The results for the experiment performed at 30 °C are shown in **Table 1**.

Table 1

Time / s	Volume of gas produced / cm^3
0	0
10	15
20	25
30	30
40	28
50	35
60	35
70	35

On the grid below, draw a graph to represent the results displayed in **Table 1**.

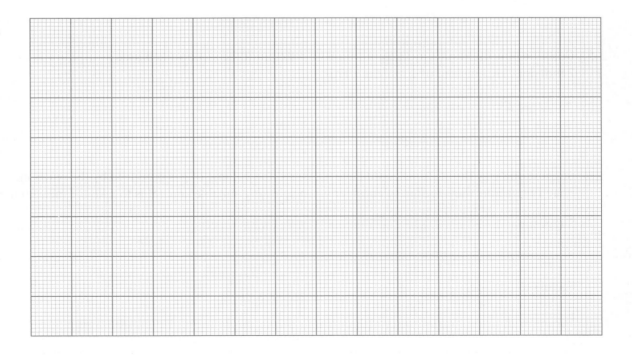

(3 marks)

1.2 On your graph, circle any outliers in the data. Suggest **one** possible reason for any outliers.

....

....
(2 marks)

1.3 Use your graph to determine the time at which the reaction finished. Justify your answer.

Time: ....

Justification: ....

....
(2 marks)

1.4 **Table 2** shows the initial rates of reaction that the students calculated
when they performed the reaction at different temperatures.

Table 2

Temperature of the reaction / °C	Initial rate of reaction / cm^3 s^{-1}
30	1.8
40	3.7
50	7.3
60	13.6
70	24.5

Describe the trend in the results shown in **Table 2**.

....

....
(1 mark)

1.5 Describe how the results in **Table 2** would be different if the students had used
2 mol dm^{-3} HCl instead of 1 mol dm^{-3} HCl.

....

....
(1 mark)

1.6 Suggest **one** way the students could have measured the volume of gas produced by the reaction.
State **two** factors they needed to consider when selecting suitable apparatus to take the measurement.

Suggestion: ....

....

Factors to consider

1. ....

2. ....
(3 marks)

2 The reaction between carbon monoxide and water vapour is an important reaction for the production of hydrogen gas in industry. The equation for the reaction is shown below.

$$CO_{(g)} + H_2O_{(g)} \rightleftharpoons CO_{2(g)} + H_{2(g)} \qquad \Delta H = -41 \text{ kJ mol}^{-1}$$

2.1 State Le Chatelier's principle.

....

....
(1 mark)

2.2 Give **two** conditions which must be met for a reaction to be described as being at equilibrium.

1. ....

....

2. ....

....
(2 marks)

2.3 **Table 3** shows the equilibrium concentrations for this reaction at temperature **X**.
Use this data to calculate the value of K_c for this reaction.
Give your answer to an appropriate number of significant figures.

Table 3

Species	CO	H_2O	CO_2	H_2
Equilibrium concentration / mol dm^{-3}	0.031	0.048	0.12	0.17

$K_c = $ ....
(3 marks)

2.4 When the reaction was performed at temperature **Y**, the value of K_c was higher than at temperature **X**. State which of temperature **X** or temperature **Y** is higher. Justify your answer.

....

....

....
(3 marks)

Score

21

Kinetics, Equilibria and Redox Reactions — 3

1   Hydrogen gas (H_2) can be used as a fuel. One possible method for producing hydrogen gas in bulk involves splitting apart water (H_2O) using energy from light. This process is a redox reaction. The half-equations for the reaction are shown below.

$$2H_2O_{(l)} \rightarrow O_{2(g)} + 4H^+_{(aq)} + 4e^-$$

$$2H^+_{(aq)} + 2e^- \rightarrow H_{2(g)}$$

1.1   With reference to the half-equations shown above,
      explain why this process can be described as a redox reaction.

      ....

      ....

      ....

      ....

      (3 marks)

1.2   Give the overall equation for this reaction.

      ....

      (1 mark)

1.3   Define the term activation energy.

      ....

      (1 mark)

      This reaction has a very high activation energy and so it cannot occur without the presence of a catalyst.

1.4   Explain how the presence of a catalyst makes the reaction possible.

      ....

      ....

      (1 mark)

1.5   State why it is possible for a single catalyst to be used many times.

      ....

      (1 mark)

1.6   One of the catalysts that can be used for this reaction is bismuth vanadate ($BiVO_4$),
      which can be produced from the oxides Bi_2O_3 and V_2O_5.
      Determine the oxidation state of bismuth in Bi_2O_3.

      Oxidation state = ...

      (2 marks)

2   Catalytic converters are used in cars to remove toxic gases from exhaust emissions. One of the reactions that occurs in a catalytic converter is the oxidation of carbon monoxide, CO, to carbon dioxide, CO_2. The overall equation for this reaction is shown below.

$$2CO_{(g)} + O_{2(g)} \rightarrow 2CO_{2(g)}$$

2.1   Give **one** reason why collisions between carbon monoxide and oxygen molecules do not always lead to a reaction.

....
(1 mark)

2.2   State whether carbon is oxidised or reduced in the reaction above. Explain your answer.

....

....
(1 mark)

2.3   Define the term catalyst.

....

....
(2 marks)

Figure 1 shows a Maxwell-Boltzmann distribution for the above reaction taking place in a catalytic converter just after the engine of the car is switched on.

Figure 1

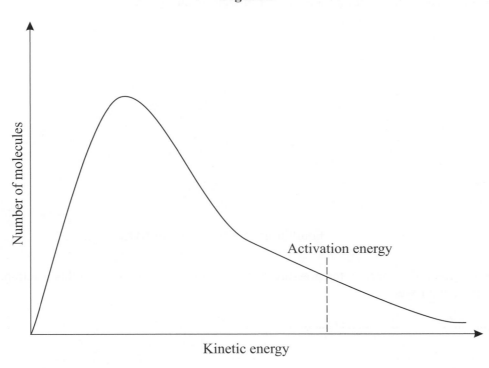

2.4   On **Figure 1**, draw a line to indicate where the activation energy for this reaction would be outside of the catalytic converter. Label your line with the letter **A**.

(1 mark)

2.5   On **Figure 1**, sketch the curve for the reaction in the catalytic converter after the engine of the car has warmed up. Label your curve with the letter **X**.

(2 marks)

2.6 Modern catalytic converters contain heating coils so that they can be heated up very quickly after the engine is switched on. Older catalytic converters do not have these heating coils.

Use your knowledge of collision theory to explain why modern catalytic converters release less carbon monoxide than older catalytic converters.

....

....

....

....

....

....

....

(5 marks)

3 Nitrogen can react with oxygen to produce nitrogen monoxide according to the equation below.

$$N_{2(g)} + O_{2(g)} \rightleftharpoons 2NO_{(g)}$$

3.1 In one reaction, the value of K_c was found to be 2.00×10^2 and the equilibrium concentrations of nitrogen and oxygen were 0.0250 mol dm^{-3} and 0.0125 mol dm^{-3}, respectively.

Calculate the equilibrium concentration of nitrogen monoxide.
Give your answer to an appropriate number of significant figures.

Equilibrium concentration of NO = ... mol dm^{-3}

(3 marks)

3.2 State the effect of increasing the pressure on the position of equilibrium in this reaction.
Explain your answer.

....

....

....

(2 marks)

Kinetics, Equilibria and Redox Reactions — 4

1   Under certain conditions, methane (CH_4) can react to give acetylene (C_2H_2) and hydrogen gas.
The equation for this reaction is shown below.

$$2CH_{4(g)} \rightleftharpoons 3H_{2(g)} + C_2H_{2(g)} \qquad \Delta H = +377 \text{ kJ mol}^{-1}$$

A chemical company is considering whether it would be feasible to use this reaction to
produce large amounts of acetylene industrially.

1.1   A scientist suggests that performing the reaction at high pressure would increase the rate of the reaction.
Explain why doing this would decrease the yield of acetylene.

....

....

....

(2 marks)

1.2   Describe and explain the factors that the company would need to consider when
choosing an appropriate temperature for this reaction in an industrial setting.

....

....

....

....

....

....

....

....

....

....

....

....

....

....

(6 marks)

1.3   Write the expression for the equilibrium constant, K_c, for this reaction.

....

....

(1 mark)

1.4 A scientist performed a test experiment. They placed 1.00 moles of methane in a heat-proof reaction vessel with a total volume of 3.00 dm³. The reaction vessel was then placed in a furnace at a very high temperature.

After an equilibrium was established, the equilibrium mixture contained 0.372 moles of acetylene.

Calculate the value of K_c for this reaction using the information given above.
Give units with your answer.

$$K_c = \text{..}$$

(7 marks)

1.5 Explain how the value of K_c would change if the same reaction was performed at a lower temperature.

....

....

....

....

(2 marks)

1.6 State how changing the initial concentration of methane would affect the value of K_c for this reaction.

....

(1 marks)

EXAM TIP

Remember, the rate and the position of equilibrium are separate. Equilibrium is the point at which the rate of the reverse reaction becomes equal to the rate of the forward reaction — it doesn't matter how high (or low) that rate is. If conditions favour the forward reaction, more of the product will be made before the reverse reaction 'catches up' (and vice versa).

Score

19

Thermodynamics — 1

All chemical reactions and processes involve some sort of energy change, or they just wouldn't happen. Thermodynamics is the study of those energy changes, so it's pretty important stuff...

For each of questions 1-4, give your answer by ticking the appropriate box.

1   Which statement gives the correct definition for the enthalpy change of atomisation of an element?

   A   The enthalpy change when 1 mole of an element in its
       standard state is converted to gaseous atoms.   ☐

   B   The enthalpy change when all the bonds of the same
       type in 1 mole of gaseous molecules are broken.   ☐

   C   The enthalpy change when 1 mole of gaseous atoms is
       formed from an element in its standard state.   ☐

   D   The enthalpy change when 1 mole of gaseous 1+ ions
       is formed from 1 mole of gaseous atoms.   ☐

                                                                    (1 mark)

2   A reaction is endothermic and is accompanied by a positive entropy change.
    Which statement best describes the feasibility of the reaction?

   A   It is never feasible.   ☐

   B   It is feasible below a certain temperature.   ☐

   C   It is always feasible.   ☐

   D   It is feasible above a certain temperature.   ☐

                                                                    (1 mark)

3   Which statement best describes the reason why silver iodide is insoluble in water?

   A   Its enthalpy of solution is exothermic.   ☐

   B   Its enthalpy of solution is endothermic.   ☐

   C   Both ions have small hydration enthalpies.   ☐

   D   The compound has a small lattice dissociation enthalpy.   ☐

                                                                    (1 mark)

4   The lattice enthalpy of formation of calcium chloride is -2258 kJ mol^{-1}, the enthalpy
    of solution is -81 kJ mol^{-1} and the enthalpy of hydration of a Cl$^-$ ion is -364 kJ mol^{-1}.
    What is the enthalpy of hydration of a calcium ion?

   A -1611 kJ mol^{-1} ☐

   B $+1449$ kJ mol^{-1} ☐

   C -1975 kJ mol^{-1} ☐

   D $+2905$ kJ mol^{-1} ☐

                                                                    (1 mark)

5   **Figure 1** shows a Born-Haber cycle for calcium oxide.

Figure 1

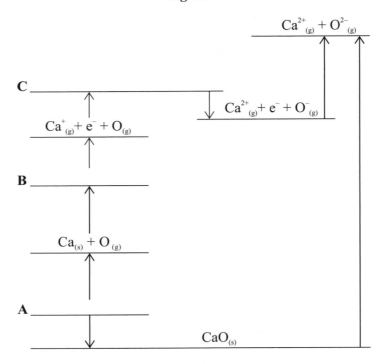

5.1   Complete **Figure 1** by writing expressions to show the changes in the species involved on each of the three blank lines labelled **A**, **B** and **C**.

(3 marks)

5.2   Use the data in **Table 1** to calculate the enthalpy of atomisation of oxygen.

Table 1

Enthalpy change	$\Delta H^{\ominus}$ / kJ mol^{-1}
Enthalpy of formation of calcium oxide	−635
Lattice dissociation enthalpy of calcium oxide	+3513
Enthalpy of atomisation of calcium	+193
First electron affinity of oxygen	−142
First ionisation energy of calcium	+590
Second electron affinity of oxygen	+844
Second ionisation energy of calcium	+1150

Enthalpy of atomisation of oxygen = ... kJ mol^{-1}

(3 marks)

6   Magnesium chloride and sodium chloride are both soluble metal chlorides.

6.1   Define the term enthalpy of solution.

....

....

(2 marks)

6.2   Write a symbol equation that represents the process of dissolving magnesium chloride.

....

(1 mark)

6.3   Use the data in **Table 2** to calculate the enthalpy of solution of magnesium chloride.

Table 2

Enthalpy change	$\Delta H^{\ominus}$ /kJ mol^{-1}
Enthalpy of hydration of Mg^{2+}	-1920
Enthalpy of hydration of Cl^-	-364
Lattice dissociation enthalpy of magnesium chloride	$+2526$

Enthalpy of solution of magnesium chloride = ... kJ mol^{-1}

(2 marks)

6.4   The enthalpy of solution of sodium chloride is slightly endothermic at 298 K.
      Explain why sodium chloride is reasonably soluble in water at room temperature.

....

....

....

....

(3 marks)

6.5   The lattice dissociation enthalpy of sodium chloride is +787 kJ mol^{-1}. Use your knowledge
      of the bonding in a lattice to explain the difference between this value and the value
      for the lattice dissociation enthalpy of magnesium chloride given in **Table 2**.

....

....

....

(2 marks)

7   Nitrogen monoxide reacts with oxygen to form nitrogen dioxide.

$$2NO_{(g)} + O_{2(g)} \rightarrow 2NO_{2(g)} \qquad\qquad \Delta H^{\ominus} = -114.0 \text{ kJ mol}^{-1}$$

7.1   Explain whether you would expect the entropy change for this reaction to be positive or negative.
Use the reaction equation to justify your answer.

....

....

....

(2 marks)

7.2   **Table 3** shows the standard entropies of the substances involved in the reaction.

Table 3

Substance	NO	O_2	NO_2
$S^{\ominus}$ / J K^{-1} mol^{-1}	210.8	205.3	240.0

Use the data in **Table 3** to determine a value for the entropy change of the reaction.

Entropy change = ... J K^{-1} mol^{-1}

(2 marks)

7.3   Use the value you calculated in question **7.2** and the given enthalpy change for
the reaction to explain whether this reaction is feasible at all temperatures.

....

....

....

(2 marks)

7.4   At standard pressure, nitrogen dioxide condenses at 21.2 °C.
Explain the effect that condensation has on its entropy.

....

....

....

(2 marks)

If a question involves lattice enthalpies, check whether you're dealing with lattice enthalpy of <u>formation</u> or lattice enthalpy of <u>dissociation</u> before you start calculating. Forming a lattice is <u>exothermic</u> — it releases energy — so lattice enthalpy of <u>formation</u> is always <u>negative</u>. You have to <u>put energy in</u> to break a lattice apart, and so lattice enthalpy of <u>dissociation</u> is always <u>positive</u>.

Score

28

Thermodynamics — 2

1 Lithium fluoride is an ionic solid with a structure similar to that of sodium chloride. Some thermodynamic data about lithium fluoride is given in **Table 1**.

Table 1

Enthalpy change	$\Delta H^{\ominus}$ / kJ mol^{-1}
Enthalpy of formation of lithium fluoride	−612
Enthalpy of atomisation of lithium	+161
First ionisation energy of lithium	+519
Enthalpy of atomisation of fluorine	+79
Lattice enthalpy of formation of lithium fluoride	−1022

1.1 Define the term first electron affinity.

....

....

(2 marks)

1.2 Explain why the first electron affinity of fluorine is exothermic.

....

....

(2 marks)

1.3 Use the data in **Table 1** to construct a Born-Haber cycle and calculate a value for the first electron affinity of fluorine.

First electron affinity of fluorine = ... kJ mol^{-1}

(6 marks)

48

1.4 Explain how the bond dissociation enthalpy of fluorine is related to the enthalpy of atomisation of fluorine. Include equations to justify your answer.

....

....

....

....

(4 marks)

2 Carbon, in the form of graphite, reacts with oxygen to produce carbon dioxide.
$$C_{(s)} + O_{2(g)} \rightarrow CO_{2(g)}$$

Table 2 shows some thermodynamic data relating to the reaction.

Table 2

Substance	$\Delta_f H$ / kJ mol^{-1}	$S^{\ominus}$ / J K^{-1} mol^{-1}
C	0	5.70
O$_2$	0	205.3
CO$_2$	−394	214.0

2.1 Explain why carbon has a much lower entropy under standard conditions than oxygen.

....

....

....

(2 marks)

2.2 Use the data in Table 2 to deduce the enthalpy change for the reaction.

....

(1 mark)

2.3 Use your answer to question 2.2, and the data in Table 2, to determine a value for the free energy change of the reaction at 298 K.

Free energy change = ... J mol^{-1}

(4 marks)

3   Many metals are extracted from their ores using carbon.

The reaction between aluminium oxide and carbon is shown in the equation below.

$$Al_2O_{3(s)} + 3C_{(s)} \rightarrow 2Al_{(s)} + 3CO_{(g)}$$

Table 3 shows some thermodynamic data relating to the reaction.

Table 3

Substance	$\Delta_f H$ / kJ mol^{-1}	$S^{\ominus}$ / J K^{-1} mol^{-1}
Al_2O_3	−1676	50.9
Al	0	28.3
C	0	5.70
CO	−110.5	198

3.1   Use the data in **Table 3** to calculate a value for the free energy change of the reaction at 277 °C.
Give your answer to an appropriate number of significant figures.

Free energy change = ... J mol^{-1}

(6 marks)

3.2   Use your answer to question **3.1** to deduce whether the reaction is feasible at 277 °C.
Give a reason for your answer.

....

....

(1 marks)

3.3   Determine a value for the minimum temperature at which the reaction is feasible.

Minimum temperature = ... °C

(2 marks)

3.4   Suggest **one** reason why reduction with carbon is not used to extract aluminium metal from its oxide.

....

(1 mark)

4   Lattice enthalpies can be calculated theoretically, or can be determined experimentally.
Table 4 shows theoretical and experimental lattice dissociation enthalpies for two compounds.

Table 4

Compound	Theoretical lattice dissociation enthalpy / kJ mol^{-1}	Experimental lattice dissociation enthalpy / kJ mol^{-1}
NaCl	+766	+787
MgI$_2$	+1944	+2327

4.1   Compare the theoretical and experimental values of lattice dissociation enthalpy for each compound given in **Table 4** and explain the difference observed in each case.

....

....

....

....

....

....

....

....

....

....

....

(6 marks)

4.2   The experimental lattice formation enthalpy for NaCl is −787 kJ mol^{-1}. Describe and explain the relationship between lattice dissociation enthalpy and lattice formation enthalpy.

....

....

....

....

....

....

(4 marks)

It's easy to trip up over units when you're calculating free energy change. Unless you're told to use a particular unit, it doesn't matter whether you give your final answer in kJ mol^{-1} or J mol^{-1}, but you'll usually be given ΔH in kJ mol^{-1} and ΔS in J K^{-1} mol^{-1}, so you'll need to convert one of them before you can plug them into the equation for ΔG.

Score

41

Rate Equations and K_p — 1

This section might feel like déjà vu, but don't worry, you're not going mad — you've already met a few of these ideas in Unit 1: Section 5. Head back there and make sure you're feeling confident before getting started here.

For each of questions 1-4, give your answer by ticking the appropriate box.

1   The rate equation for the reaction between two compounds, A and B, is: Rate = $k[A]^2[B]$.
What would happen to the rate of reaction if the concentrations of both A and B were tripled?

    A   It would increase by a factor of 3.   ☐

    B   It would increase by a factor of 27.   ☐

    C   It would increase by a factor of 18.   ☐

    D   It would increase by a factor of 9.   ☐

                                                                           (1 mark)

2   Four concentration-time graphs for chemical reactions are shown in **Figure 1**.

Figure 1

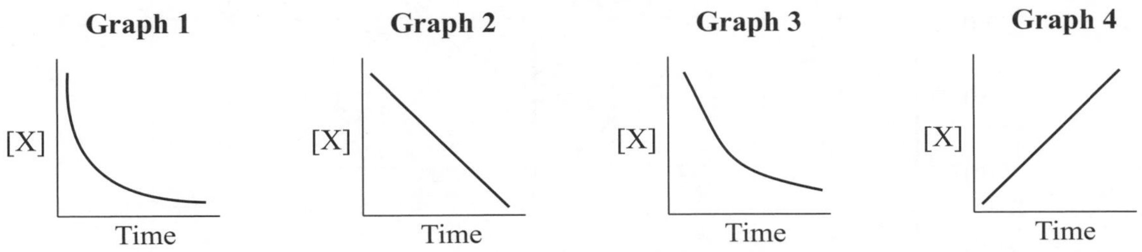

Graph 1   **Graph 2**   **Graph 3**   **Graph 4**

Which graph correctly shows a reaction in which increasing the concentration of the reactant X would **not** affect the rate of the reaction.

    A   Graph 1   ☐   **B**   Graph 2   ☐

    C   Graph 3   ☐   **D**   Graph 4   ☐

                                                                             (1 mark)

3   The equilibrium constant for the reversible dissociation of N_2O_4 into two molecules of NO_2 is 6.03×10^3 atm at 550 K. The partial pressure of N_2O_4 in a sealed container held at 550 K is found to be 1.78×10^3 atm. What is the partial pressure of NO_2 in the container?

    A 4.25×10^3 atm   ☐   **B** 3.56×10^3 atm   ☐

    C 3.39×10^3 atm   ☐   **D** 3.28×10^3 atm   ☐

                                                                              (1 mark)

4   A scientist heats a sample of gaseous chloroethane. At a certain temperature, chloroethane molecules start to decompose, forming ethane and hydrogen chloride. The activation energy for the reaction is 254.4 kJ mol^{-1}, the rate constant is 1.37×10^{-4} s^{-1} and the Arrhenius constant is 4.00×10^{14} s^{-1}.

Use the Arrhenius equation ($k = Ae^{\frac{-E_a}{RT}}$) to calculate the temperature at which the decomposition reaction happens. (The gas constant, R = 8.31 J K^{-1} mol^{-1}.)

    A   330 K   ☐   **B**   1250 K   ☐

    C   720 K   ☐   **D**   500 K   ☐

                                                                              (1 mark)

5   The rate of reaction between magnesium and hydrochloric acid can be monitored by measuring the volume of hydrogen gas produced over time. In an experiment, a small piece of magnesium ribbon is added to an excess of hydrochloric acid.

5.1   Draw a labelled diagram to show an experimental set-up that could be used to collect and measure the volume of hydrogen gas produced over time.

(3 marks)

Figure 2 shows the results of the experiment.

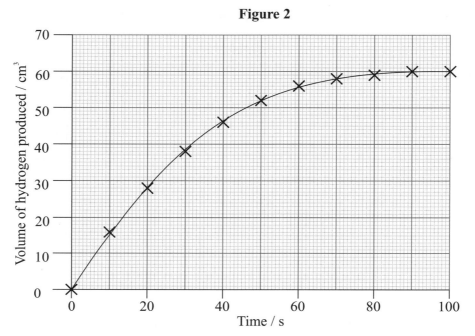

Figure 2

5.2   Use **Figure 2** to determine the initial rate of the reaction.
       Give units with your answer.

Initial rate = ...

(4 marks)

5.3   State and explain how the rate of reaction changes as the reaction proceeds.

....

....

(2 marks)

If you're asked to find a rate of reaction from a curved graph, don't panic. You just need to draw a tangent to the curve at the time you're interested in — that's a straight line with the same gradient as the curve at that particular time. Then just find the gradient of your tangent. Easy.

Score

13

Rate Equations and K_p — 2

1   Sodium thiosulfate ($Na_2S_2O_3$) reacts with hydrochloric acid to produce a mixture of products. The equation for the reaction is:

$$Na_2S_2O_{3(aq)} + 2HCl_{(aq)} \rightarrow 2NaCl_{(aq)} + S_{(s)} + SO_{2(g)} + H_2O_{(l)}$$

A student measured the time taken for a fixed amount of solid sulfur to form at different concentrations of sodium thiosulfate. **Table 1** shows the results of the experiment.

Table 1

Concentration of $Na_2S_2O_{3(aq)}$ / mol dm⁻³	Time taken / s	Rate of reaction / $\times 10^{-3}$ s⁻¹
0	0	0
0.200	404	
0.400	199	
0.600	137	
0.800	103	

1.1   Complete **Table 1** by using the equation $\text{Rate} = \dfrac{1}{\text{Time taken}}$ to calculate the missing rates of reaction.

(2 marks)

1.2   On the grid below, draw a graph to show how the rate of reaction changes with increasing concentration of sodium thiosulfate. Include a line of best fit in your answer.

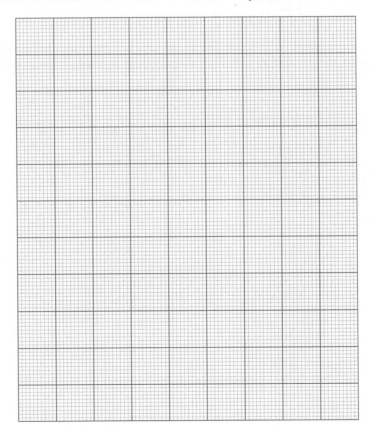

(3 marks)

1.3 Use the graph you drew in question **1.2** to determine the order of reaction with respect to sodium thiosulfate. Justify your answer.

....

....

....

(2 marks)

1.4 A series of similar experiments showed that the reaction is zero order with respect to hydrochloric acid. Use this information, along with your answer to question **1.3**, to write the rate equation for this reaction.

....

(1 mark)

2   The Haber process and the Contact process are important methods for the production of industrial chemicals.

The Haber process is a reversible reaction used to manufacture ammonia gas. The equation for the reaction is:

$$N_{2(g)} + 3H_{2(g)} \rightleftharpoons 2NH_{3(g)} \qquad \Delta H = -92.4 \text{ kJ mol}^{-1}$$

2.1 Write an expression for K_p for this reaction.

....

(1 mark)

2.2 An equilibrium mixture at a pressure of 200 atm is found to contain 15.0 moles of nitrogen, 30.0 moles of hydrogen and 22.0 moles of ammonia.

Use this information to calculate a value for K_p for the reaction under these conditions. Give your answer to an appropriate number of significant figures. Give units with your answer.

$K_p =$ ....

(6 marks)

2.3 Predict how increases in the pressure and temperature, and the addition of a catalyst, would affect the position of equilibrium and the value of K_p for this reaction. Justify your predictions.

....

....

....

....

....

....

....

....

....

....

....

(6 marks)

The Contact process is used in the manufacture of sulfuric acid.
The second step involves the reversible reaction shown in the equation below.

$$2SO_{2(g)} + O_{2(g)} \rightleftharpoons 2SO_{3(g)}$$

A mixture of sulfur dioxide and oxygen was sealed in a container and allowed to reach equilibrium at a constant temperature. The partial pressure of SO_3 was found to be 96 kPa and the partial pressure of O_2 was found to be 40 kPa. The value for K_p under these conditions is 0.056 kPa^{-1}.

2.4 Use this information to calculate the partial pressure of sulfur dioxide in the equilibrium mixture.

Partial pressure of SO_2 = ... kPa

(3 marks)

2.5 Calculate the total pressure of the reaction mixture.

Total pressure = ... kPa

(1 mark)

Score

25

Rate Equations and K_p — 3

1 A student carried out a series of experiments to measure the initial rate of reaction between two reactants, **E** and **F**, at various initial concentrations.

Table 1 shows the results of the experiments.

Table 1

Experiment	Initial [E] / mol dm^{-3}	Initial [F] / mol dm^{-3}	Initial rate of reaction / mol dm^{-3} s^{-1}
1	0.0800	0.0600	8.00×10^{-4}
2	0.0800	0.0900	12.0×10^{-4}
3	0.120	0.0900	18.0×10^{-4}

1.1 Use the data shown in **Table 1** to determine the order of reaction with respect to each of the reactants **E** and **F**. Justify your answer.

....

....

....

....

(2 marks)

1.2 Write the rate equation for the reaction.

....

(1 mark)

1.3 Deduce the overall order of the reaction.

....

(1 mark)

1.4 Use the data from experiment 1 in **Table 1** to calculate the value of the rate constant, k. Give your answer to the appropriate number of significant figures. Give units with your answer.

$k =$ ....

(4 marks)

1.5 The experiment was repeated a fourth time. The initial concentrations of reactants E and F were 0.200 mol dm^{-3} and 0.500 mol dm^{-3}, respectively. Use your value for the rate constant from question **1.4** to calculate the initial rate of the reaction for this repeat.

Initial rate of reaction = ... mol dm^{-3} s^{-1}

(1 mark)

2 An initial rate method can be used to determine the rate of the following reaction:

$$CH_3COCH_{3(aq)} + I_{2(aq)} \xrightarrow{\text{HCl catalyst}} CH_3COCH_2I_{(aq)} + HI_{(aq)}$$

The concentration of each reagent is varied in separate experiments and the time taken for the iodine colour to just disappear measured. **Table 2** shows the results of experiment 1. Water is added to allow the total volume to be kept constant in subsequent experiments.

Table 2

Expt.	Volume of 1.0 mol dm^{-3} CH$_3$COCH$_3$ / cm^3	Volume of 0.004 mol dm^{-3} I$_2$ / cm^3	Volume of 1.0 mol dm^{-3} HCl / cm^3	Volume of H$_2$O / cm^3	Time / s
1	10	4	10	26	210
2					

The reaction is first order with respect to both CH$_3$COCH$_3$ and HCl and zero order with respect to I$_2$.

2.1 Complete **Table 2** by suggesting volumes of reagents that the student could use to show that the reaction is first order with respect to propanone. Include the expected result of the experiment in your answer.

(3 marks)

2.2 Write the rate equation for this reaction.

....

(1 mark)

2.3 Calculate a value for the rate constant, k, using the data in **Table 2**.
The rate for this experiment was found to be 1.5×10^{-6} mol dm^{-3} s^{-1}.
Give your answer to an appropriate number of significant figures.
Give units with your answer.

$k =$ ....

(5 marks)

2.4 **Figure 1** shows a proposed rate-determining step for the reaction.

Figure 1

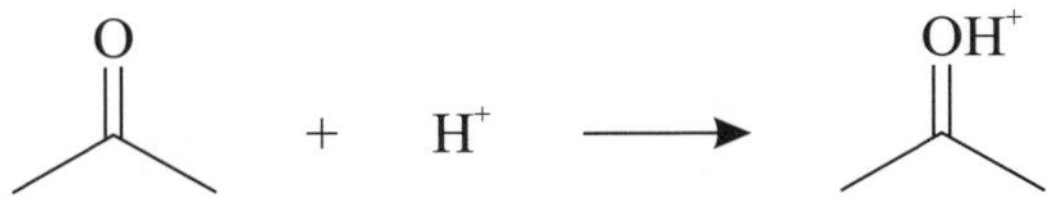

Explain how the form of the rate equation provides evidence that this is the rate-determining step.

....

....

....

....

(3 marks)

3 Iodide ions can be oxidised by iodate(V) ions in acidic solution. The equation for the reaction is:

$$IO_{3\ (aq)}^{-} + 5I^{-}_{(aq)} + 6H^{+}_{(aq)} \rightarrow 3I_{2(aq)} + 3H_2O_{(l)}$$

An experiment to determine the activation energy for this reaction was carried out.
The processed results are shown in **Table 3**.

Table 3

Temperature / K	$\frac{1}{T}$ / (×10^{-3} K)	k / s^{-1}	ln$k$
673	1.49	1.01×10^{-4}	−9.20
704	1.42	5.00×10^{-4}	−7.60
740	1.35	3.08×10^{-3}	−5.78
775	1.29	1.50×10^{-2}	−4.20

The Arrhenius equation can be used to determine the activation energy for any chemical reaction as long as the values of temperature and rate constant, k, are known.

$$\ln k = \frac{-E_a}{RT} + \ln A$$

3.1 Explain how the Arrhenius equation can be used with the data given in **Table 3** to calculate the activation energy for this reaction.

....

....

....

....

....

(5 marks)

3.2 Use your knowledge of collision theory to explain how the value of the rate constant, k, would be affected by an increase in temperature.

....

....

....

....

(4 marks)

3.3 Iodide ions can also be oxidised by peroxydisulfate ions, $S_2O_8^{2-}$. The activation energy for this reaction is 44.9 kJ mol^{-1} and the rate constant is 1.54×10^{-6} mol^{-1} dm^3 s^{-1}. Use this information to calculate the Arrhenius constant, A, for the reaction at 298 K. (The gas constant, R = 8.31 J K^{-1} mol^{-1}.)

A = ... mol^{-1} dm^3 s^{-1}

(2 marks)

The various forms of the Arrhenius equation can look a bit daunting, what with all those exponentials and logs, but the good news is you'll always be given it if you need it in the exam. Make sure you get plenty of practice rearranging it beforehand though — you'll be less likely to make a mistake when it matters if you're already familiar with the different rearrangements.

Score

32

Electrode Potentials and Cells — 1

If I were you, I'd make sure I was feeling nice and comfortable with redox reactions and half-equations before I started this section — there'll be a lot of them coming your way over the next few pages...

For each of questions 1-4, give your answer by ticking the appropriate box.

1 Which of the following would **not** be used in a standard hydrogen electrode?

    A   A 2 mol dm^{-3} solution of HCl ☐

    B   A temperature of 298 K ☐

    C   A platinum electrode ☐

    D   Hydrogen gas at a pressure of 100 kPa ☐

(1 mark)

2 Which species acts as the oxidising agent in the following electrochemical cell?

        Cu | Cu^{2+} || Fe^{3+}, Fe^{2+} | Pt   EMF = +0.43 V

    A   Pt ☐   **B**   Cu^{2+} ☐

    C   Fe^{3+} ☐   **D**   Fe^{2+} ☐

(1 mark)

3 **Table 1** shows some standard electrode potentials.

Table 1

Electrode half-equation	E°/V
$Al^{3+} + 3e^- \rightleftharpoons Al$	−1.66
$2H^+ + 2e^- \rightleftharpoons H_2$	0.00
$Fe^{3+} + e^- \rightleftharpoons Fe^{2+}$	+0.77
$Cl_2 + 2e^- \rightleftharpoons 2Cl^-$	+1.36

Which of the species shown in **Table 1** could reduce hydrogen ions?

    A   Both Fe^{2+} and Cl$^-$ ☐   **B**   Al^{3+} only ☐

    C   Al only ☐   **D**   Both Al^{3+} and Fe^{3+} ☐

(1 mark)

4 What is the EMF of the following electrochemical cell?

        Zn | Zn^{2+} || Cr^{3+}, Cr^{2+} | Pt

    Zn^{2+} + 2e$^-$ $\rightleftharpoons$ Zn E° = −0.76 V   Cr^{3+} + e$^-$ $\rightleftharpoons$ Cr^{2+} E° = −0.41 V

    A   −0.35 V ☐   **B**   −1.17 V ☐

    C   +1.17 V ☐   **D**   +0.35 V ☐

(1 mark)

5   **Figure 1** shows a typical alkaline fuel cell. Hydrogen and oxygen react to produce electricity and water.

Figure 1

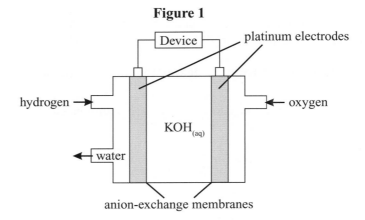

The half-equations for the reactions taking place in the fuel cell are:

$$2H_2O + 2e^- \rightleftharpoons H_2 + 2OH^- \qquad E^\circ = -0.83 \text{ V}$$
$$O_2 + 2H_2O + 4e^- \rightleftharpoons 4OH^- \qquad E^\circ = +0.40 \text{ V}$$

5.1   Draw the conventional representation for this cell. State symbols are **not** required in your answer.

....

(2 marks)

5.2   Calculate a value for the EMF of the fuel cell shown in **Figure 1**.

EMF = ... V

(1 mark)

5.3   Explain why it is not necessary to recharge a fuel cell.

....

(1 mark)

5.4   State which substance acts as the electrolyte in the cell.

....

(1 mark)

5.5   State **one** advantage and **one** disadvantage of using fuel cells to power cars,
      rather than internal combustion engines.

Advantage: ....

....

Disadvantage: ....

....

(2 marks)

EXAM TIP

You need to be confident with what goes where in the conventional representation of a cell —
you could be asked to draw one or to use one to help you work out the half-equations for the
cell. Remember, the half-cell where oxidation occurs goes on the left. The half-cell where reduction
occurs goes on the right. Don't forget to draw a salt bridge to separate the two half-cells.

Score

11

Electrode Potentials and Cells — 2

1   A student is investigating reactions in electrochemical cells. The student has access to the half-cells **A-G** shown in **Table 1**. Platinum electrodes were used in half-cells where inert electrodes were required.

Table 1

Half-cell	Electrode half-equation	$E^{\ominus}$ / V
A	$Zn^{2+}_{(aq)} + 2e^- \rightleftharpoons Zn_{(s)}$	−0.76
B	$Fe^{2+}_{(aq)} + 2e^- \rightleftharpoons Fe_{(s)}$	−0.44
C	$2H^+_{(aq)} + 2e^- \rightleftharpoons H_{2(g)}$	0.00
D	$Cu^{2+}_{(aq)} + 2e^- \rightleftharpoons Cu_{(s)}$	+0.34
E	$I_{2(aq)} + 2e^- \rightleftharpoons 2I^-_{(aq)}$	+0.54
F	$Fe^{3+}_{(aq)} + e^- \rightleftharpoons Fe^{2+}_{(aq)}$	+0.77
G	$MnO_4^-{}_{(aq)} + 8H^+_{(aq)} + 5e^- \rightleftharpoons Mn^{2+}_{(aq)} + 4H_2O_{(l)}$	+1.51

1.1   The student connects some of the half-cells together as shown in **Table 2**.
Complete **Table 2** by writing the equations, including state symbols, for the overall reactions that occur.

Table 2

Half-cells	Reaction equation
A and **C**	
B and **D**	
E and **F**	
B and **G**	

(4 marks)

1.2   Draw conventional representations, including state symbols, for the following combinations of half-cells:

A and **C**: ....

B and **D**: ....

E and **F**: ....

(6 marks)

1.3   Calculate a value for the EMF of the reaction that occurs when half-cells **B** and **G** are connected.

EMF = ... V

(1 mark)

1.4 Draw a labelled diagram to show an experimental set-up that the student could use to measure the standard cell potential for the following cell:

$$Fe_{(s)} \mid Fe^{2+}_{(aq)} \mid\mid I_{2(aq)}, I^-_{(aq)} \mid Pt$$

State the temperature at which the student should take their measurements.

Temperature: ....

(6 marks)

1.5 The student records a standard cell potential of 0.98 V. The uncertainty in this reading is ±0.005 V. Calculate the percentage uncertainty in the student's measurement of the standard cell potential.

Percentage uncertainty = ... %

(1 mark)

2 **Figure 1** shows a rechargeable lead acid cell being discharged to power a motor.

Figure 1

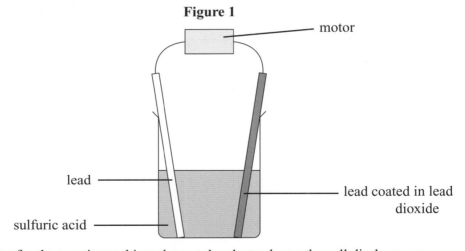

The half-equations for the reactions taking place at the electrodes as the cell discharges are:

$$Pb + SO_4^{2-} \rightarrow PbSO_4 + 2e^-$$
$$PbO_2 + SO_4^{2-} + 4H^+ + 2e^- \rightarrow PbSO_4 + 2H_2O$$

2.1 On **Figure 1**, identify and label the positive and negative electrodes during discharge. Draw an arrow to show the direction of electron flow across the motor during discharge.

(2 marks)

2.2 Combine these half-equations to show a full equation for the cell reaction during **discharge**. Deduce the full equation for the cell reaction during **recharge**.

Discharge: ....

Recharge: ....

(2 marks)

2.3 Describe the processes that occur when the cell in **Figure 1** is recharged.
Include in your answer the relevant half-equations, and identify the electrode at which each reaction occurs.

....

....

....

....

(4 marks)

Lithium cells are another type of rechargeable battery.

2.4 Write half-equations for the reactions which occur in a lithium cell during charging.

....

....

(2 marks)

2.5 Suggest why, in everyday use, the EMF produced by a lithium battery may be different to the EMF that is calculated using standard electrode potentials.

....

....

(1 mark)

3 An electrochemical cell containing acidified hydrogen peroxide in both half-cells is shown below.

$$Pt \mid H_2O_2 \mid O_2 \mid\mid H_2O_2, H_2O \mid Pt \qquad EMF = +1.09\ V$$

3.1 Write a half-equation for the half-cell in which hydrogen peroxide acts as an oxidising agent.

....

(1 mark)

3.2 Write a half-equation for the half-cell in which hydrogen peroxide acts as a reducing agent.

....

(1 mark)

3.3 Combine your half-equations from questions **3.1** and **3.2** to give an equation for the overall cell reaction.

....

(1 mark)

3.4 $E°$ for the $Pt \mid H_2O_2 \mid O_2$ half-cell is +0.68 V.
Calculate $E°$ for the $H_2O_2, H_2O \mid Pt$ half-cell.

$E° = $ V

(2 marks)

In your exam, you could be asked how you'd set up an electrochemical cell to measure its EMF. One thing you can do to really improve the accuracy of your results is to clean the electrodes with emery paper before you pop them into the solutions, and again before taking any repeat measurements. That'll get rid of any impurities that might affect the reactions in the half-cells.

Score

34

Acids, Bases and pH — 1

You'll need all your concentration to find the solutions to this section — it's not as basic as it seems...

For each of questions 1-5, give your answer by ticking the appropriate box.

1   Which of the following is an example of a strong monoprotic acid?

     A   Nitric acid (HNO_3)   ☐

     B   Ethanoic acid (CH_3COOH)   ☐

     C   Sulfuric acid (H_2SO_4)   ☐

     D   Ethanedioic acid ($C_2H_2O_4$)   ☐

                                              (1 mark)

2   A sample of 0.050 mol dm^{-3} hydrochloric acid undergoes complete dissociation in water. What is the pH of the resultant solution?

     A   3.0   ☐   **B**   1.3   ☐

     C   1.0   ☐   **D**   1.5   ☐

                                              (1 mark)

3   A basic buffer solution is made up of which of the following?

     A   A weak acid and one of its salts   ☐

     B   A strong acid and one of its salts   ☐

     C   A weak base and one of its salts   ☐

     D   A strong base and one of its salts   ☐

                                              (1 mark)

4   An acid has a K_a value of 2.24×10^{-5} mol dm^{-3}. What is the pK_a value of the acid?

     A   4.65   ☐   **B**   10.7   ☐

     C   1.00   ☐   **D**   4.29   ☐

                                              (1 mark)

5   Calcium hydroxide is a strong base. At 298 K the value of K_w is 1.00×10^{-14} mol^2 dm^{-6}. What is the pH of a 0.0200 mol dm^{-3} solution of calcium hydroxide at this temperature?

     A   12.0   ☐   **B**   12.3   ☐

     C   12.6   ☐   **D**   13.0   ☐

                                              (1 mark)

6   The Brønsted-Lowry theory can be used to explain the reactions of acids and bases.

Sodium hydroxide is an example of a Brønsted-Lowry base.

6.1   State the meaning of the term Brønsted-Lowry base.

....

(1 mark)

Hydrochloric acid and sulfuric acid are examples of strong Brønsted-Lowry acids.

6.2   Explain the difference between strong and weak acids.

....

....

(2 marks)

6.3   Write an equation to show how hydrochloric acid acts as a strong acid when added to water.

....

(1 mark)

6.4   Calculate the pH of a 0.0500 mol dm^{-3} solution of sulfuric acid.

pH = ...

(2 marks)

6.5   A second solution of sulfuric acid has a pH of 1.75.
Calculate the concentration of this solution.

Concentration = ... mol dm^{-3}

(2 marks)

7   Acid-base titrations can be used to determine the concentration of an acidic or basic solution. Carbonic acid, H_2CO_3, is a diprotic acid. A student found the concentration of a solution of carbonic acid by titrating it against a standard solution of sodium hydroxide, NaOH.

7.1   The student prepared the standard solution of sodium hydroxide by dissolving 1.20 g of solid sodium hydroxide in 200 cm^3 of distilled water. Calculate the concentration of the standard solution.

Concentration = ... mol dm^{-3}

(2 marks)

The student pipetted 25.0 cm³ of the carbonic acid solution into a conical flask and added a few drops of phenolphthalein indicator solution. Sodium hydroxide solution was added slowly from a burette until the carbonic acid was fully neutralised and the end point of the titration was reached.

The results of the student's titration are shown in **Table 1**.

Table 1

	Rough	Run 1	Run 2	Run 3
Initial burette reading / cm³	0.00	0.05	0.00	0.10
Final burette reading / cm³	23.60	23.50	23.40	23.55
Titre value / cm³	23.60	23.45	23.40	23.45

7.2 Use the results from **Table 1** and your answer to question **7.1** to calculate the concentration of the carbonic acid solution.

Concentration = ... mol dm⁻³

(5 marks)

7.3 The uncertainty in the mean titre value is ±0.15 cm³.
Calculate the percentage uncertainty in the mean titre value.
Give your answer to an appropriate number of significant figures.

Percentage uncertainty = ... %

(2 marks)

7.4 Suggest **one** way in which the student could reduce the percentage uncertainty in this mean titre value.

....

....

(1 mark)

Score

23

Acids, Bases and pH — 2

1   Carboxylic acids, such as propanoic acid, are weak acids.

1.1   Write an equation to show how propanoic acid (CH_3CH_2COOH) acts as a weak acid when added to water.

....
(1 mark)

The pH of a weak acid can be calculated using the acid dissociation constant, K_a.

1.2   Deduce the K_a expression for propanoic acid.

....
(1 mark)

A solution of propanoic acid was prepared by dissolving 12.0 g of propanoic acid in 150 cm³ of distilled water. The K_a value for propanoic acid is 1.34×10^{-5} mol dm⁻³.

1.3   Calculate the pH of the resultant solution of propanoic acid.

pH = ...
(5 marks)

2   The ionic product of water can be used to calculate the pH of solutions of strong bases.

2.1   Give the expression for the ionic product of water.

....
(1 mark)

68

The dissociation of water is an equilibrium process. The value of K_w varies with temperature.

2.2 As temperature increases, the position of equilibrium shifts to the right.
Explain the effect of increasing temperature on the value of K_w.

....

....

(2 marks)

At a temperature of 298 K the value of K_w is 1.00×10^{-14} mol^2 dm^{-6}.

2.3 Calculate the pH of a 0.800 mol dm^{-3} solution of the strong base potassium hydroxide at 298 K.

pH = ...

(3 marks)

When the temperature was increased to 373 K, the same solution
of potassium hydroxide was found to have a pH of 12.19.

2.4 Calculate the value of K_w for the solution at this higher temperature.

K_w = ... mol^2 dm^{-3}

(2 marks)

3 A student is conducting an experiment to investigate how pH changes during an acid-base reaction. They have been provided with 50 cm^3 of 1.0×10^{-5} mol dm^{-3} potassium hydroxide solution, 25 cm^3 of 1.0×10^{-5} mol dm^{-3} butanoic acid solution and a calibrated pH meter. Butanoic acid is a weak acid similar to ethanoic acid.

3.1 Explain why it is necessary to calibrate the pH meter before use.

....

....

(1 mark)

3.2 Describe the method that could be used by the student in their investigation.
Include all apparatus and relevant practical details in your answer.

....

....

....

....

....

....

....

....

....

....

....

(6 marks)

3.3 On the axes provided below, sketch the pH curve you would expect to be produced during the reaction.
Assume the equivalence point occurs after 25 cm^3 of potassium hydroxide solution has been added.

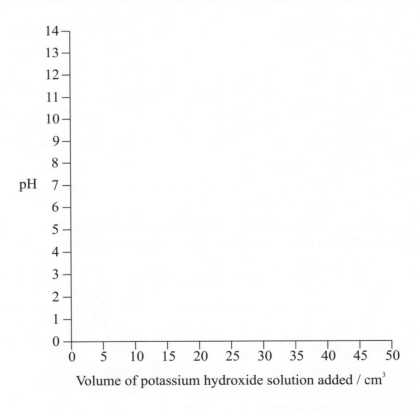

(3 marks)

Even if you're confident you know what you're doing, it's always a good idea to write out your working in full. That way if you do slip up and end up with the wrong numbers, the examiner will still be able to understand what you're trying to do and give you some marks for it. If you're worried any stage of your working is unclear, you can just add in a brief note to explain it.

Score

25

Acids, Bases and pH — 3

1   An acidic buffer solution was produced by adding a solution of propanoic acid containing 5.0×10^{-4} moles in a volume of 25 cm³ to a solution of sodium propanoate containing 5.0×10^{-3} moles in a volume of 25 cm³.

1.1   Write an equation for the dissociation of sodium propanoate.

....

(1 mark)

1.2   The K_a value for propanoic acid is 1.34×10^{-5} mol dm⁻³.
Calculate the pH of the acidic buffer solution produced.

pH = ...

(6 marks)

1.3   A small amount of dilute hydrochloric acid was added to the buffer solution.
State and explain the effect that this would have on the pH of the solution.

....

....

....

....

(3 marks)

1.4   Give **two** applications of buffer solutions in everyday life.

1. ....

2. ....

(2 marks)

2   The pH changes which occur during an acid-base titration can be measured and used to produce a pH curve.

Figure 1 shows a typical pH curve for a titration involving a strong acid and a weak base.

Figure 1

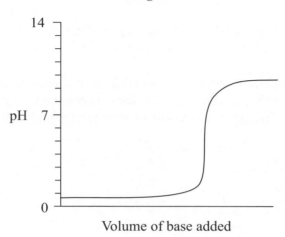

Indicators are chemicals which are used to detect the end point of an acid-base titration. Some commonly used indicators, along with their pH ranges and colours in acidic and basic solutions, are shown in **Table 1**.

Table 1

Indicator	Colour in acidic solution	Colour in basic solution	pH range
Methyl orange	Red	Yellow	3.10 - 4.40
Phenolphthalein	Colourless	Pink	8.30 - 10.00
Phenol red	Yellow	Red	6.80 - 8.20

2.1   Explain how a pH curve can be used to determine the most suitable indicator to use in an acid-base titration.

....

....

....

(2 marks)

2.2   Use **Figure 1** and the data provided in **Table 1** to select the most appropriate indicator to use in a strong acid/weak base titration. Give the colour change that would occur at the end point of the titration.

Indicator: ....

Colour change: ....

(1 mark)

2.3   Explain why an indicator cannot be used to determine the equivalence point in a titration between a weak acid and a weak base.

....

....

(1 mark)

The value of the acid dissociation constant, K_a, for a weak acid such as butanoic acid ($CH_3CH_2CH_2COOH$) can be determined from the pH curve produced during a reaction of the weak acid with a strong base.

2.4 Write an equation for the neutralisation reaction that occurs when butanoic acid is titrated with aqueous sodium hydroxide, NaOH.

....
(1 mark)

In a titration involving 0.0500 mol dm^{-3} butanoic acid and 0.0500 mol dm^{-3} sodium hydroxide, the equivalence point was reached after 25.0 cm^3 of the sodium hydroxide had been added.

2.5 At the half-neutralisation point, enough sodium hydroxide had been added to neutralise exactly half of the butanoic acid originally present. Calculate the concentrations of the acid and its salt at the half-neutralisation point. Give your answers to an appropriate number of significant figures.

Concentration of acid = ... mol dm^{-3}

Concentration of salt = ... mol dm^{-3}
(6 marks)

2.6 Write an expression for K_a for butanoic acid.

....
(1 mark)

The pH at the half-neutralisation point was 4.80.

2.7 Use this information and your answers to questions **2.5** and **2.6** to calculate the value of K_a for butanoic acid

K_a = ... mol dm^{-3}
(2 marks)

> **EXAM TIP**
> For questions involving K_a, it's always a good idea to start by writing out the expression for K_a for the acid you're interested in. That way you can see what data you have, what data you need, and how you need to rearrange the expression. You won't always just be given numbers to plug in, sometimes you might need to use the reaction equation to help you with your calculation.

Score

26

Inorganic Chemistry — 1

Have you heard the story of the student who stayed up all night practising inorganic chemistry? They found him wandering the streets at sunrise, blabbering about atomic radii. That's what you get for not taking periodic breaks.

For each of questions 1-5, give your answer by ticking the appropriate box.

1   Which of the following is the strongest oxidising agent?

  A F_2 ☐   **B** Cl_2 ☐

  C Br_2 ☐   **D** I_2 ☐

(1 mark)

2   Why do the melting points of the elements in Group 2 decrease going down the group?

  A   The strength of the metallic bonding increases.   ☐

  B   The number of delocalised electrons decreases.   ☐

  C   The attraction between the metal ions and the delocalised electrons decreases.   ☐

  D   The nuclear charge increases.   ☐

(1 mark)

3   Which of the following compounds contains elements
     from each of the s, p and d blocks of the periodic table?

  A $KAl(SO_4)_2$ ☐   **B** $CuCrO_4$ ☐

  C $KMnO_4$ ☐   **D** $Na_2B_4O_7$ ☐

(1 mark)

4   Which of the following electron arrangements is that of a d block element?

  A $1s^2\ 2s^2\ 2p^6\ 3s^2\ 3p^6\ 3d^{10}\ 4s^2\ 4p^5$ ☐

  B $1s^2\ 2s^2\ 2p^6\ 3s^2\ 3p^6\ 3d^8\ 4s^2$ ☐

  C $1s^2\ 2s^2\ 2p^6\ 3s^2\ 3p^6$ ☐

  D $1s^2\ 2s^2\ 2p^6\ 3s^2\ 3p^6\ 3d^{10}\ 4s^2\ 4p^6\ 5s^1$ ☐

(1 mark)

5   Which of the following statements about Group 2 elements is correct?

  A   The first ionisation energy increases going down the group.   ☐

  B   The second ionisation energy is less than the first ionisation energy.   ☐

  C   The first ionisation energy of a Group 2 element is greater
           than that of the Group 1 element in the same period.   ☐

  D   The first ionisation energy of a Group 2 element is less
           than that of the Group 3 element in the same period.   ☐

(1 mark)

74

6 The atomic radii of the Period 3 elements are shown in **Figure 1**.

Figure 1

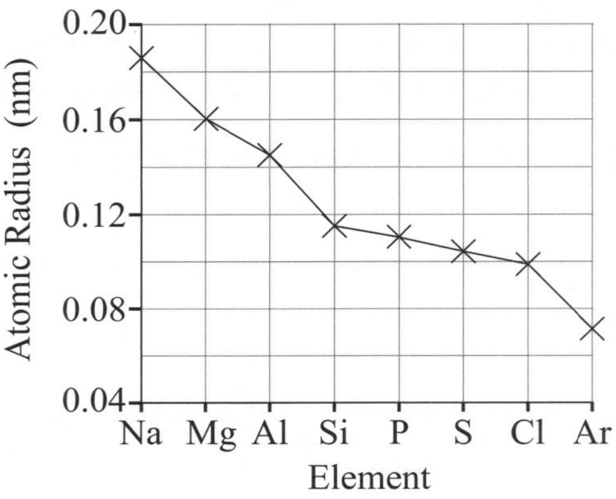

6.1 List all of the elements shown in **Figure 1** that are in the p block of the periodic table.

....

....
(1 mark)

6.2 Write the electron configuration of phosphorus, P.

....
(1 mark)

6.3 Explain the trend in atomic radii shown in **Figure 1**.

....

....

....

....
(3 marks)

7 Group 2 metals are in the s block of the periodic table.

7.1 Explain, with reference to their electron configurations, why Group 2 metals are classified as s block elements.

....
(1 mark)

7.2 State and explain the trend in the reactivity of Group 2 metals with water.

....

....
(2 mark)

7.3 Describe **one** similarity and **one** difference in the observations that you would expect to make when pieces of calcium and barium are added to water.

Similarity: ....

Difference: ....
(2 marks)

7.4 Equal molar amounts of strontium and calcium were added to two test tubes containing water. A reaction occurs. Which of the resulting solutions would have the highest pH? Explain your answer.

....

....
(2 marks)

7.5 Describe a test that could be used to confirm the presence of strontium ions in a solution of strontium chloride. In your answer include any observations that you would expect to make.

....

....

....

....

....

....

....

(5 marks)

8 A student has a two unlabelled bottles containing sodium carbonate and sodium sulfate solutions. He carries out a sulfate test on each solution by adding a few drops of barium chloride solution.

8.1 Identify **one** mistake that the student made when carrying out the sulfate test, and explain the effect that this mistake would have on the test.

....

....

....

(3 marks)

8.2 Describe a test that could have been used to confirm the presence of carbonate ions in the sodium carbonate solution.

....

....

....

(3 marks)

The student has a solution of sodium bromide. He carries out a test to confirm that the solution contains sodium bromide, and not sodium iodide. The first part of the test involved the formation of a silver halide.

8.3 Describe the test that the student used.

....

....

....

....

....

....

(5 marks)

9   There are trends in the properties of the halogens.

9.1   Explain why chlorine has a lower boiling point than iodine.

....

....

(2 marks)

9.2   State and explain the trend in the reducing ability of the halide ions.

....

....

....

(3 marks)

Halide ions can be oxidised in displacement reactions.

9.3   Describe briefly why chlorine is able to oxidise bromide ions, but iodine cannot.

....

....

(1 mark)

9.4   Write an ionic equation for the reaction of chlorine with a solution containing bromide ions.

....

(1 mark)

Group 1 metal halides can react with concentrated sulfuric acid to form hydrogen halides.

9.5   Write a balanced equation for the reaction of sodium fluoride with concentrated sulfuric acid.

....

(1 mark)

Some of the hydrogen halides produced during reactions like these can undergo further reactions with sulfuric acid. The products of these reactions depend on the reducing power of the halide. Some information about the products of the reactions of HBr and HI with sulfuric acid is shown in **Table 1**.

Table 1

Hydrogen halide	Reaction products
HBr	
HI	I_2, SO_2, H_2O, H_2S

9.6   Complete **Table 1** by filling in the products for the reaction of HBr with concentrated sulfuric acid.

(1 mark)

9.7   Write a balanced equation for the reaction of HI with concentrated sulfuric acid, where H_2S is the only sulfur-containing product.

....

(1 mark)

EXAM TIP — In the exam you might be asked to predict the properties of an element that you haven't come across before. For example, you could be given some information about the properties of some of the elements in Group 7, and asked to predict the properties of astatine. Knowing the trends down the group makes questions like this a lot easier — so make sure you learn 'em.

Score

43

Inorganic Chemistry — 2

1   The solubilities of some Group 2 compounds in water are shown in **Table 1**.

Table 1

Compound	Solubility
$Mg(NO_3)_2$	Soluble
$Mg(OH)_2$	Sparingly soluble
$MgSO_4$	Soluble
$Ba(NO_3)_2$	Soluble
$Ba(OH)_2$	Moderately soluble
$BaSO_4$	Insoluble
$Ca(OH)_2$	Slightly soluble

1.1   A student has an aqueous solution of $Ba(NO_3)_2$. He plans to carry out a reaction to show that $BaSO_4$ is insoluble in water. Suggest a reagent that the student could use, and write an ionic equation for the reaction.

Reagent: ....

Equation: ....

(2 marks)

1.2   Suggest what you would observe if solid $Mg(NO_3)_2$ was added to an aqueous solution with a pH of 10.

....

(1 mark)

1.3   Suggest how a pH meter could be used to show that $Ba(OH)_2$ is more soluble than $Ca(OH)_2$.

....

....

....

(3 marks)

Group 2 elements and their compounds have a wide range of applications.
Many of these uses depend on the solubility of the element or compound involved.

1.4   Describe how $BaSO_4$ is used in medical X-ray imaging.

....

....

....

(3 marks)

1.5   Name a Group 2 compound that is used to remove sulfur dioxide (SO_2) from flue gases in power stations. Write an overall symbol equation for the reaction between SO_2 and the compound you have named.

Compound: ....

Equation: ....

(2 marks)

1.6 Name a Group 2 metal or compound that is used for the following applications:

Antacid medicines: ....

Neutralising acidic soils: ....

Extracting titanium from $TiCl_4$: ....

(3 marks)

2   Compounds containing chlorine are often used to disinfect water.
     Some reactions of these compounds are shown in **Figure 1**.

Figure 1

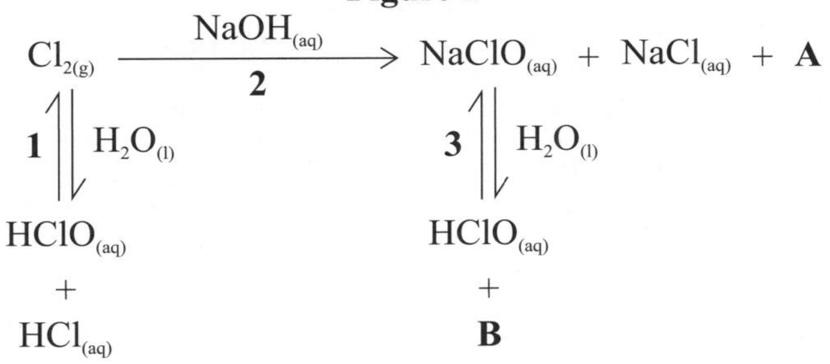

$$Cl_{2(g)} \xrightarrow[\textbf{2}]{NaOH_{(aq)}} NaClO_{(aq)} + NaCl_{(aq)} + \textbf{A}$$

$$\textbf{1} \Big\Updownarrow H_2O_{(l)} \qquad\qquad \textbf{3} \Big\Updownarrow H_2O_{(l)}$$

$HClO_{(aq)}$ $HClO_{(aq)}$

$+$ $+$

$HCl_{(aq)}$ **B**

2.1 Write balanced equations for reactions **2** and **3**.

Reaction 2: ....

Reaction 3: ....

(2 marks)

2.2 Write an ionic equation for reaction **1**.

....

(1 mark)

2.3 Which of the reactions in **Figure 1** form a mixture of products
in which chlorine is in more than one oxidation state?

....

(1 mark)

2.4 Explain why the use of chlorine to treat outdoor swimming pools may not be as efficient
as using solid sodium chlorate(I) (NaClO).

....

....

....

....

....

(4 marks)

2.5 Describe **two** disadvantages of using chlorine to treat public drinking water supplies.

1. ....

....

2. ....

....

(2 marks)

3   The trend in the melting points across Period 3 is shown in **Figure 2**.

Figure 2

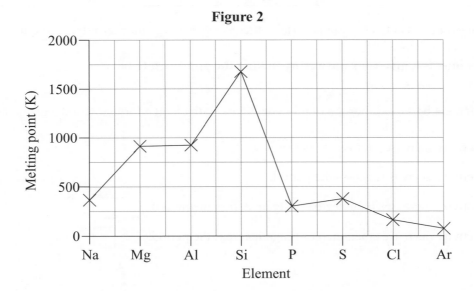

Describe and explain the patterns and variations in the melting points of the Period 3 elements shown in **Figure 2**. In your answer include ideas about the structure and bonding of the elements.

....

....

....

....

....

....

....

....

....

....

....

....

....

....

....

(6 marks)

If you're faced with a question in the exam asking you to explain the trends down a group or across a period, don't panic. Take your time to read the question carefully and make sure you understand what it's asking — you don't want to start talking about the boiling points in Group 7 when you've been asked to describe the melting points in Group 2...

Score

30

More Inorganic Chemistry — 1

They think it's all over... it's not yet. Yes that's right, there's *more* inorganic chemistry, and quite a lot of it...

For each of questions 1-4, give your answer by ticking the appropriate box.

1   Which statement best describes the trend in reactivity with oxygen for the Period 3 elements Na-S?

   A   Reactivity increases across the period.

   B   Reactivity decreases across the period.

   C   Reactivity increases then decreases again across the period.

   D   Reactivity decreases then increases again across the period.

   (1 mark)

2   Aqueous Fe^{3+} ions are reacted with an excess of aqueous sodium hydroxide. What is the product formed?

   A $[Fe(OH)_6]^{3-}$

   B $Fe(OH)_3(H_2O)_3$

   C $[Fe(OH)_4(H_2O)_2]^-$

   D $[Fe(OH)_4]^{3-}$

   (1 mark)

3   **Table 1** shows some electron configurations. Which row or rows of **Table 1** are correct?

Table 1

	Species	Electron configuration
1	Cu	$1s^2\ 2s^2\ 2p^6\ 3s^2\ 3p^6\ 3d^9\ 4s^2$
2	Cr	$1s^2\ 2s^2\ 2p^6\ 3s^2\ 3p^6\ 3d^5\ 4s^1$
3	Mn^{2+}	$1s^2\ 2s^2\ 2p^6\ 3s^2\ 3p^6\ 3d^5$

   A   1 and 3 only   **B**   2 only

   C   2 and 3 only   **D**   1, 2 and 3

   (1 mark)

4   VO_2^+ ions can be reduced to V^{2+} using zinc metal in solution. In addition to VO_2^+, how many coloured vanadium species are produced over the course of the reduction reaction?

   A   One   **B**   Two

   C   Three   **D**   Four

   (1 mark)

5   Transition metals such as cobalt are capable of forming a wide range of complex ions.

5.1 State the full electron configurations of cobalt and zinc.
     Use the electron configurations to explain why cobalt is regarded as a transition metal but zinc is not.

     ....

     ....

     ....

     ....
                                                                                                            (4 marks)

5.2 Give the name of the type of bonding responsible for the formation of transition metal complexes.

     ....
                                                                                                            (1 mark)

5.3 State the meaning of the term ligand.

     ....

     ....
                                                                                                            (1 mark)

5.4 Draw a diagram to show the three-dimensional shape of $[CoCl_4]^{2-}$. Label the bond angle(s) in your diagram.

                                                                                                            (2 marks)

     In aqueous solution, $[CoCl_4]^{2-}$ ions exist in equilibrium with $[Co(H_2O)_6]^{2+}$ ions.

5.5 Write an equation for this equilibrium reaction.

     ....
                                                                                                            (1 mark)

5.6 Explain how differences between the ligands in this reaction lead to a change in both
     the co-ordination number and the total oxidation state of the complex ion.

     ....

     ....

     ....

     ....
                                                                                                            (2 marks)

5.7 State a ligand which can substitute with the water in $[Co(H_2O)_6]^{2+}$ without causing
     a change in the co-ordination number or the total oxidation state.

     ....
                                                                                                            (1 mark)

5.8 Co^{2+} ions can also form the complex $[Co(EDTA)]^{2-}$, which is much more stable than $[Co(H_2O)_6]^{2+}$. State the name given to the effect which produces this increase in stability.

....

(1 mark)

6 **Figure 1** shows the melting points of four of the first five Period 3 oxides.

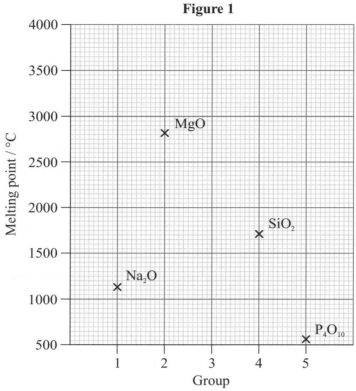

6.1 Complete **Figure 1** by plotting the approximate melting point of Al_2O_3.

(1 mark)

6.2 Explain why MgO has a higher melting point than Na_2O.

....

....

(2 marks)

6.3 Explain why SiO_2 and P_4O_{10} have very different melting points, despite both substances being covalently bonded.

....

....

....

....

....

(4 marks)

There's less new information than you might think in this section — you just need to think about stuff you already know in slightly different ways. Everything you learnt about structure and bonding back in Year 1 comes in really handy, as do electron configurations, redox reactions, isomerism... Pull all that together, and you'll be writing some really fantastic exam answers.

Score

24

More Inorganic Chemistry — 2

1 A student is investigating copper complex ions. Starting with a sample of solid copper(II) sulfate, they carry out the series of reactions shown in **Figure 1**.

Figure 1

$CuSO_{4(s)} \xrightarrow{\text{excess of water}}$ pale blue solution **A** $\xrightarrow{\text{conc. HCl}} [CuCl_4]^{2-}_{(aq)} \xrightarrow{\text{heat with Cu metal}} [CuCl_4]^{3-}_{(aq)}$

1.1 Give the formula of the copper complex present in solution **A**.
State the shape of the complex.

Formula: ....

Shape: ....

(2 marks)

1.2 Give the oxidation state of Cu in $[CuCl_4]^{3-}_{(aq)}$.

....

(1 mark)

1.3 Suggest the role played by copper metal in the reaction to form $[CuCl_4]^{3-}_{(aq)}$ from $[CuCl_4]^{2-}_{(aq)}$.

....

(1 mark)

1.4 The solution of $[CuCl_4]^{2-}_{(aq)}$ ions is yellow. Explain why different copper complexes produce differently coloured solutions.

....

....

....

....

....

....

(3 marks)

2 MgO, SO_2, P_4O_{10} and Al_2O_3 are all oxides of Period 3 elements.

2.1 Explain, in terms of its structure and bonding, why MgO has a high melting point.

....

....

....

....

(3 marks)

2.2 A sample of MgO reacts with water to form a solution with pH 9. Write an equation for this reaction.

....
(1 mark)

2.3 Explain why the solution formed in question 2.2 is only weakly alkaline.

....

....
(2 marks)

2.4 MgO can be formed by the reaction of magnesium metal with steam.
Write a equation for this reaction. Include state symbols in your answer.

....
(2 marks)

2.5 State the products formed when magnesium metal reacts with cold water.

....
(1 mark)

2.6 SO_2 is a colourless gas at room temperature. State the type of structure SO_2 has.

....
(1 mark)

2.7 A sample of SO_2 reacts with water to give a solution with pH 2. Write an equation for this reaction.
Write a second equation to show how the solution behaves as an acid.
Include state symbols in your equations.

....

....
(2 marks)

2.8 Sulfur has a second oxide, SO_3. Give the equation for the reaction to form
SO_3 from SO_2 and identify the catalyst used for this reaction in industry.

Equation: ....

Catalyst: ....
(2 marks)

2.9 Write an equation for the reaction of P_4O_{10} with aqueous sodium hydroxide.
State the type of reaction occurring.

Equation: ....

Type of reaction: ....
(2 marks)

2.10 Al_2O_3 is insoluble in water but dissolves in both aqueous sodium hydroxide and aqueous sulfuric acid.
Give the name used to describe this behaviour of the oxide.

....
(1 mark)

2.11 Write equations for the reactions of Al_2O_3 with sodium hydroxide and with sulfuric acid.

....

....
(2 marks)

3 Iron is a transition metal that has two stable ions, Fe^{2+} and Fe^{3+}. In aqueous solution, they become hydrated to form the complex ions $[Fe(H_2O)_6]^{2+}$ and $[Fe(H_2O)_6]^{3+}$.

3.1 State the full electron configuration of an Fe^{2+} ion.

....

(1 mark)

3.2 State whether a solution containing $[Fe(H_2O)_6]^{3+}$ ions has a higher or lower pH than a solution containing an equal concentration of $[Fe(H_2O)_6]^{2+}$ ions. Justify your answer.

....

....

....

(3 marks)

3.3 State what you would observe when ammonia is added to a solution containing $[Fe(H_2O)_6]^{2+}$ ions and to a solution containing $[Fe(H_2O)_6]^{3+}$ ions. Give the formula of the iron-containing species formed in each case.

$[Fe(H_2O)_6]^{2+}$: ....

....

$[Fe(H_2O)_6]^{3+}$: ....

....

(4 marks)

3.4 $[Fe(H_2O)_6]^{2+}$ ions will oxidise to $[Fe(H_2O)_6]^{3+}$ if left in contact with air. Suggest **one** way of ensuring that accurate observations of the reaction of $[Fe(H_2O)_6]^{2+}$ with ammonia can be made.

....

....

(1 mark)

If a solution containing ethanedioate ions ($C_2O_4^{2-}$) is added to a solution containing $[Fe(H_2O)_6]^{3+}$, a ligand substitution reaction occurs to form the complex ion $[Fe(C_2O_4)_3]^{3-}$.

3.5 Write an equation for this ligand substitution reaction.

....

(1 mark)

3.6 Describe how the ethanedioate ion acts as a bidentate ligand.

....

....

(1 mark)

3.7 This ligand substitution reaction is reversible, but the equilibrium lies so far to the right that it is often thought of as irreversible. Explain why the equilibrium strongly favours the formation of $[Fe(C_2O_4)_3]^{3-}$.

....

....

....

(2 marks)

Haemoglobin contains Fe^{2+} ions. The Fe^{2+} ion forms a complex ion with 6 co-ordinate bonds.

3.8 Outline how this complex ion is involved in the transport of oxygen in the body.

....

....

....

(2 marks)

3.9 Explain why carbon monoxide is toxic when inhaled.

....

....

....

(2 marks)

4   Fe^{2+} ions are oxidised by $Cr_2O_7^{2-}$ ions according to the equation:

$$6Fe^{2+} + Cr_2O_7^{2-} + 14H^+ \rightarrow 6Fe^{3+} + 2Cr^{3+} + 7H_2O$$

A 2.00 g sample of iron tablets containing Fe^{2+} was dissolved in excess dilute sulfuric acid and the solution made up to 250 cm^3 in a volumetric flask. 25.0 cm^3 of this solution was pipetted into a conical flask and titrated against a 0.0200 mol dm^{-3} solution of acidified potassium dichromate(VI). 23.85 cm^3 of the potassium dichromate(VI) solution was required for complete oxidation.

Calculate the percentage of iron in the iron tablets.
Give your answer to an appropriate number of significant figures.

Percentage of iron = ...%

(6 marks)

Score

49

More Inorganic Chemistry — 3

1   Metal ions in solution react in characteristic ways with some common reagents.

1.1   Explain how an aqueous solution of Cu^{2+} ions could be used to determine the identities of three unlabelled samples of the bases $NH_{3(aq)}$, $NaOH_{(aq)}$ and $Na_2CO_{3(aq)}$.

....

....

....

....

....

(4 marks)

1.2   Describe what you would observe as aqueous NaOH is added dropwise to an aqueous solution of Al^{3+} ions until the NaOH is in excess. Write equations for the reactions that lead to these observations.

....

....

....

....

....

(4 marks)

2   The catalyst used in the Haber Process is described as heterogeneous.

2.1   Identify this catalyst.

....

(1 mark)

2.2   State what is meant by the term 'heterogeneous', when describing a catalyst.

....

(1 mark)

2.3   State what is meant by the term 'active sites' when applied to a catalyst.

....

....

(1 mark)

2.4   Explain how heterogeneous catalysts may be poisoned by impurities in the reactants.

....

....

....

(2 marks)

2.5 Explain how catalyst poisoning can increase the cost of a chemical process.

....

....

(1 mark)

The reaction between peroxodisulfate and iodide ions is catalysed by Fe^{2+} ions which act as a homogeneous catalyst. The equation for the uncatalysed reaction is:

$$S_2O_8^{2-} + 2I^- \rightarrow 2SO_4^{2-} + I_2$$

2.6 Suggest why this reaction has a high activation energy, making it slow in the absence of a catalyst.

....

....

(1 mark)

2.7 Write equations to show how Fe^{2+} ions are able to catalyse this reaction.

....

....

(2 marks)

3   The half-equation for the reduction of acidified potassium manganate(VII) is:
$$MnO_4^- + 8H^+ + 5e^- \rightarrow Mn^{2+} + 4H_2O$$

Acidified potassium manganate(VII), $KMnO_{4(aq)}$, can oxidise 2+ ions of a particular metal, **X**, in aqueous solution. A 25.0 cm³ sample of a 0.160 mol dm⁻³ solution of X^{2+} was titrated against a 0.0300 mol dm⁻³ solution of acidified potassium manganate(VII). 26.7 cm³ of the potassium manganate(VII) solution was required for complete oxidation.

Determine the oxidation state of the metal **X** following the oxidation reaction.

Oxidation state = ...

(5 marks)

More Inorganic Chemistry — 4

1 Cisplatin is a complex with the formula $Pt(NH_3)_2Cl_2$ that is used as an anti-cancer drug. Only the cis isomer will inhibit cell division.

1.1 Draw a diagram to show the trans isomer of $Pt(NH_3)_2Cl_2$.

(1 mark)

1.2 Another platinum complex which has been investigated for anti-cancer properties has the formula $PtCl_4(NH_3)_2$. This also exists as two isomers. Draw the three-dimensional structures of both isomers below and label each as cis or trans.

(3 marks)

1.3 The NH_3 ligands in cisplatin can be substituted for the ligand $NH_2CH_2CH_2NH_2$. Write an equation for this reaction.

....

(1 mark)

2 In the ligand substitution reaction shown below, a colour change is observed. The initial solution is pink, then turns purple as concentrated HCl is added, then turns blue in excess HCl indicating the formation of the complex ion $[CoCl_4]^{2-}$.

$$[Co(H_2O)_6]^{2+} + 4Cl^- \rightleftharpoons [CoCl_4]^{2-} + 6H_2O$$

2.1 Explain, with reference to the visible light spectrum, why the solution of $[CoCl_4]^{2-}$ appears blue in colour.

....

....

....

(2 marks)

2.2 Name a piece of apparatus that can be used to determine the concentration of a solution of coloured ions such as $[CoCl_4]^{2-}$ by measuring its absorption of light.

....

(1 mark)

Table 1 shows the standard redox potentials for Co^{2+} and Cu^{2+} ions.

Table 1

Half-equation	Standard redox potential / V
$Co^{2+} + 2e^- \rightleftharpoons Co$	−0.28
$Cu^{2+} + 2e^- \rightleftharpoons Cu$	+0.34

2.3 State and explain how the information in the table tells you which of these ions is less stable.

....

(1 mark)

2.4 A student carries out an experiment to measure the redox potential of Co^{2+} ions.
They use a solution of $[CoCl_4]^{2-}$ in their experiment. Explain why the student's result
is different to the value for the redox potential of Co^{2+} shown in **Table 1**.

....

....

(2 marks)

2.5 The Cu^{2+} ions in a $CuSO_4$ solution form $[Cu(H_2O)_6]^{2+}$ complex ions. $[Cu(H_2O)_6]^{2+}$ ions strongly absorb
visible light at a wavelength of 670 nm. Use this information to calculate a value for the energy gap,
ΔE, in $[Cu(H_2O)_6]^{2+}$ ions. Give your answer to an appropriate number of significant figures.
($h = 6.63 \times 10^{-34}$ J s, $c = 3.00 \times 10^8$ m s^{-1})

$\Delta E =$ .... J

(3 marks)

Adding sodium hydroxide and ammonia to silver nitrate solution results in the formation
of Tollens' reagent, a colourless solution containing the complex ion $[Ag(NH_3)_2]^+$.

2.6 Identify the shape of this silver-containing complex.

....

(1 mark)

2.7 Suggest why Tollens' reagent is colourless.

....

....

....

(2 marks)

2.8 Describe the reaction of Tollens' reagent with aldehydes.
Explain how this reaction can be used to distinguish between aldehydes and ketones.

....

....

....

....

(2 marks)

3 Hydrated ethanedioic acid has the formula $C_2O_4H_2.xH_2O$, meaning that for every 1 mole of $C_2O_4H_2$ present in a sample, there are x moles of H_2O. The value of x can be determined by reacting a solution of $C_2O_4H_2.xH_2O$ with acidified potassium manganate(VII) solution. The equation for this reaction is:

$$5C_2O_4^{2-} + 2MnO_4^- + 16H^+ \rightarrow 10CO_2 + 2Mn^{2+} + 8H_2O$$

3.1 A 1.20 g sample of solid hydrated ethanedioic acid is dissolved in sulfuric acid and the solution made up to 250 cm³ with distilled water in a volumetric flask. 25.0 cm³ samples are taken from this solution and titrated against 0.0200 mol dm⁻³ $KMnO_4$ solution. An average of 19.10 cm³ of $KMnO_4$ solution is required to reach the equivalence point of the titration.

Determine the value of x in the formula $C_2O_4H_2.xH_2O$.

$x =$ ....

(6 marks)

3.2 This reaction is an autocatalysis reaction. Explain how this affects the rate of reaction over time. You should include an explanation of the initial rate of reaction and write equations to illustrate your answer.

....

....

....

....

....

....

(4 marks)

EXAM TIP

If you're unsure how to approach a calculation question, think about the data you've been given, and the kind of calculations you would usually use that data for. Even if you don't get to the end of the question, you might pick up some marks for making a start, or it might just become more obvious what you need to do next.

Score

29

The Basics of Organic Chemistry — 1

Organic chemistry is pretty tricky, but fear not — this section covers all the basics. Have a go at these questions, and you'll be a master of organic chemistry faster than you can say "smashed avocado with a side of chia seeds".

1 A student measured the time taken for a precipitate to form when a solution of silver nitrate was added to test tubes containing equal volumes and concentrations of 1-chlorobutane, 1-iodobutane and 1-bromobutane dissolved in ethanol. Her results are shown in **Table 1**.

Table 1

Halogenoalkane	Time taken for precipitate to form / s
1-chlorobutane	588
1-iodobutane	
1-bromobutane	88

Predict how long it took for a precipitate to form in the test tube containing 1-iodobutane.

A	330 seconds	☐	**B**	50 seconds	☐
C	120 seconds	☐	**D**	810 seconds	☐

(1 mark)

2 What is the molecular formula of an alkane that contains 16 hydrogen atoms per molecule?

A	C_4H_8	☐	**B**	C_5H_8	☐
C	C_7H_{16}	☐	**D**	C_8H_{16}	☐

(1 mark)

3 The structures of four alkenes are shown in **Figure 1**.

Figure 1

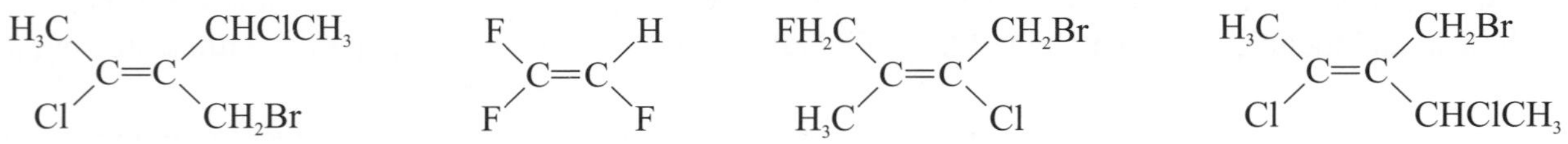

Which of the alkenes in **Figure 1** is a Z isomer?

A	M	☐	**B**	N	☐
C	O	☐	**D**	P	☐

(1 mark)

4 Which of the following molecules does **not** exhibit E/Z stereoisomerism?

A	3-methylpent-2-ene	☐	**B**	2-methylbut-2-ene	☐
C	3-methylhex-2-ene	☐	**D**	3-methylhex-3-ene	☐

(1 mark)

5 Hex-1-ene is a hydrocarbon with the molecular formula C_6H_{12}.
Four isomers of hex-1-ene are shown in **Table 2**.

Table 2

Isomer	Displayed formula	IUPAC name
A	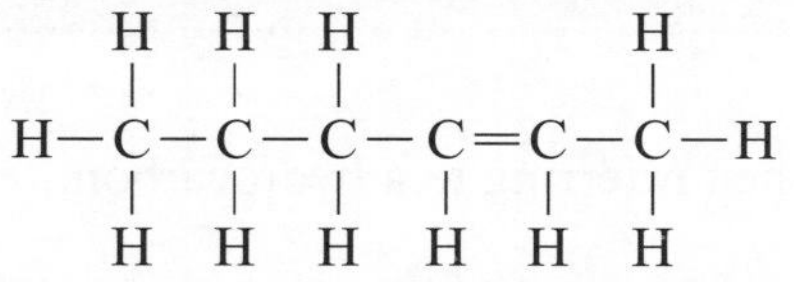 H—C—C—C—C=C—C—H (with H atoms)	hex-2-ene
B	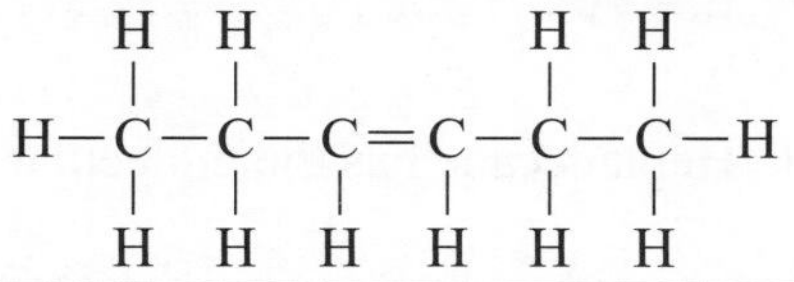 H—C—C—C=C—C—C—H (with H atoms)	hex-3-ene
C		2,3-dimethylbut-1-ene
D	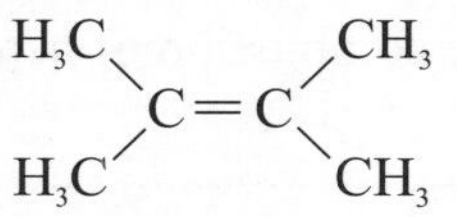 H_3C, H_3C \C=C/ CH_3, CH_3	

5.1 Write the letter of an isomer in **Table 2** that is a position isomer of hex-1-ene.

....
(1 mark)

5.2 Draw the displayed formula of isomer **C**.

(1 mark)

5.3 Write the IUPAC name of isomer **D**.

....
(1 mark)

5.4 Draw the skeletal formula of a functional group isomer of hex-1-ene.

(1 mark)

6   Crude oil fractions contain saturated hydrocarbons belonging to the alkane homologous series.

6.1   State **two** features of a homologous series.

....

....

(2 marks)

6.2   State what is meant by the term 'saturated' when referring to a hydrocarbon.

....

(1 mark)

Heptadecane is an alkane present in crude oil. Heptadecane has the molecular formula $C_{17}H_{36}$.

6.3   State what is meant by the term molecular formula.

....

(1 mark)

6.4   Give the balanced symbol equation for the complete combustion of heptadecane.

....

(1 mark)

6.5   Name the solid pollutant that may be formed during the incomplete combustion of heptadecane.

....

(1 mark)

Heptadecane can be cracked to form more useful products. Octane (C_8H_{18}) is produced during this process.

6.6   Write a balanced equation to show the thermal cracking of heptadecane to form
one molecule each of octane and butene, and one other alkene only.

....

(1 mark)

Catalytic cracking is another process used to decompose long chain alkanes.

6.7   State the conditions used in catalytic cracking.

....

(2 marks)

6.8   Suggest **two** reasons why catalytic cracking is less expensive to carry out than thermal cracking.

1. ....

....

2. ....

....

(2 marks)

EXAM TIP   There are quite a few definitions to learn in chemistry, but it's definitely worth memorising them.
If you know your stuff, you'll be able to answer any questions that ask you for definitions
quickly and easily in your exams. That will give you more time to answer the trickier questions.

Score

19

The Basics of Organic Chemistry — 2

1   1,2-dichlorobut-1-ene ($C_4H_6Cl_2$) exists as a pair of stereoisomers.

1.1   Draw the Z isomer of 1,2-dichlorobut-1-ene.

(1 mark)

1.2   Explain why 1,2-dichlorobut-1-ene can exhibit E/Z stereoisomerism.

....

....

....

(2 marks)

1.3   Draw and name an isomer of $C_4H_6Cl_2$, other than 1,2-dichlorobut-1-ene, which exhibits E/Z stereoisomerism. Your answer only needs to show the structure of **one** of the possible stereoisomers.

Name: ....

(2 marks)

1.4   Name an isomer of $C_4H_6Cl_2$ which is an alkene that does **not** exhibit E/Z stereoisomerism.

....

(1 mark)

2   Pentane is a hydrocarbon found in the petrol fraction of crude oil.
     When pentane burns in a limited supply of oxygen, incomplete combustion takes place.

2.1   Write a balanced equation for the incomplete combustion of pentane
     to produce a poisonous gas and one other product.

....

(1 mark)

2.2   State how car exhausts are adapted to remove the poisonous gas from exhaust gases.

....

(1 mark)

2.3 Sulfur dioxide is a gaseous pollutant that may be found in the gases released by cars and power stations. Give **one** reason why sulfur dioxide may be present.

....

....

(2 marks)

2.4 Explain how sulfur dioxide gas can be removed from power station flue gases using calcium carbonate.

....

....

....

(3 marks)

3 Describe how propene can be produced from crude oil by fractional distillation and thermal cracking. Include in your answer an example equation showing decane ($C_{10}H_{22}$) being cracked to produce propene.

....

....

....

....

....

....

....

....

....

....

....

....

....

....

....

(6 marks)

When you're faced with a question that asks you to describe a process, tackle it methodically. It's a good idea to spend a moment jotting down what you want to cover and in what order. That way, your answer will be well structured and you're less likely to forget important pieces of information. (Cross out your plan afterwards though, so the examiner knows not to mark it.)

Score

19

The Basics of Organic Chemistry — 3

1   1-chloropropane ($CH_3CH_2CH_2Cl$) can react in a nucleophilic substitution reaction with ethanolic ammonia (NH_3) to form the primary amine propylamine.

   1.1   Explain why 1-chloropropane reacts with a solution of ethanolic ammonia but propane does not.

   ....

   ....
                                                                                                    (2 marks)

   1.2   State what is meant by the term 'nucleophile'.

   ....
                                                                                                    (1 mark)

   1.3   Draw the mechanism for the reaction of 1-chloropropane with ethanolic ammonia to form propylamine. Write a balanced symbol equation for the reaction.

   Equation: ....
                                                                                                    (6 marks)

   1.4   Explain why a mixture of products containing different numbers of carbon atoms might form in the reaction.

   ....

   ....
                                                                                                    (1 mark)

   1.5   Explain how the rate of reaction would be different if the reaction was carried under the same conditions but 1-fluoropropane was used instead of 1-chloropropane.

   ....

   ....
                                                                                                    (2 marks)

2   Trichloromethane ($CHCl_3$) can be formed by the reaction of dichloromethane (CH_2Cl_2) with chlorine (Cl_2) in a free radical substitution reaction involving chlorine free radicals.

   2.1   State the condition required for the reaction to start.

   ....
                                                                                                    (1 mark)

98

2.2 Write equations to show each step in the reaction mechanism.
Include the name of each step in your answer.

....

....

....

....

....

....

....

....

(7 marks)

2.3 Write an equation to show why tetrachloroethane ($C_2H_2Cl_4$) might be found in the reaction mixture.

....

(1 mark)

2.4 The breakdown of ozone, O_3, in the upper atmosphere is catalysed by chlorine free radicals.

Write equations to show how chlorine free radicals catalyse the breakdown of ozone to form oxygen, O_2.
In your answer you should include an overall equation for the reaction and an explanation of why
chlorine radicals are described as a catalyst for this reaction.

....

....

....

....

....

(4 marks)

3 When 2-bromobutane is heated with potassium hydroxide, KOH, under certain conditions
an elimination reaction occurs. But-1-ene is one possible product of this reaction.

3.1 Draw the mechanism for the reaction of 2-bromobutane with potassium hydroxide to produce but-1-ene.

(4 marks)

Unit 3 : Section 1 — The Basics of Organic Chemistry

3.2 State the role of OH⁻ in this reaction.

....

(1 mark)

3.3 State the conditions, other than heating under reflux, that are required for this reaction to take place.

....

(1 mark)

3.4 Another possible product of this reaction is an alkene that exists as a pair of stereoisomers. Explain what is meant by the term 'stereoisomers'.

....

....

(2 marks)

3.5 Draw **one** of the stereoisomers of this alkene.

(1 mark)

3.6 2-bromobutane can also react with KOH when heated to produce an alcohol. Name the mechanism of this reaction and state the required reaction conditions, other than heating under reflux.

Mechanism: ....

Conditions: ....

(2 marks)

4 A possible two-step synthesis of an organic molecule, **B**, is shown in **Figure 1**.

Figure 1

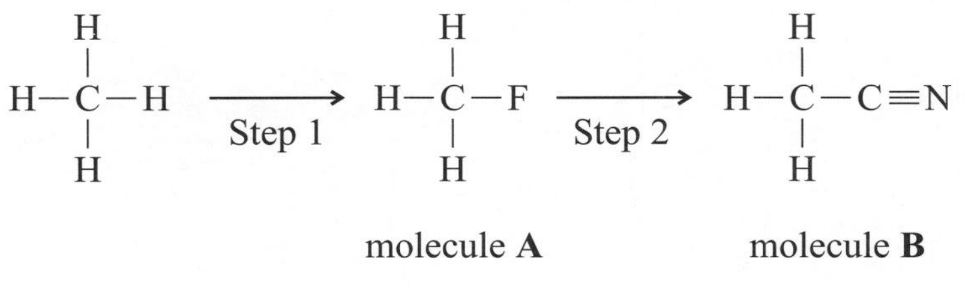

4.1 Give the name of the mechanism occurring in **step 1**.

....

(1 mark)

4.2 Write the IUPAC name of molecule **A**.

....

(1 mark)

4.3 Suggest the reagents and conditions needed for **step 2**.

....

....

(3 marks)

4.4 Draw and name the mechanism occurring in **step 2**.

Name of mechanism: ....

(3 marks)

5 Diethylamine, $(CH_3CH_2)_2NH$, can be synthesised using ethylamine and a bromoalkane. Ethylamine reacts with bromoalkanes in a similar way to ammonia reacting with bromoalkanes. The skeletal formula of diethylamine is shown in **Figure 2**, below.

Figure 2

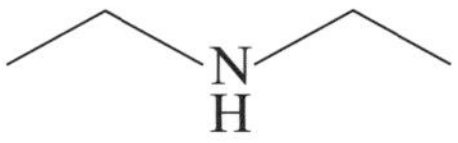

Suggest the reagents and conditions needed for the synthesis of diethylamine from ethylamine and a bromoalkane. Draw the mechanism for the reaction.

Reagents and conditions: ....

....

Mechanism:

(8 marks)

EXAM TIP

Don't panic if you're faced with drawing the mechanism for the reaction of an unfamiliar compound. Start by having a good look at the structure of the molecule — the functional group that it has should let you figure out what kind of mechanism you should be drawing.

Score

52

Alkenes and Alcohols — 1

Be warned, there are more organic molecules in this section than you can shake a stick at. But please note that the mechanism for the reaction when you shake a stick at an alkene and an alcohol isn't on the A-level syllabus.

For each of questions 1-4, give your answer by ticking the appropriate box.

1 Which of the following methods would **not** produce ethanol?

A Fermentation of a sugar ☐

B Hydrating ethene in the presence of an acid catalyst ☐

C Heating ethanal with acidified potassium dichromate ☐

D Reacting ethene with cold concentrated sulfuric acid, followed by hydrolysis ☐

(1 mark)

2 Which of the following species is **not** an example of an electrophile?

A H^+ ☐   B H_2O ☐   C HCl ☐   D NH_3 ☐

(1 mark)

3 Which of the following structures shows an alcohol which can be oxidised but not dehydrated?

A   H—C—C—C—OH ☐   B   H—C—C—C—C—H ☐

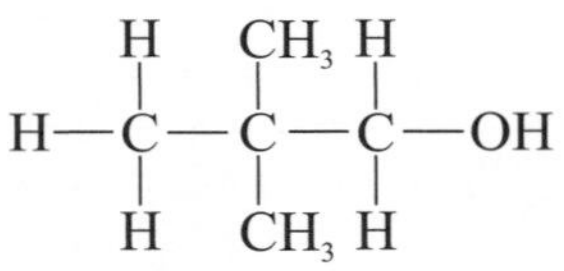

C   H—C—C—C—H ☐   D   H—C—C—C—C—H ☐

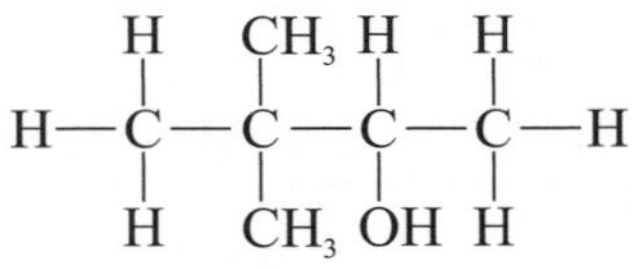

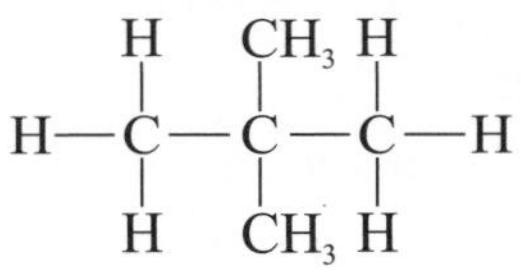

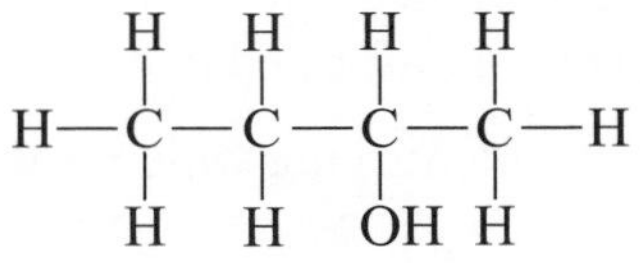

(1 mark)

4 The molecule shown below is reacted with hydrogen bromide.

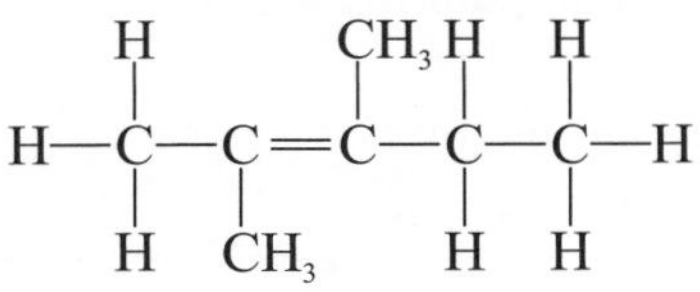

H—C—C=C—C—C—H

Which of the following are the most likely products of this reaction?

A 4-bromo-3,4-dimethylpentane and 3-bromo-3,4-dimethylpentane ☐

B 3-bromo-2,3-dimethylpentane and 2-bromo-2,3-dimethylpentane ☐

C 3-bromo-2-methylpentane and 2-bromo-2-methylpentane ☐

D 2-bromo-3,4-dimethylpentane and 3-bromo-2,3-dimethylpentane ☐

(1 mark)

5 Isoamylene can be formed by the dehydration of a tertiary alcohol, **A**, using an acid catalyst. This reaction produces a mixture containing isoamylene and another alkene, **B**. The synthesis of isoamylene and alkene **B** from alcohol **A** is shown in **Figure 1**.

Figure 1

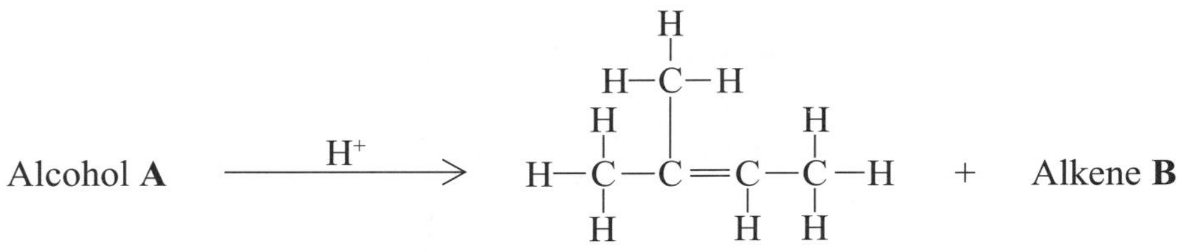

Alcohol **A** $\xrightarrow{\text{H}^+}$

isoamylene

+ Alkene **B**

5.1 Give the IUPAC name of isoamylene.

....
(1 mark)

5.2 Draw the structures of alcohol **A** and alkene **B**, and give their names.

Structure of A: Structure of B:

Name of A: ....   Name of B: ....
(4 marks)

Isoamylene reacts with hydrogen chloride. Two products are formed during the reaction. The two products are not formed in equal quantities.

5.3 Name the products, identifying which is the major product and which is the minor product.

Major product: ....

Minor product: ....
(2 marks)

5.4 Explain why the products of the reaction between isoamylene and hydrogen chloride are not produced in equal quantities.

....

....

....

....
(3 marks)

Alkenes and Alcohols — 2

1   The apparatus shown in **Figure 1** can be used to oxidise an alcohol to an aldehyde.

Figure 1

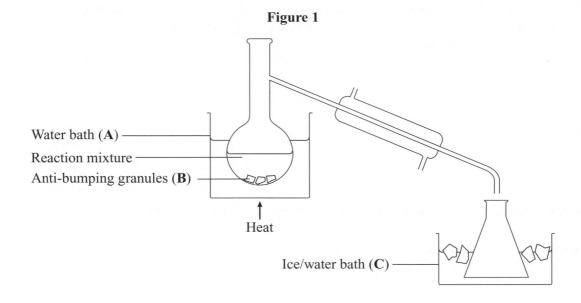

Water bath (**A**)
Reaction mixture
Anti-bumping granules (**B**)
Heat
Ice/water bath (**C**)

1.1   The reaction mixture contains ethanol, sulfuric acid and an oxidising agent.
      Suggest a suitable oxidising agent for this reaction.

      ....
                                                                                                        (1 mark)

1.2   Identify the method shown in **Figure 1** and explain how it allows a pure sample of an aldehyde
      to be prepared from an alcohol.

      ....

      ....
                                                                                                        (2 marks)

1.3   Suggest the purpose of the parts of the practical set up labelled **A** to **C**.

      A ....

      B ....

      C ....
                                                                                                        (3 marks)

1.4   Describe and give reasons for any changes in the set-up that would allow the alcohol
      to be oxidised to a carboxylic acid.

      ....

      ....

      ....

      ....
                                                                                                        (4 marks)

1.5 Write an equation to show how methanol is oxidised to methanoic acid.
You should represent the oxidising agent as [O] in your answer.

....
(1 mark)

1.6 A student tried to distinguish between methanal and methanoic acid using Tollens' reagent,
but found that both compounds produced a silver mirror. By reference to the structure of
methanoic acid shown below, suggest a reason why it gave a positive result with Tollens' reagent.

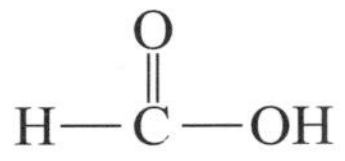

$$H-\overset{\overset{\displaystyle O}{\|}}{C}-OH$$

....
(1 mark)

2 Addition polymers can be formed from alkenes in polymerisation reactions.

2.1 Explain what is meant by the term polymerisation.

....

....
(2 marks)

2.2 Describe briefly the process by which alkenes form addition polymers.

....

....
(2 marks)

The structures of low density poly(ethene) (LDPE) and high density poly(ethene) (HDPE) are shown in
Figure 2. LDPE is used to make plastic food wrap, whereas HDPE is used in plastic storage boxes.

Figure 2

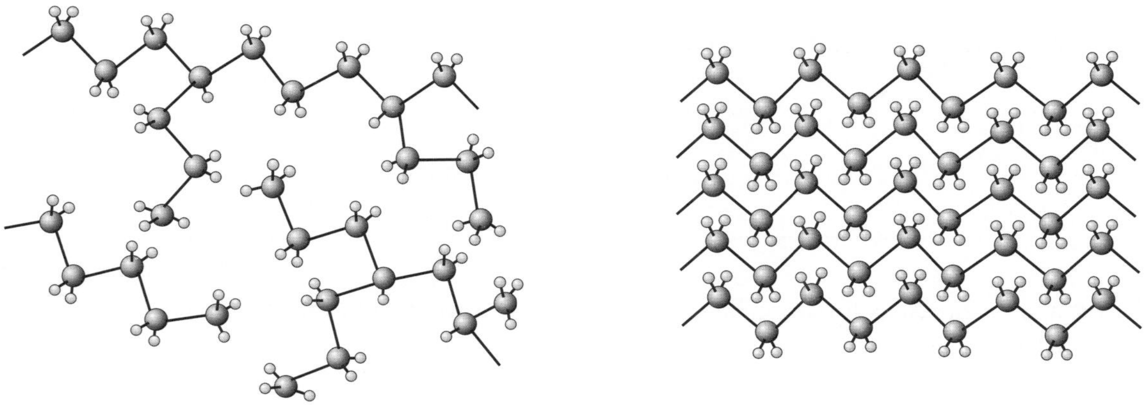

LDPE   **HDPE**

2.3 Explain how the structures of these polymers give rise to the properties that make them suitable for each use.

....

....
(2 marks)

2.4 Suggest **two** reasons why both LDPE and HDPE are unreactive.

....

....

(2 marks)

2.5 A section of a polymer is shown in **Figure 3**.

Figure 3

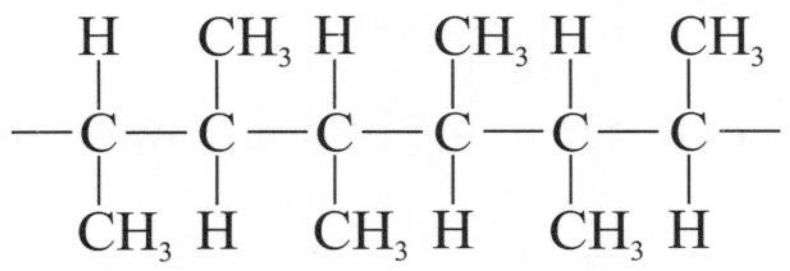

Draw and name the monomer used to form the polymer shown in **Figure 3**.

Name: ....

(2 marks)

Styrene acrylonitrile resin (SAN) is a copolymer, used in place of polystyrene where a greater thermal resistance is required. A copolymer is a polymer made from more than one type of monomer.
The repeating unit of SAN is shown in **Figure 4**.

Figure 4

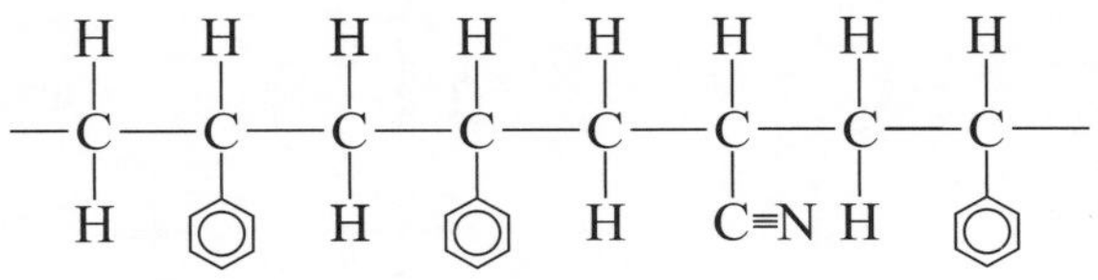

2.6 Draw the displayed formulas of the **two** monomers from which SAN is made.

(2 marks)

2.7 Deduce the ratio in which these monomers are combined in the polymer.

ratio = ... : ....

(1 mark)

EXAM TIP

Make sure you're really familiar with the experimental set-up of all the required practicals. You might be asked to draw one in the exam, and you need to get all the details right to get top marks. Learn what each bit of equipment is for, and how you're supposed to draw it.

Score

25

Alkenes and Alcohols — 3

1   Excess 1-methylcyclohexene reacts with bromine water in the reaction shown below.

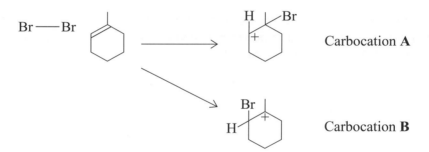

1.1   Describe the change you would expect to see in the bromine water during the reaction.

....
                                                                                                   (1 mark)

1.2   Explain why alkenes are attacked by electrophiles.

....
                                                                                                   (1 mark)

The mechanism involves the formation of a carbocation intermediate.
There are two possible carbocations, **A** and **B**, that can be formed.

1.3   Draw curly arrows on the diagram below to show how the carbocation intermediates are formed.

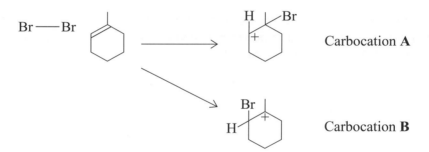

                                                                                                   (2 marks)

1.4   State and explain which of the carbocations, **A** or **B**, is most likely to be formed.

....

....
                                                                                                   (1 mark)

1.5   1-methylcyclohexene also reacts with hydrogen bromide.
      Draw the skeletal formulas of the **two** products formed in this reaction.

                                                                                                   (2 marks)

1.6 1-methylcyclohexene reacts with concentrated sulfuric acid to produce an alkyl hydrogen sulfate. The alkyl hydrogen sulfate can then undergo a reaction to produce an alcohol. State the reagent and conditions for this reaction.

....

....

(2 marks)

2 Linalool, geraniol and myrcene are molecules found in many essential oils. Linalool is an ingredient in up to three-quarters of all perfumed hygiene products. The structures of linalool, geraniol and myrcene are shown in **Figure 1**.

Figure 1

Linalool

Geraniol

Myrcene

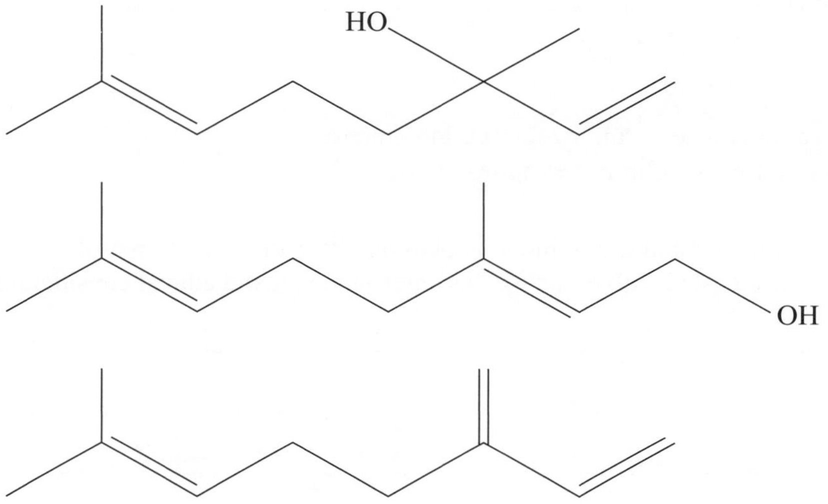

2.1 How many carbon atoms are there in one linalool molecule?

....

(1 mark)

2.2 Linalool and geraniol differ in their reaction with acidified potassium dichromate. Describe any differences you would observe and give reasons for your answer.

....

....

....

(3 marks)

Linalool and geraniol can undergo dehydration reactions.

2.3 Linalool can be dehydrated to form myrcene but geraniol cannot. Explain how you can deduce this from the structures of the three compounds.

....

....

....

(2 marks)

2.4 Draw and name the mechanism for the dehydration of linalool to produce myrcene.
You may use R_1, R_2, etc. to represent any side chains which do not participate in the reaction.

Name of mechanism: ....

(5 marks)

3 Bioethanol is a fuel made during by fermenting glucose.
It is used in countries with limited supplies of crude oil.

Evaluate the production and use of bioethanol as an alternative fuel to petrol.
You should refer to costs involved, as well as environmental and ethical considerations in your answer.

....

....

....

....

....

....

....

....

....

....

....

....

(6 marks)

EXAM TIP
There are lots of mechanisms to learn in this part of the course. Instead of just learning where the curly arrows need to go, it's a good idea to try to learn what each arrow shows as well. If you've got a solid understanding of how the reaction mechanism actually works, it'll make it easier to answer any tricky exam questions about the mechanisms for unfamiliar reactions.

Score

26

Organic Analysis — 1

It's all very well carrying out all these organic reactions, but how can you be sure you've actually ended up with the products you wanted? That's where organic analysis comes in, and jolly useful it is too.

For each of questions 1-4, give your answer by ticking the appropriate box.

1 Which of the following compounds will produce an observable change when added to Tollens' reagent?

   A $CH_3CH_2COCH_2CH_3$ ☐

   B CH_2CH_2 ☐

   C CH_3CH_2CHO ☐

   D CH_3COOH ☐

   (1 mark)

2 Which of the following compounds could be distinguished from the other three using molecular ion data from low resolution mass spectrometry?

   A $NH_2CH_2CH_2NH_2$ ☐

   B $CH_3CH_2CH_2OH$ ☐

   C CH_3COCH_3 ☐

   D CH_3COOH ☐

   (1 mark)

3 The precise atomic masses of carbon, hydrogen and oxygen are shown in **Table 1**.

Table 1

Element	C	H	O
Precise atomic mass / g mol^{-1}	12.0107	1.0079	15.9994

Use the data from **Table 1** to calculate the precise molecular mass of pentanal.

   A 86.1319 g mol^{-1} ☐   **B** 85.1240 g mol^{-1} ☐

   C 88.1477 g mol^{-1} ☐   **D** 84.1161 g mol^{-1} ☐

   (1 mark)

4 The infrared spectrum of compound **X** shows peaks at wavenumbers of 1700-1725 cm^{-1} and 3240-3280 cm^{-1}. Use the data sheet on pages 192-194 to help you determine which of the following functional groups could have caused these peaks.

   A N–H and C=O ☐

   B C=O and O–H ☐

   C C–O and O–H ☐

   D C=C and C=O ☐

   (1 mark)

5 A student is using chemical tests to identify the functional groups in four unknown organic compounds, **A**, **B**, **C** and **D**. All four compounds are colourless liquids.

5.1 It is thought that compound **A** may be a carboxylic acid.
Outline how the student could use sodium carbonate to confirm that compound **A** is a carboxylic acid.
Include the names of all reagents used, the equation for the reaction of the carboxylic acid that occurs and expected observations. Use RCOOH to represent the carboxylic acid in your equation.

....

....

....

....

....

....

(4 marks)

5.2 A sample of compound **B** was placed in a test tube. A small amount of Fehling's solution was added to the test tube and the test tube was heated using a water bath.
Suggest why a hot water bath and not a Bunsen flame was used to heat the test tube.

....

(1 mark)

5.3 After heating the test tube for a few minutes, a red precipitate was formed.
State what can be deduced from this observation about the identity of compound **B**.

....

(1 mark)

The tests used on compounds **A** and **B** produced no visible results when used on compounds **C** and **D**, so two further tests were carried out. The results of these tests are shown in **Table 2**.

Table 2

Organic compound	Shaking with bromine water	Addition of sodium metal
C	Bromine water decolourised	No visible change
D	No visible change	Quick fizzing and gas produced ignites with a squeaky pop sound

5.4 Use the information above and the results shown in **Table 2** to deduce the functional groups present in compounds **C** and **D**. Justify your deductions for each compound.

....

....

....

....

(4 marks)

Make sure you learn the exact descriptions of colour changes in chemical tests that the examiners are after. Bromine water goes colourless, NOT clear, and Fehling's solution forms a red or orange-red precipitate, so don't go saying it's vermilion or terracotta or anything fancy...

Score

14

Organic Analysis — 2

1 High resolution mass spectrometry was used to find the precise molecular masses of two unidentified organic compounds, **F** and **G**.

Compound **F** is known to be either pentane (C_5H_{12}) or butanone (C_4H_8O).

1.1 The precise molecular mass of compound **F** was found to be 72.1054 g mol^{-1}. The precise atomic masses of carbon, hydrogen and oxygen are 12.0107 g mol^{-1}, 1.0079 g mol^{-1} and 15.9994 g mol^{-1}, respectively. Use this information to calculate the precise molecular masses of pentane and butanone and hence determine the identity of compound **F**.

Identity of compound **F**: ....

(2 marks)

Compound **G** is either butanal or butanone. Butanal and butanone are isomers with the same molecular formula and therefore the same precise molecular mass. This means that high resolution mass spectroscopy could not be used to identify compound **G**.

1.2 An infrared spectrum was produced for compound **G**. Peaks were detected at wavenumbers of approximately 1720 cm^{-1} and 2950 cm^{-1}. Explain why this is not sufficient information to determine whether compound **G** is butanal or butanone.

....

....

....

....

....

(2 marks)

1.3 Outline the method for a chemical test involving Tollens' reagent that could be used to determine the identity of compound **G**. Include all steps needed and any expected observations.

....

....

....

....

....

....

(4 marks)

2 Compound **H** is an alcohol with molecular formula $C_4H_{10}O$. **Figure 1** shows the names and displayed formulas of the four possible structures of compound **H**.

Figure 1

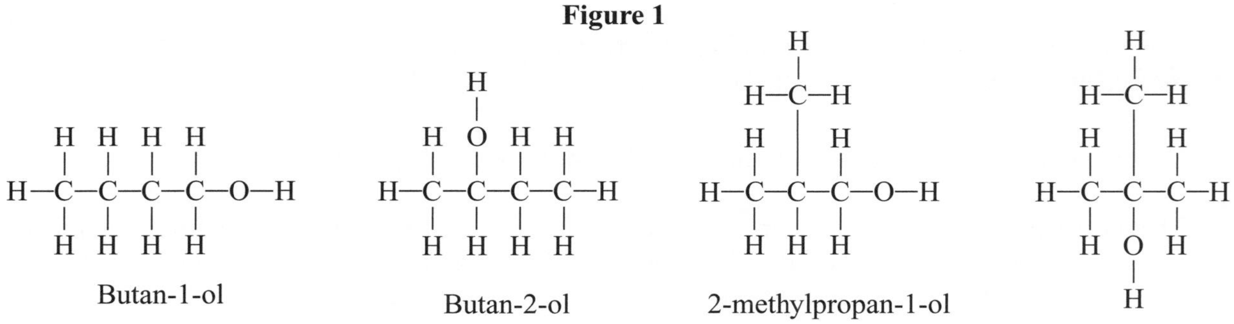

Butan-1-ol

Butan-2-ol

2-methylpropan-1-ol

2-methylpropan-2-ol

Outline the method by which chemical tests could be used to determine that compound **H** is butan-2-ol, and not any of the other structures shown in **Figure 1**.
Include the names of all reagents used and all expected observations.

....

....

....

....

....

....

....

....

....

....

....

....

(6 marks)

3 Infrared spectroscopy is a commonly used method of analysing compounds.

3.1 Explain how the infrared spectra for water vapour, carbon dioxide and methane could be used to compare their ability to act as greenhouse gases.

....

....

....

....

....

(3 marks)

3.2 Explain how the fingerprint region can be used to identify an unknown compound.

....

....

....

(2 marks)

Compound **I** is one of butanol, butanal or butylamine. It was analysed using infrared spectroscopy to determine its identity. **Figure 2** shows the spectrum produced.

Figure 2

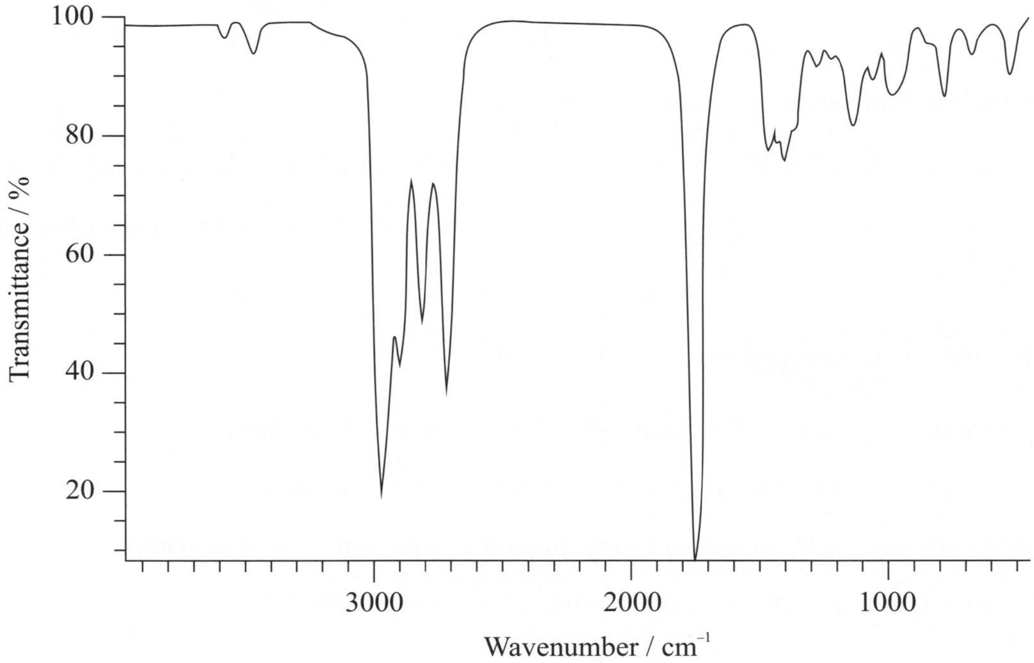

3.3 Use **Figure 2** and the infrared absorption data given on the data sheet on pages 192-194 to identify compound **I** as either butanol, butanal or butylamine. Fully justify your answer.

....

....

....

....

....

....

(4 marks)

In infrared spectra, some of the wavenumber ranges for different bonds overlap, so make sure you pay attention to which molecules you've been asked to identify, and any clues you've been given, like the M_r or results of any chemical tests. You wouldn't want to start talking about N–H bonds if you're supposed to be picking between an alcohol and an alkane, that would just be embarrassing...

Score

23

Isomerism and Carbonyl Compounds — 1

You've already met aldehydes, ketones and carboxylic acids — now it's time to look at their reactions in more detail. And while you're about it there's yet another type of isomerism for you to reflect on...

For each of questions 1-4, give your answer by ticking the appropriate box.

1   The structure shown in **Figure 1** is tested using Tollens' reagent, Na_2CO_3 and acidified $K_2Cr_2O_7$.

Figure 1

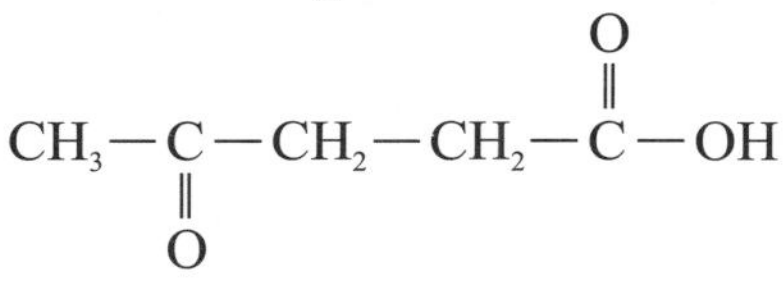

$$CH_3-\underset{\underset{O}{\|}}{C}-CH_2-CH_2-\overset{\overset{O}{\|}}{C}-OH$$

Which of the tests would give positive results?

A   Tollens' reagent only ☐   **B**   Both Tollens' reagent and Na_2CO_3 ☐

C Na_2CO_3 only ☐   **D**   Both Na_2CO_3 and acidified $K_2Cr_2O_7$ ☐

(1 mark)

2   Which of the following statements is **not** correct?

A   An alcohol acts as a nucleophile when it reacts with an acyl chloride. ☐

B   Water reacts with an acyl chloride to produce a carboxylic acid. ☐

C   A carboxylic acid is produced when ammonia reacts with an acid anhydride. ☐

D   An amine reacts with an acid anhydride to produce an ester. ☐

(1 mark)

3   Which of the following compounds is formed from the reaction of a carboxylic acid with butane-1,4-diol?

A $CH_3-\overset{\overset{O}{\|}}{C}-O-CH_2-CH_2-CH_2-O-\overset{\overset{O}{\|}}{C}-CH_3$ ☐

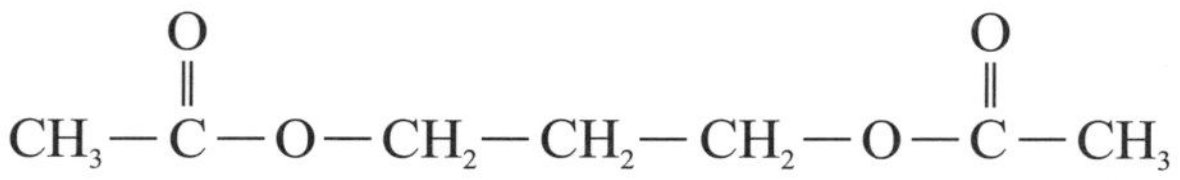

B $CH_3-O-\overset{\overset{O}{\|}}{C}-CH_2-CH_2-CH_2-CH_2-\overset{\overset{O}{\|}}{C}-O-CH_3$ ☐

C $CH_3-O-\overset{\overset{O}{\|}}{C}-CH_2-CH_2-CH_2-CH_2-O-\overset{\overset{O}{\|}}{C}-CH_3$ ☐

D $CH_3-\overset{\overset{O}{\|}}{C}-O-CH_2-CH_2-CH_2-CH_2-O-\overset{\overset{O}{\|}}{C}-CH_3$ ☐

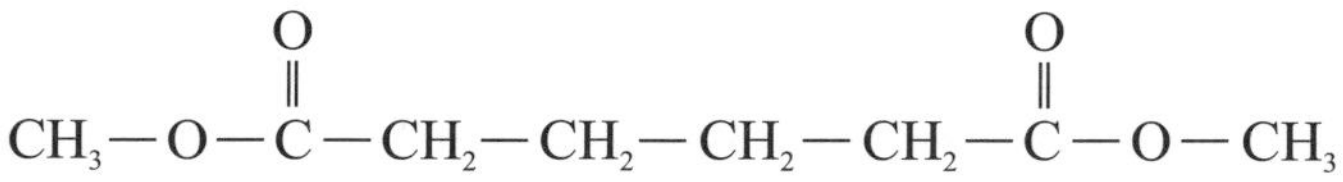

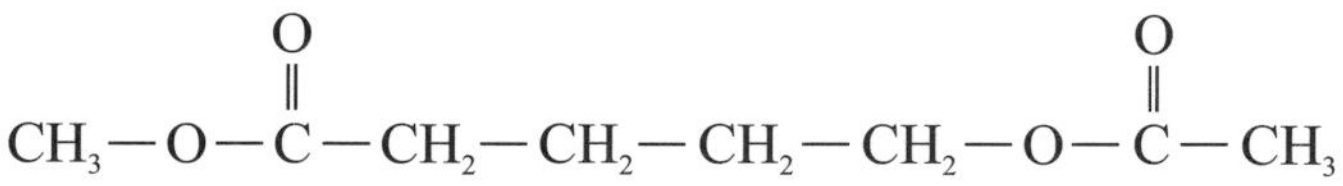

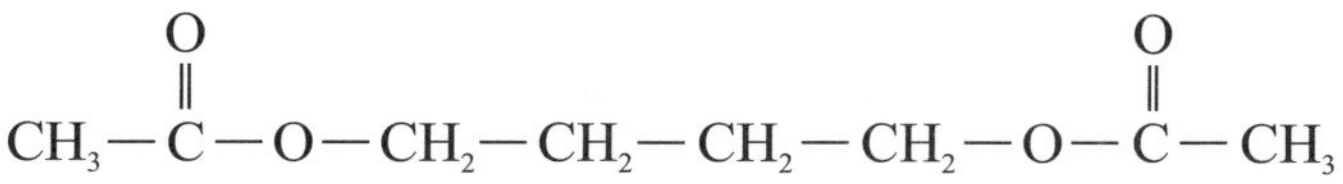

(1 mark)

4   Which of the following pairs of reagents produces a racemic mixture when reacted together?

A   Methanal and HCN ☐   **B**   Ethanal and $NaBH_4$ ☐

C   Ethanal and HCN ☐   **D**   Propanone and $NaBH_4$ ☐

(1 mark)

5   Ester **A** can be prepared by reacting propan-1-ol with either a carboxylic acid, an acid anhydride or an acyl chloride.

5.1   In one reaction, ester **A** was prepared by reacting propan-1-ol with ethanoic anhydride, $(CH_3CO)_2O$. Write an equation for this reaction.

....
(1 mark)

5.2   Give the IUPAC name for ester **A**.

....
(1 mark)

5.3   In a different reaction, ester **A** was prepared by reacting propan-1-ol with ethanoyl chloride. Name and draw the mechanism for this reaction.

Name of mechanism: ....

Mechanism:

(5 marks)

5.4   In industry, the reaction using an acid anhydride is preferred over the reaction using an acyl chloride. Give **two** reasons for this.

1. ....

2. ....
(2 marks)

Ester **B** has the molecular formula $C_5H_{10}O_2$. A student is carrying out a reaction to produce ester **B** from a branched chain carboxylic acid and methanol.

5.5   Using structural formulas, write an equation for this reaction.

....
(2 marks)

5.6   The student carries out the reaction under reflux. Explain the purpose of reflux.

....

....
(1 mark)

5.7 Explain why it is likely that the carboxylic acid will still be present in the product mixture.

....

....
(2 marks)

5.8 Suggest why the product mixture in the flask may appear to consist of two layers.

....

....
(1 mark)

6   **Figure 2** shows the structure of N-phenylethanamide, a drug originally used in the 19th century to reduce fever and pain.

Figure 2

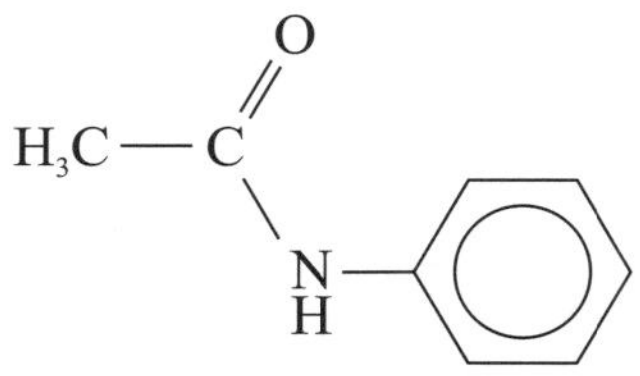

$$H_3C - C \overset{O}{\underset{\underset{H}{N}}{\big\|}} \bigcirc$$

A scientist is preparing a sample of N-phenylethanamide. They start by reacting a solution of sodium ethanoate with phenylammonium chloride to form phenylamine, ethanoic acid and sodium chloride.

6.1 Write a symbol equation for this reaction.

....
(1 mark)

6.2 Phenylamine is toxic. Suggest **two** safety precautions, other than wearing a lab coat and goggles, that should be taken by the scientist when carrying out this procedure.

1. ....

2. ....
(2 marks)

The scientist then reacts the phenylamine produced with ethanoic anhydride.
The products of this reaction are N-phenylethanamide and ethanoic acid.

6.3 The reaction between an amine and an acid anhydride proceeds in a similar way to the reaction between an amine and an acyl chloride. Suggest a mechanism for the reaction between phenylamine and ethanoic anhydride that produces N-phenylethanamide as the main organic product.

(4 marks)

6.4 After the crude product has been obtained, the scientist filters the reaction mixture under reduced pressure. Draw a labelled diagram to show how they should set up apparatus to carry out this procedure.

(2 marks)

6.5 The scientist purifies their sample of N-phenylethanamide by recrystallisation. They dissolve the sample in the minimum quantity of hot solvent and filter through a funnel to remove insoluble impurities. They then leave the solution to cool and form crystals of the product. Describe the steps needed to complete the recrystallisation process. Explain the purpose of each step.

....

....

....

....

(4 marks)

After drying, the pure sample was weighed and the percentage yield of N-phenylethanamide calculated.

6.6 Suggest **one** practical reason why the yield of this reaction may be less than 100%.

....

(1 mark)

6.7 Suggest **one** practical reason why the yield of this reaction may be higher than expected.

....

(1 mark)

The melting point range of the sample was determined in order to assess its purity.

6.8 Explain how you would determine the melting point range of the sample.

....

....

....

(2 marks)

6.9 Give **two** ways in which impurities in the sample would affect the melting point range.

1. ....

2. ....

(2 marks)

Isomerism and Carbonyl Compounds — 2

1   Lactones are cyclic esters widely used in food flavourings and fragrances. They can be hydrolysed in acidic or alkaline conditions to produce a single product. The structure of a lactone is shown in **Figure 1**.

Figure 1

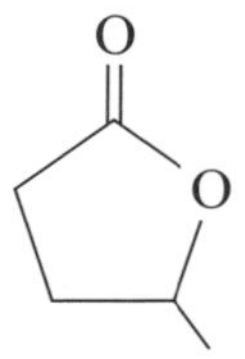

1.1   The hydrolysis of lactones is a reversible reaction. Write an equation for the acid-catalysed hydrolysis of the lactone shown in **Figure 1**. Use skeletal formulas to represent any organic reactants and products.

(1 mark)

1.2   State, in terms of reaction conditions, how would you ensure that the equilibrium was shifted to the right.

....

(1 mark)

1.3   The product can be separated from the reaction mixture by distillation.
Draw a labelled diagram to show how you would set up apparatus to carry out this distillation.

(3 marks)

1.4   Give the structural formula of the product that would be formed if the ester were hydrolysed in a solution of NaOH.

....

(1 mark)

1.5   Suggest a reagent that could be used to convert the product of alkaline hydrolysis into the product formed by acid hydrolysis.

....

(1 mark)

2   Biodiesel can be produced from fats. An example of a fat of palmitoleic acid is shown in **Figure 2**.

Figure 2

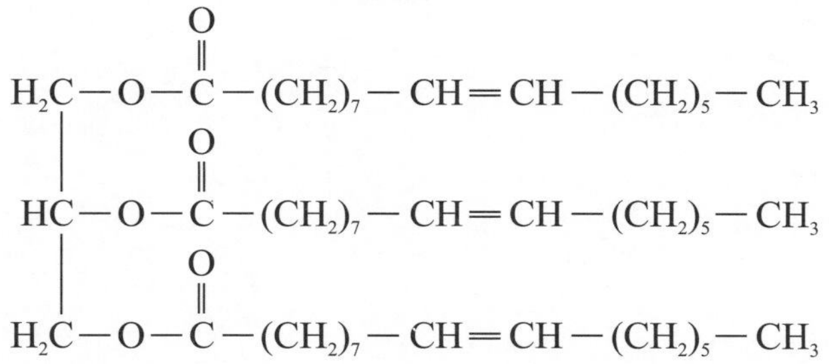

$$H_2C-O-\overset{\displaystyle O}{\overset{\|}{C}}-(CH_2)_7-CH=CH-(CH_2)_5-CH_3$$
$$HC-O-\overset{\displaystyle O}{\overset{\|}{C}}-(CH_2)_7-CH=CH-(CH_2)_5-CH_3$$
$$H_2C-O-\overset{\displaystyle O}{\overset{\|}{C}}-(CH_2)_7-CH=CH-(CH_2)_5-CH_3$$

2.1   Identify the reagent and reaction conditions needed to produce biodiesel from the fat shown in **Figure 2**.

Reagent: ....

Reaction conditions: ....
(2 marks)

2.2   Draw the structures of the **two** products of the reaction to produce biodiesel from the fat shown in **Figure 2**.

(2 marks)

The fat shown in **Figure 2** can also react with aqueous NaOH to produce a soap and **one** other product.

2.3   Give the structural formula of the soap that would be produced in this reaction.

....
(1 mark)

2.4   Deduce the IUPAC name of the other product of the reaction.

....
(1 mark)

3   Butan-2-ol is a secondary alcohol that exists as a pair of optical isomers.

3.1   State what is meant by the term optical isomers.

....
(1 mark)

3.2   Draw diagrams to show the three-dimensional structures of the two optical isomers of butan-2-ol.

(1 mark)

Unit 3 : Section 4 — Isomerism and Carbonyl Compounds

120

3.3 Butan-2-ol can be prepared in the lab by the reduction of butanone using an aqueous solution of $NaBH_4$. Name and draw the mechanism for this reaction.

Name of mechanism: ....

Mechanism:

(5 marks)

3.4 Butan-2-ol reacts with ethanoic acid to form the ester 1-methylpropyl ethanoate ($C_6H_{12}O_2$). Draw the displayed formula of 1-methylpropyl ethanoate.

(1 mark)

3.5 Draw the displayed formula of another branched chain ester of ethanoic acid with the molecular formula $C_6H_{12}O_2$.

(1 mark)

4   Propanone and butanone can both react with HCN to form hydroxynitriles.

Describe and explain whether each reaction produces a chiral product. Predict the optical activity of the products of each reaction, and outline how this could be determined.

....
....
....
....
....
....
....
....
....
....
(6 marks)

EXAM TIP — When you're drawing a mechanism, you need to make it clear where electrons are coming from and where they're going to. So make sure your curly arrows start and finish exactly in the middle of bonds, and on the correct atoms and lone pairs. You don't want to lose marks when you understand the mechanism perfectly, but your arrows are just a bit sloppy...

Score

28

Unit 3 : Section 4 — Isomerism and Carbonyl Compounds

Aromatic Compounds and Amines — 1

Personally, I think the structures of aromatic compounds look a bit like fried eggs. But maybe that's just me. Anyway, it's time for some questions — there's nearly 50 marks up for grabs here. Don't say I don't treat you...

For each of questions 1-4, give your answer by ticking the appropriate box.

1   Which of the following statements about dimethylbenzene ($C_6H_4(CH_3)_2$) is **not** correct?

    A   Dimethylbenzene undergoes electrophilic substitution reactions. ☐

    B   All carbon-carbon bond lengths are equal in dimethylbenzene. ☐

    C   There are four structural isomers of dimethylbenzene that contain a benzene ring. ☐

    D   It can undergo an acylation reaction to produce an aromatic ketone. ☐

        (1 mark)

Questions 2 and 3 are about the reaction scheme for the formation of N-methylaniline ($C_6H_5NHCH_3$) shown in **Figure 1**.

Figure 1

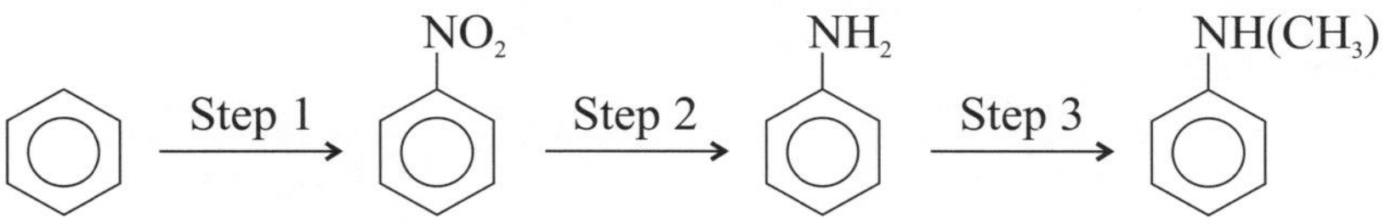

2   Which of the following reagents is **not** required in steps 1–2?

    A   Concentrated NH_3 ☐   **B**   Concentrated HNO_3 ☐

    C   Concentrated H_2SO_4 ☐   **D**   Concentrated HCl ☐

        (1 mark)

3   Step 3 can be carried out using bromomethane as the reagent. What type of reaction would this be?

    A   Electrophilic substitution ☐

    B   Reduction ☐

    C   Nucleophilic substitution ☐

    D   Electrophilic addition ☐

        (1 mark)

4   Which of the following amines is formed when methylamine is heated with bromoethane?

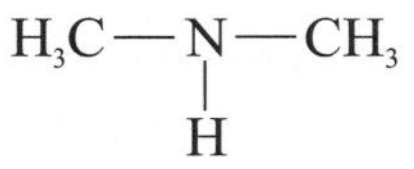

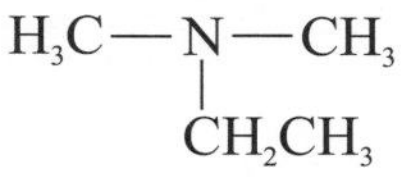

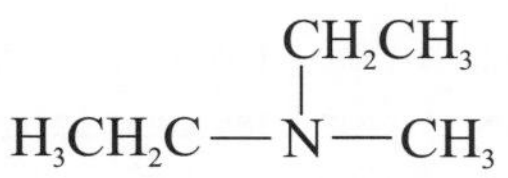

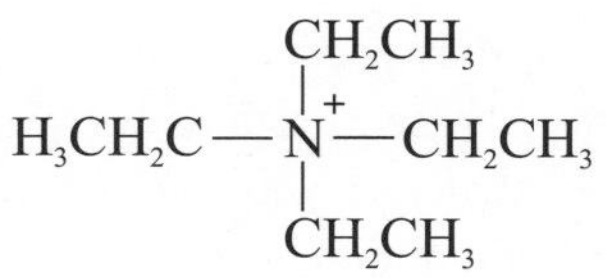

        (1 mark)

5   Benzene is a cyclic compound that can react with certain electrophiles.

5.1   Define the term electrophile.

....

(1 mark)

5.2   Explain why electrophiles do **not** undergo addition reactions with benzene under standard conditions.

....

(1 mark)

Benzene was once incorrectly thought to have the structure of the theoretical compound cyclohexa-1,3,5-triene. Both benzene and cyclohexa-1,3,5-triene have the formula C_6H_6. The hydrogenation reactions of benzene, cyclohexa-1,3,5-triene and cyclohexene are shown in **Figure 2**.

Figure 2

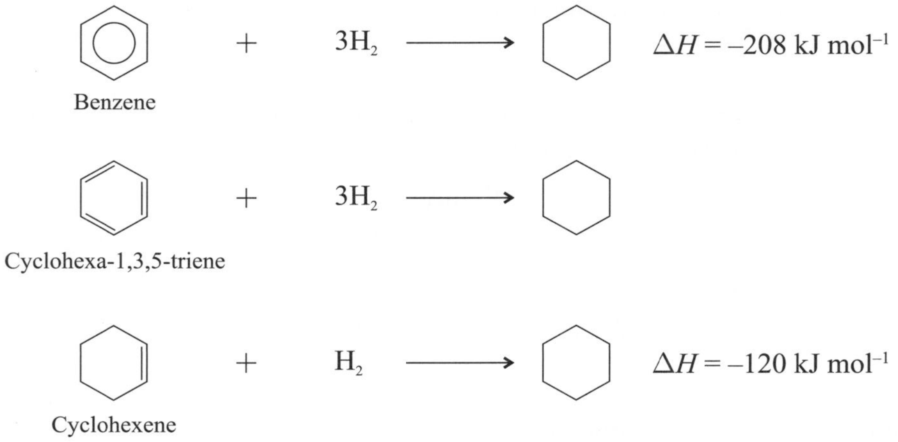

Benzene $+$ $3H_2$ $\longrightarrow$ $\Delta H = -208$ kJ mol^{-1}

Cyclohexa-1,3,5-triene $+$ $3H_2$ $\longrightarrow$

Cyclohexene $+$ H_2 $\longrightarrow$ $\Delta H = -120$ kJ mol^{-1}

5.3   Compare the structure, bonding and reactivity of benzene to that of cyclohexa-1,3,5-triene. Show how the information in **Figure 2** provides evidence that benzene does **not** have the structure of cyclohexa-1,3,5-triene.

....

....

....

....

....

....

....

....

....

....

(6 marks)

EXAM TIP   It's almost certain that you'll encounter an extended response question at some point during your chemistry exams. These questions test your chemistry knowledge (obviously), but they also test whether you can structure your answer in a logical way — so it's worth spending a bit of time having a good think about how best to order all the stuff you want to include in your answer.

Score

12

Aromatic Compounds and Amines — 2

1 Under certain conditions, benzene can react with propanoyl chloride (CH$_3$CH$_2$COCl).

1.1 Write a balanced symbol equation for the reaction between benzene and propanoyl chloride.

....
(1 mark)

1.2 Name the catalyst used in the reaction.

....
(1 mark)

1.3 Draw a mechanism for this reaction. Your answer should show the action of the catalyst and how it is re-formed at the end of the reaction.

(5 marks)

1.4 Give the full IUPAC name for the organic product formed during the reaction.

....
(1 mark)

2 A scientist is investigating the reaction of an amine with a halogenoalkane.

She adds butan-1-amine to an excess of bromomethane and heats the reaction mixture. A mixture of products is formed. One of the products is a secondary amine.

2.1 Draw and name the mechanism for the reaction to produce a secondary amine.

Name of mechanism: ....
(6 marks)

2.2 Explain why a mixture of products is formed.

....

....

(1 mark)

2.3 A quaternary ammonium salt is also produced during the experiment.
Explain why quaternary ammonium salts are often used in cleaning products.

....

....

(2 marks)

3 Multiple substitution reactions can occur when benzene is heated with a mixture of concentrated nitric and sulfuric acids.

3.1 Draw a mechanism to show the formation of 1,3-dinitrobenzene from nitrobenzene.
Include equations to show how the electrophile is generated at the start of the reaction.

(4 marks)

Methylbenzene reacts with a mixture of concentrated nitric and sulfuric acids in a similar way to benzene.

3.2 Suggest why methylbenzene is more attracted to electrophiles than benzene is.

....

....

(1 mark)

One of the products of the reaction is the aromatic compound 2-methyl-1,3,5-trinitrobenzene.

3.3 Draw the displayed formula of this product.

(1 mark)

3.4 Suggest a use for 2-methyl-1,3,5-trinitrobenzene.

....

(1 mark)

4 The structures of two amines, ethylamine and phenylamine, are shown in **Figure 1**.

Figure 1

Ethylamine Phenylamine

4.1 Explain why amines can behave as both bases and nucleophiles.

....

....

....

(2 marks)

4.2 Under certain conditions, ethylamine can react with ethanoyl chloride.
Draw the displayed formula of the nitrogen-containing product of this reaction.

(1 mark)

4.3 A scientist has two test tubes containing solutions of ethylamine and phenylamine of equal concentration.
State which solution would have a higher pH. Explain your answer.

....

....

....

....

....

(5 marks)

4.4 Ethylamine can be prepared by gently warming a solution of ammonia and chloroethane.
Suggest **one** reason why phenylamine is **not** prepared from ammonia and chlorobenzene in the same way.

....

....

(2 marks)

4.5 Ethylamine can also be prepared by the reduction of ethanenitrile.
Write an equation for this reaction. You should represent the reducing agent as [H] in your answer.

....

(1 mark)

EXAM TIP

If you get stuck halfway through drawing a mechanism, don't panic — you can sometimes work out what the next step is going to be by looking out for any way that a negative charge (or a lone pair or δ–) can attack a positive charge (or δ+). For example, if you've got a molecule with a lone pair of electrons, it's pretty likely that it'll want to attack a δ+ carbon in another molecule.

Score

35

Polymers and Proteins — 1

Things start looking a bit biological in this section, but fear not, they can all be explained through the magic of chemistry. I mean, it's not magic, it's probably the opposite of magic really, but you know what I'm getting at...

For each of questions 1-4, give your answer by ticking the appropriate box.

1   Terylene™ can be formed from the monomers benzene-1,4-dicarboxylic acid and ethane-1,2-diol. Which of the following is the correct repeating unit of Terylene™?

A   ☐   B   ☐

C   ☐   D   ☐

(1 mark)

2   Which of the following statements about polyamides is correct?

A   Polyamides are formed by a hydrolysis reaction.   ☐

B   Polyamides are formed from a diamine and a diol.   ☐

C   PVC is an example of a polyamide.   ☐

D   Water is eliminated when a polyamide is formed.   ☐

(1 mark)

3   Which of the following diagrams of the amino acid glycine shows it at its isoelectric point?

A   ☐   B   ☐

C   ☐   D   ☐

(1 mark)

4   **Figure 1** shows the skeletal formula of the amino acid serine.

Figure 1

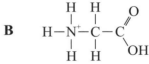

Which of the following is the correct IUPAC name for serine?

A   1-hydroxy-2-aminopropanoic acid   ☐   B   2-amino-3-carboxypropan-1-ol   ☐

C   2-amino-3-hydroxypropanoic acid   ☐   D   1-carboxy-2-aminopropan-3-ol   ☐

(1 mark)

5 Polybutylene succinate is a polymer with great potential for use in the food packaging industry. It is formed from succinic acid and butane-1,4-diol, the structures of which are shown in **Figure 2**.

Figure 2

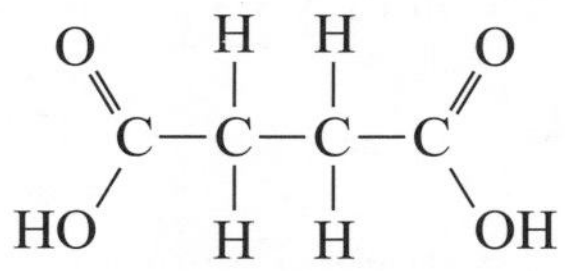

O   H H   O
 \\ | | //
  C—C—C—C
 / | | \\
HO   H H   OH

Succinic acid

   H H H H
   | | | |
HO—C—C—C—C—OH
   | | | |
   H H H H

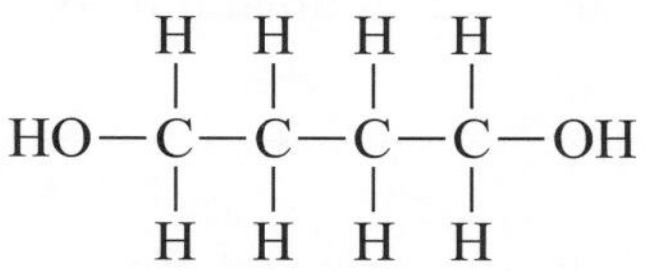

butane-1,4-diol

5.1 State the name given to polymers formed from dicarboxylic acid and diol monomers.

....
(1 mark)

5.2 Identify the compound released when polybutylene succinate is formed from succinic acid and butane-1,4-diol.

....
(1 mark)

5.3 Draw the repeating unit of polybutylene succinate.

(1 mark)

In the future, polybutylene succinate may replace typical polyalkenes like poly(ethene) in some food packaging applications, because it breaks down more easily after use. At the moment, poly(ethene) is commonly disposed of through recycling, but much is buried in landfill.

5.4 Explain why polybutylene succinate breaks down more easily than poly(ethene).

....

....

....

....

....
(4 marks)

5.5 Compare recycling and burying in landfill as methods of disposing of waste plastic. You should comment on advantages and disadvantages of both methods in your answer.

....

....

....

....

....
(3 marks)

6 α-amanitin is a toxin produced by some species of poisonous mushroom. It is a small, cyclic protein formed from 8 amino acids that are joined together in a loop. α-amanitin is toxic because it inhibits the action of the enzyme RNA polymerase, which is essential for the survival of cells.

6.1 Suggest **one** way in which α-amanitin could inhibit the action of RNA polymerase.

....

....

....

(3 marks)

A scientist is investigating the amino acids that make up the structure of α-amanitin. The scientist breaks the protein down into its constituent amino acids and uses thin-layer chromatography to identify the amino acids present.

6.2 Outline how thin-layer chromatography can be used to separate the amino acids present in a mixture. Explain which property of the amino acids allows them be separated in this way.

....

....

....

....

....

....

(4 marks)

The scientist's chromatogram is shown in **Figure 3**.

Figure 3

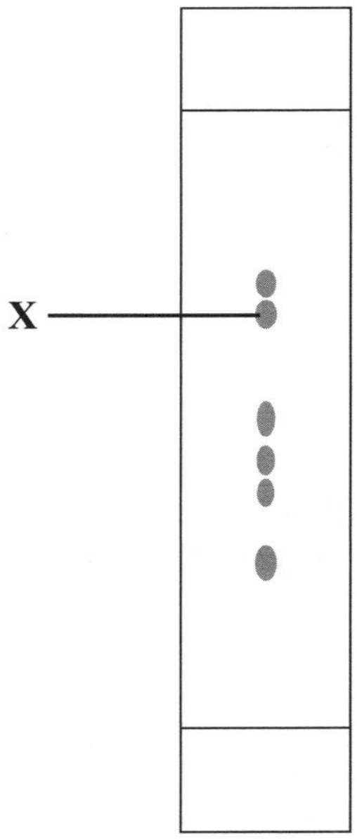

6.3 Suggest **two** methods that could have been used to make the amino acids spots on this chromatogram visible.

....

....

(2 marks)

The amino acids present in α-amanitin were totally separated during the scientist's investigation.

6.4 Use **Figure 3** to determine the number of different types of amino acid present in α-amanitin.

....

(1 mark)

Table 1 shows the R_f values of some amino acids.

Table 1

Amino acid	R_f value
Arginine	0.21
Glycine	0.26
Cysteine	0.39
Proline	0.44
Asparagine	0.50
Tryptophan	0.66
Isoleucine	0.70

6.5 Use the data in **Table 1** to identify the amino acid labelled **X** in **Figure 4**.

Amino acid **X** = ...

(3 marks)

Figure 4 shows the skeletal formula of isoleucine.

Figure 4

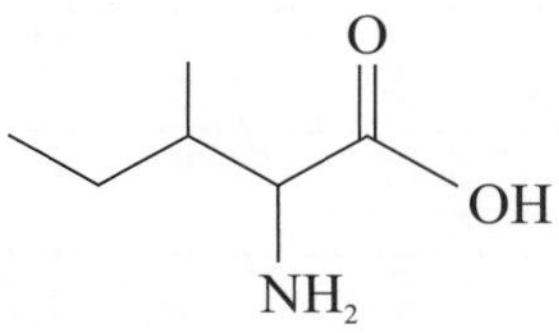

6.6 Give the IUPAC name of isoleucine.

....

(1 mark)

6.7 Draw the zwitterion of isoleucine.

(1 mark)

EXAM TIP   You'll probably be presented with some unfamiliar monomers or repeating units in the exam, but try not to panic. Just make sure that you can recognise amide and ester links and that you know how they're formed and what happens when they're broken apart. That'll see you right.

Score

[ ]

29

Polymers and Proteins — 2

1   Trypsin is an enzyme found in the small intestine. It is one of the enzymes
    responsible for the breakdown of proteins into amino acids during digestion.

1.1   Describe the structure of a protein in terms of its primary, secondary and tertiary structures.

    ....

    ....

    ....

    ....

                                                                                                        (3 marks)

Figure 1 shows two types of secondary structure.

Figure 1

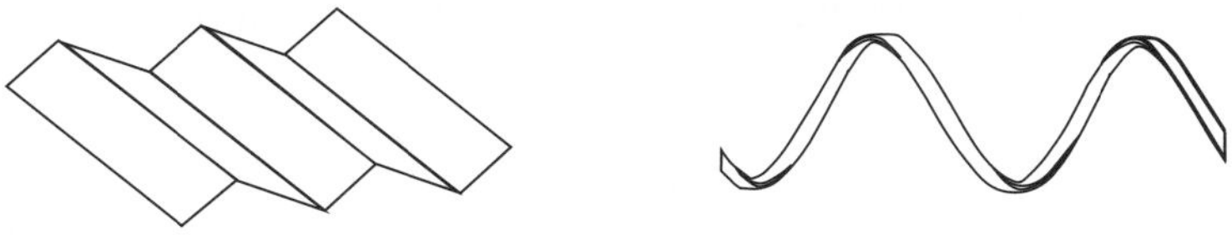

Structure **A**   Structure **B**

1.2   Identify structure **A** and structure **B**.

    A: ....   **B**: ....
                                                                                                        (2 marks)

1.3   Describe the **two** main types of bond that are responsible for stabilising the tertiary structure.

    ....

    ....

    ....

    ....

                                                                                                        (4 marks)

Trypsin preferentially breaks peptide chains at the carboxyl side of the amino acid lysine.
The structure of a peptide that might be broken up by trypsin is shown in **Figure 2**.

Figure 2

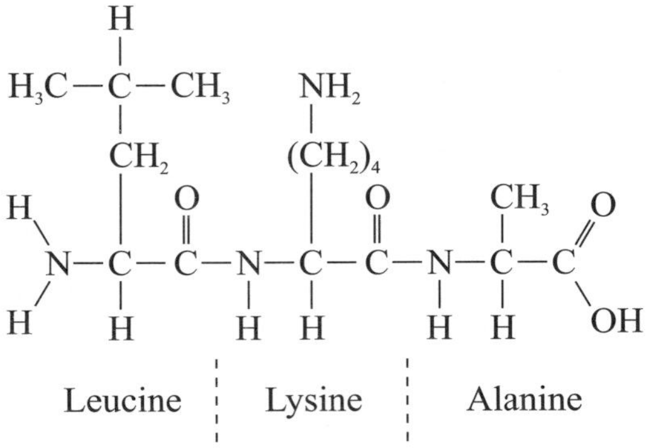

Leucine   Lysine   Alanine

1.4   Name the type of reaction that takes place when trypsin breaks up the peptide.

    ....
                                                                                                        (1 mark)

1.5 Draw the structures of the amino acid and the dipeptide that will be formed if trypsin catalyses the break-up of the peptide shown in **Figure 2**.

Amino acid: Dipeptide:

(2 marks)

1.6 Explain why the amino acid produced during the reaction is unlikely to exist as a zwitterion under the alkaline conditions found in the small intestine.

....

....

....

(2 marks)

1.7 Apart from glycine, all amino acids can exist as two different enantiomers, known as L- and D-enantiomers. The amino acids found in nature are almost all L-enantiomers. Explain why trypsin would not be able to catalyse the break-up of a similar peptide formed from the D-enantiomers of these amino acids.

....

....

....

....

(3 marks)

2   DNA is a biological condensation polymer formed by the polymerisation of monomers known as nucleotides. Each nucleotide is formed from a phosphate group, a 2-deoxyribose molecule and a nitrogenous base. The structures of the four nitrogenous bases are shown in **Figure 3**.

Figure 3

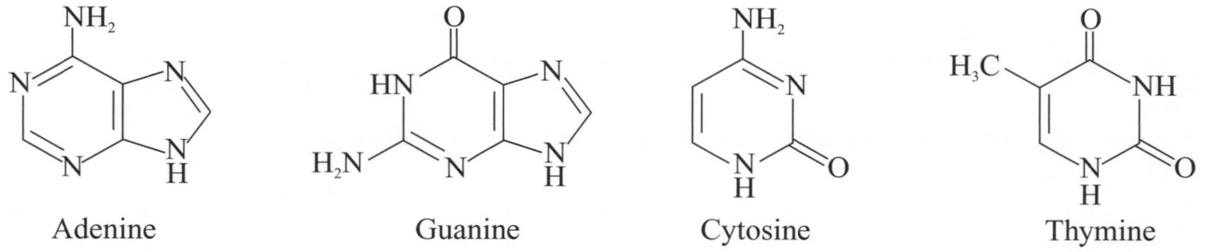

Adenine   Guanine   Cytosine   Thymine

2.1 Explain what complementary base pairing is and how it influences the structure of a DNA molecule inside a living cell.

....

....

....

....

....

....

....

(5 marks)

2.2 Use the structures in **Figure 3** to draw a diagram to show the bonding in **one** of the sets of complementary base pairs found in DNA.

(3 marks)

Mutations in DNA can lead to uncontrolled cell replication, known as cancer. Carboplatin is an anti-cancer drug which has a structure similar to that of cisplatin. Carboplatin consists of a platinum ion bonded to a cyclobutane-1,1-dicarboxylic acid ligand and two ammonia ligands. The structure of carboplatin is shown in **Figure 4**.

Figure 4

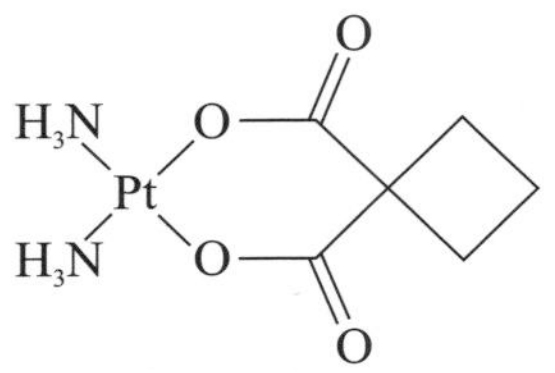

2.3 Using your knowledge of the mechanism of action of cisplatin, suggest and explain how carboplatin can inhibit the replication of cancer cells.

....

....

....

....

(4 marks)

2.4 Suggest why treatment with carboplatin often has adverse side-effects.

....

....

....

(2 marks)

3 Nomex® is a polymer with excellent flame-resistant properties. It is commonly used in the production of fire-retardant clothing, such as the hoods worn by fire-fighters and the suits worn by racing drivers. Part of the structure of Nomex® is shown in **Figure 5**.

Figure 5

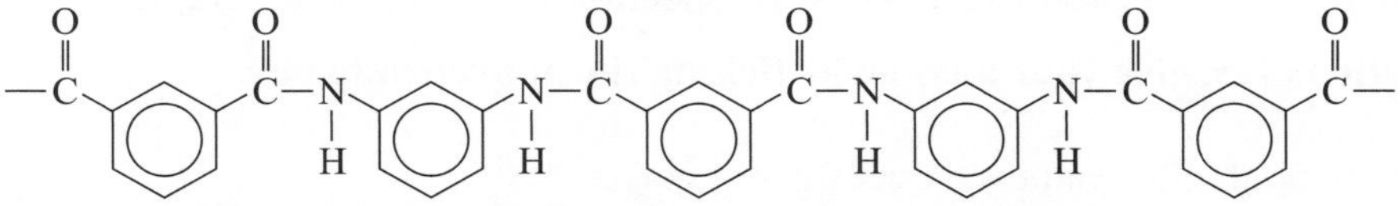

3.1 Draw the structures of the **two** monomers that polymerise to form Nomex®.

(2 marks)

3.2 Give the name of the type of bond formed between the monomers in Nomex®.

....

(1 mark)

3.3 Name the molecule that reacts with Nomex® to break it down into its constituent monomers.

....

(1 mark)

Nomex® is structurally similar to Kevlar®. Part of the structure of Kevlar® is shown in **Figure 6**.

Figure 6

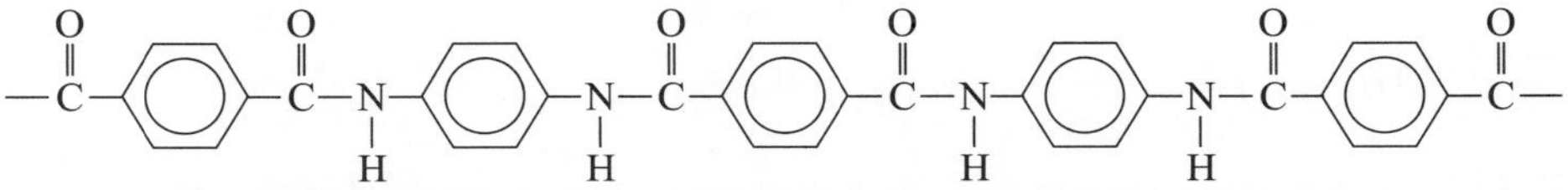

3.4 Explain in terms of intermolecular forces why condensation polymers like Kevlar® and Nomex® are generally stronger than addition polymers such as poly(ethene).

....

....

....

....

(3 marks)

3.5 By comparing the structures shown in **Figure 5** and **Figure 6**, suggest why Nomex® is not as strong as Kevlar®.

....

....

....

....

(3 marks)

EXAM TIP Intermolecular forces are super-important in condensation polymers, proteins and DNA, and examiners will want you to go into detail about the different types and how and why they form. You might want to flick back to your Year 1 notes to make sure you're fully up to speed and ready to write about them, no matter what the context of the question is.

Score

41

Further Synthesis and Analysis — 1

Time to pull everything you know about organic reactions together now for the grand finale — synthesis routes. You can check the identities of products using NMR spectroscopy or chromatography, so they feature too...

For each of questions 1-5, give your answer by ticking the appropriate box.

1   Which statement about organic synthesis is **not** correct?

    A   Acyl chlorides can be converted into primary amides in one step.

    B   Acyl chlorides can be converted into carboxylic acids in one step.

    C   Halogenoalkanes can be converted into carboxylic acids in one step.

    D   Halogenoalkanes can be converted into alcohols in one step.

(1 mark)

2   Which of the following structures has the fewest peaks in its ^{13}C NMR spectrum?

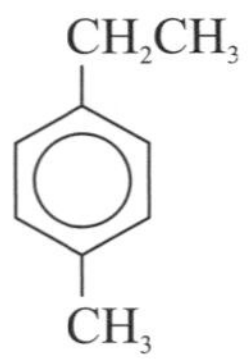

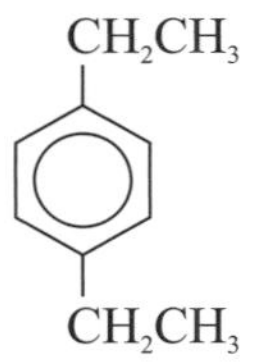

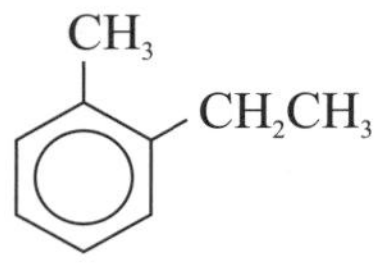

(1 mark)

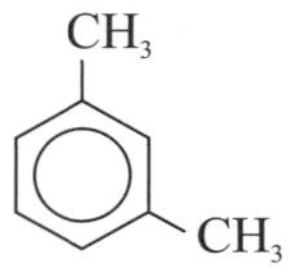

3   Which of the following dibromoalkanes has 5 peaks in its ^{1}H NMR spectrum?

    A $CH_2BrCHBrCH(CH_3)CH_3$ B $(CH_3)_2CBrCH_2CH_2Br$

    C $(CH_3)_2CHCHBrCHBrCH_3$ D $CH_3CHBrC(CH_3)_2CH_2Br$

(1 mark)

4   Which of the following processes is **not** involved in the reaction sequence shown in **Figure 1**?

Figure 1

$$CH_3-CH=CH_2 \longrightarrow C_3H_7Br \longrightarrow C_4H_7N \longrightarrow CH_3-\underset{\underset{CH_3}{|}}{CH}-CH_2-NH_2$$

    A   Substitution   B   Reduction

    C   Addition   D   Elimination

(1 mark)

5   Which of the following organic compounds shows a doublet in its ^{1}H NMR spectrum?

    A   3-chloro-butan-2-one

    B   propanoic acid

    C   ethane-1,2-diamine

    D   2-methylpropan-2-ol

(1 mark)

6 Chromatography can be used to separate and identify the components in a mixture of chemicals.

6.1 Describe how gas chromatography can be used to separate a mixture of volatile compounds.
In your answer you should include details of the mobile and stationary phases in gas chromatography.
You should also explain how the data obtained can be used to identify the components of the mixture.

....

....

....

....

....

....

....

....

....

....

....

(6 marks)

A student was given a test tube that contained a mixture of amino acids.
They were asked to separate and identify the amino acids using thin-layer chromatography (TLC).
The student was provided with a TLC plate coated with silica gel and a solvent containing butanol,
which is a respiratory irritant. The chromatogram they produced is shown in **Figure 2**.

Figure 2

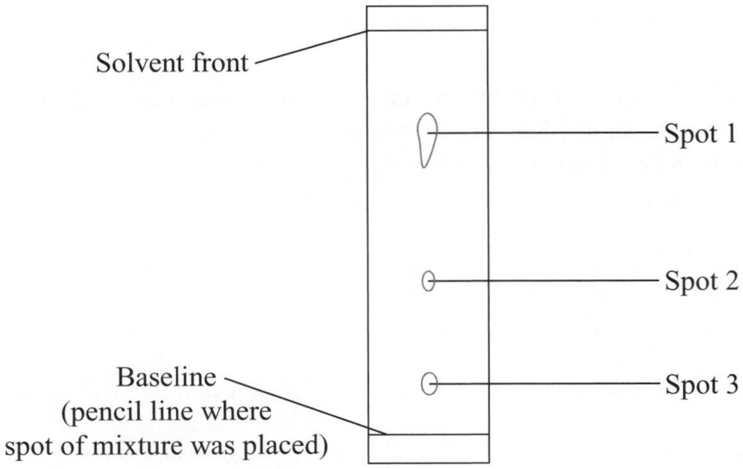

Table 1 shows the data the student used to identify the amino acids present in the mixture.

Table 1

Amino acid	Data book R_f value
Alanine	0.38
Leucine	0.73
Glutamine	0.13

6.2 Suggest **one** safety precaution the student should have taken during the experiment. Explain why this precaution should be taken.

....

....

(2 marks)

6.3 When the solvent had almost reached the top of the plate, the plate was removed from the developing tank and a pencil line was quickly drawn to mark the solvent front. Suggest why this step should be carried out quickly.

....

....

(1 mark)

6.4 When the plate was dry, the student located the position of the amino acid spots, and drew around them with a pencil. Suggest how the student located the spots and why it was necessary to draw around them using a pencil.

....

....

....

(2 marks)

6.5 Calculate the R_f value of spot 2.
Use your value and the data provided in **Table 1** to identify the amino acid present in spot 2.

Amino acid: ....

(4 marks)

6.6 The student decided to redo the experiment, but this time they placed spots of pure leucine, alanine and glutamine on the same plate, beside the spot of the amino acid mixture. Explain why this may be a better method of identifying the amino acids present than comparing their R_f values with those in a data book.

....

....

....

....

(2 marks)

6.7 Suggest why it is not possible to use the method described in question **6.6** in all cases.

....

....

(1 mark)

7 Organic chemists design multi-step processes that are used to produce chemicals on an industrial scale. They aim to devise processes that are as safe as possible and that keep waste to a minimum.

7.1 Describe **two** ways in which a synthetic pathway could be designed to minimise waste.

....

....

(2 marks)

Consider the three-step process shown in **Figure 3**.

Figure 3

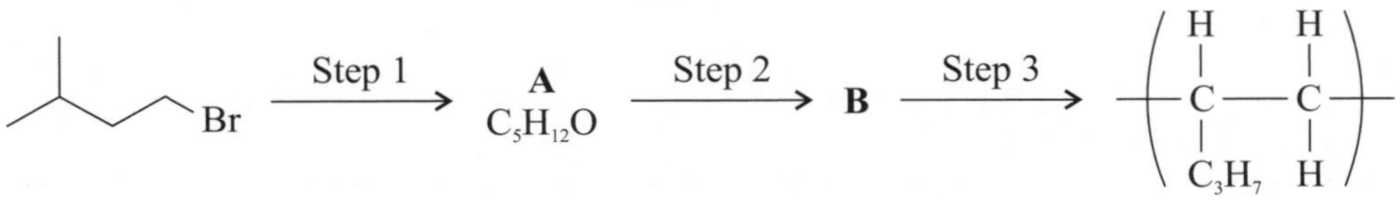

7.2 Draw diagrams to show the structures of compounds **A** and **B**.

A **B**

(2 marks)

7.3 Give the IUPAC name of compound **B**.

....

(1 mark)

7.4 Give the reagent and conditions used in Step 1.

....

....

(2 marks)

7.5 Identify the type of reaction occurring in Step 3.

....

(1 mark)

7.6 The process shown in **Figure 3** is not the shortest route from the starting material to the product. Suggest how the process could be completed in fewer steps, including any reagents and conditions required.

....

....

....

....

(4 marks)

EXAM TIP	There are some things you just have to sit and learn, and the reagents and conditions for organic reactions is one of them. Not only can you pick up marks for rattling them off, they could also help you spot the types of reaction occurring in a process. Use any method that helps to get them to stick — flashcards, sticky notes on the fridge, mnemonics, a soulful revision ballad...	Score 35

Further Synthesis and Analysis — 2

1 ^{1}H and ^{13}C NMR spectroscopy are techniques frequently used by organic chemists to determine the structures of molecules they have synthesised.

1.1 Tetramethylsilane (TMS) is used as a standard substance in ^{1}H NMR. Draw the displayed formula of TMS. Explain why the structure of TMS makes it suitable for use as a standard substance in ^{1}H NMR.

....

....

....

(3 marks)

1.2 Suggest a suitable solvent for a compound being analysed using ^{1}H NMR. Justify your choice.

....

....

(2 marks)

Three compounds containing a benzene ring are shown in **Figure 1**.

Figure 1

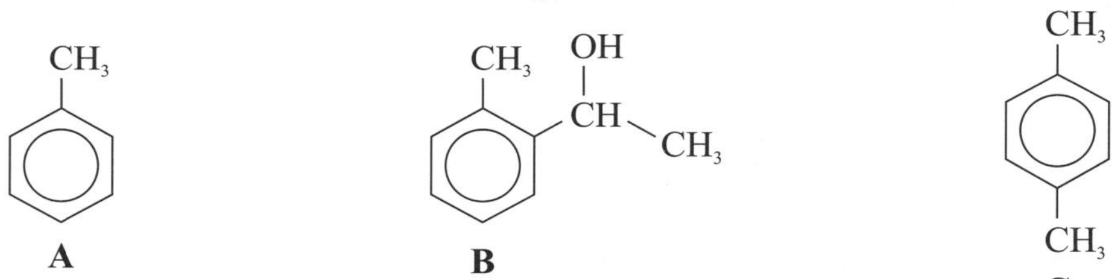

A   **B**   **C**

1.3 State the number of peaks in the ^{13}C NMR spectra of compound **A** and compound **C**.

Compound **A** ....

Compound **C** ....

(2 marks)

1.4 A ^{1}H NMR spectrum is produced for compound **B**. Using the data sheet on p.192-194, give the chemical shift range in which you would expect to find the peak caused by the hydrogen atom in the OH group.

....

(1 mark)

Compound **B** can be prepared from compound **A** in a two-step synthesis, as shown in **Figure 2**.

Figure 2

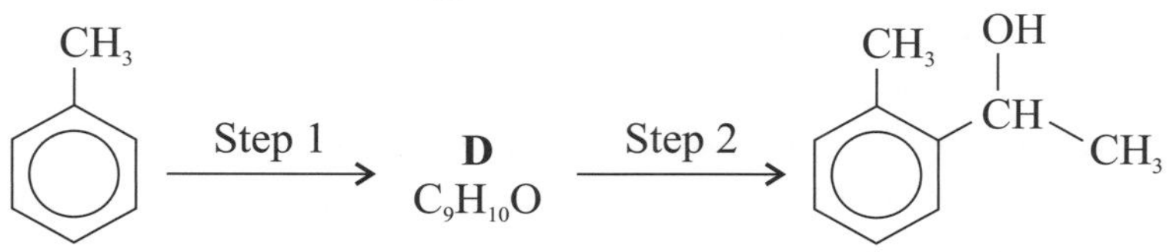

1.5 Compound **D** is an aromatic ketone. Draw a diagram to show the structure of compound **D**.

(1 mark)

1.6 Give reagents and conditions for Step 1 and Step 2.

Step 1 ....

....

Step 2 ....

....

(5 marks)

1.7 Identify the type of reaction occurring in Step 2.

....

(1 mark)

1.8 Although less toxic than benzene, compound **A** is harmful by inhalation. Give **one** reason why chemists should always try to choose the least hazardous starting materials for an organic synthesis.

....

(1 mark)

2 **Figure 3** shows the structures of two esters, **A** and **B**. They both have the molecular formula $C_4H_8O_2$. Both esters have a ^1H NMR spectrum with three peaks and a ^{13}C NMR spectrum with four peaks.

Figure 3

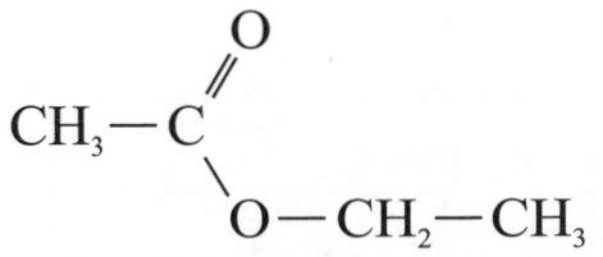

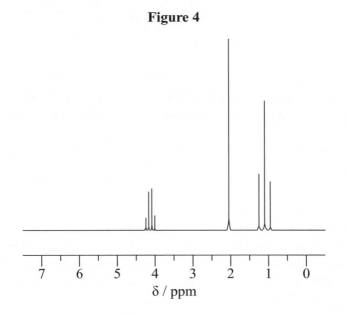

Ester **A** 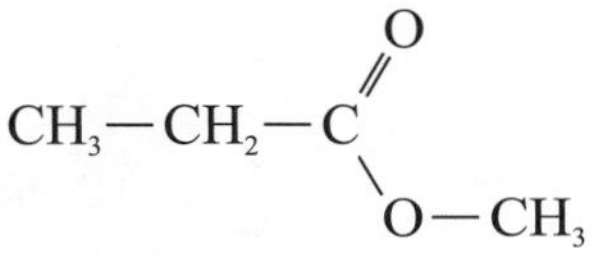   Ester **B**

Figure 4 shows the ^1H NMR spectra for **one** of these esters.

Figure 4

δ / ppm

2.1 Explain the splitting patterns observed and the positions of the peaks in the spectrum in **Figure 4**. Identify which of the esters, **A** or **B**, created this spectrum and explain your reasoning.

(6 marks)

2.2 A third isomer with molecular formula $C_4H_8O_2$ also has three peaks in its ^1H NMR spectrum. Draw the displayed formula of this ester.

(1 mark)

Table 1 shows data from the ^{13}C NMR spectra for esters **A** and **B**.

Table 1

Peak number	δ / ppm	
	A	**B**
1	15	10
2	23	28
3	60	52
4		

2.3 Using the data sheet on pages 192-194, complete **Table 1** by giving the chemical shift range in which you would expect to find peak 4 for each ester. Justify your suggestions.

(2 marks)

EXAM TIP

OK, it's true, NMR is definitely a tricky subject. Don't panic though — just work through the information you've got logically. Jot down what you can tell about the molecule from the number of peaks and their chemical shifts (and for ^1H NMR the splitting patterns and integration ratios too). Then just join all those pieces together and you should see a molecule emerge...

Score

25

Further Synthesis and Analysis — 3

1 Compounds **A** and **B** are both branched chain organic molecules containing 7 carbon atoms.

Compound **A** has the molecular formula $C_7H_{14}O_3$.
The structure of compound **A** is shown in **Figure 1**.

Figure 1

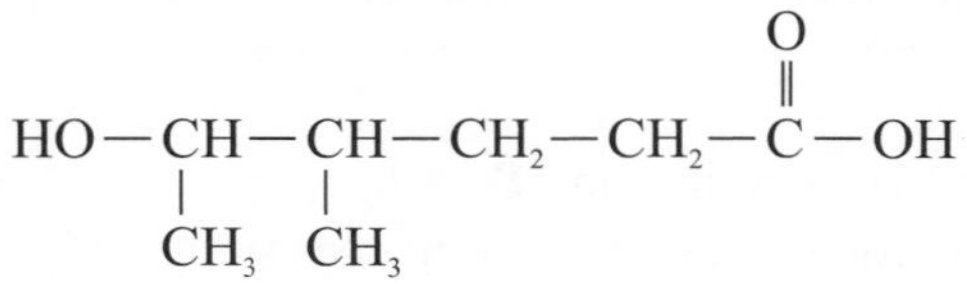

$$HO-\underset{\underset{CH_3}{|}}{CH}-\underset{\underset{CH_3}{|}}{CH}-CH_2-CH_2-\overset{\overset{O}{\|}}{C}-OH$$

1.1 State how many peaks would be seen in the ^1H NMR spectrum of compound **A**.

....
(1 mark)

1.2 Compound **A** was oxidised by heating it under reflux with an oxidising agent.
Identify a suitable reagent for this oxidation reaction.

....
(1 mark)

1.3 The oxidation product of this reaction, compound **C**, has the molecular formula $C_7H_{12}O_3$.
Draw the structure of compound **C**.

(1 mark)

1.4 State how many peaks would be seen in the ^{13}C NMR spectrum of compound **C**.

....
(1 mark)

Compound **C** can be treated with another reagent to produce compound **D**.
Compound **D** has the molecular formula $C_8H_{13}O_3N$.

1.5 Suggest a reagent that could be used to convert compound **C** into compound **D**.

....
(1 mark)

1.6 The added carbon atom causes compound **D** to have an additional peak in its ^{13}C NMR spectrum.
Use the data sheet on pages 192-194 to suggest the chemical shift range in which you would find this peak.

....
(1 mark)

Compound **B** is a carbonyl compound with the molecular formula $C_7H_{14}O$.
It cannot be oxidised under normal laboratory conditions.

Data from the ^1H NMR spectrum of compound **B** is shown in **Table 1**.

Table 1

δ / ppm	2.4	1.1	0.9
Integration ratio	2	3	9
Splitting pattern	Quartet	Triplet	Singlet

1.7 Deduce the displayed formula of compound **B**.
Use all the information provided and explain your reasoning fully.

....

....

....

....

....

....

....

....

....

....

....

....

....

....

(8 marks)

EXAM
TIP

NMR chemical shift values can be really useful if you're trying to work out functional groups a molecule contains. There's often some overlap between chemical shift values for carbons and hydrogens in different environments though, so you might get other information to help you work out what functional group you're dealing with (like an IR spectrum or reaction details).

Score

14

Mixed Questions — 1

I hope you had a large helping of your whole grain, wheat-based, high-fibre breakfast cereal this morning, because this section will test you on material from Units 1, 2 and 3. It's time to bring it all together.

For each of questions 1-5, give your answer by ticking the appropriate box.

1   Which of the following statements about chemical reactions is correct?

    A   Magnesium reacts more vigorously than barium with water. ☐

    B   Increasing the amount of a reactant decreases the area under the Maxwell-Boltzmann distribution curve for the reaction. ☐

    C   Reactant molecules move slower at higher temperatures. ☐

    D   The peak of the curve on a Maxwell-Boltzmann distribution represents the most likely energy of any single molecule. ☐

    (1 mark)

2   What is the chemical equation for the 3rd ionisation energy of sulfur?

    A $S_{(g)} \rightarrow S^{3+}_{(g)} + 3e^-$ ☐   **B** $S^{2+}_{(g)} \rightarrow S^{3+}_{(g)} + e^-$ ☐

    C $S^{3+}_{(g)} + e^- \rightarrow S^{2+}_{(g)}$ ☐   **D** $S^{3+}_{(g)} \rightarrow S^{4+}_{(g)} + e^-$ ☐

    (1 mark)

3   What is the oxidation state of hydrogen in MgH_2?

    A   +2 ☐   **B**   +1 ☐

    C   −1 ☐   **D**   −2 ☐

    (1 mark)

4   Which of the following are the conditions used in catalytic cracking?

    A   High temperature and high pressure, with a zeolite catalyst. ☐

    B   Low temperature and slight pressure, with an acidified dichromate catalyst. ☐

    C   Low temperature and high pressure, with a phosphoric acid catalyst. ☐

    D   High temperature and slight pressure, with a zeolite catalyst. ☐

    (1 mark)

5   Which of the following would be produced if 2-bromo-pentan-3-ol was heated with aqueous NaOH?

    A   2,3-dibromopentane ☐   **B**   2-bromo-pentane-2,3-diol ☐

    C   pentane-2,3-diol ☐   **D**   2-bromo-pentan-3-one ☐

    (1 mark)

6 A student is planning to use calorimetry to measure the molar enthalpy change that occurs when a solution of sodium hydroxide is neutralised by an excess of a solution of nitric acid.

The equation for the neutralisation reaction is:

$$HNO_3 + NaOH \rightarrow NaNO_3 + H_2O$$

The student begins by making a 100 cm^3 standard solution of sodium hydroxide with a concentration of 1.20 mol dm^{-3}.

6.1 Calculate the mass of solid sodium hydroxide required to make the standard solution.

mass = ... g

(2 marks)

The student adds 50.0 cm^3 of nitric acid solution to a polystyrene cup and records the temperature. She then adds 30.0 cm^3 of the sodium hydroxide solution and measures the highest temperature that the solution reached. The difference between the temperature measurements was 6.05 K.

6.2 Calculate the number of moles of nitric acid that reacted.

number of moles = ...

(1 mark)

6.3 Calculate the molar enthalpy change for the neutralisation reaction.
(The specific heat capacity of water, c = 4.18 J g^{-1} K^{-1})

molar enthalpy change = ... kJ mol^{-1}

(3 marks)

6.4 Describe an improvement to the way the student collected and used the data that would have increased the accuracy of the value for the temperature change.

....

....

....

....

....

(5 marks)

7   A student is investigating the rate of the reaction between calcium and water.

She uses the following method:

1. Add 150 cm^3 of water to a conical flask.
2. Add 142 mg of calcium to the conical flask and connect a 100 cm^3 gas syringe.
3. Use a stopwatch to record the time taken for 80 cm^3 of gas to be produced.

The reaction was carried out at a pressure of 101 kPa and a temperature of 298 K.

7.1   The reaction of calcium with water is an example of a redox reaction.
Write a half-equation for the oxidation process occurring during the reaction.

....
(1 mark)

7.2   Give the oxidation state of hydrogen in a molecule of water.

....
(1 mark)

7.3   Calculate the maximum mass of calcium that the student could safely use with her method.
(The gas constant, $R = 8.31$ J K^{-1} mol^{-1})

mass = ... mg
(4 marks)

7.4   Suggest why the amount of gas collected during the experiment may be less than the
amount of gas produced during the reaction.

....

....
(1 mark)

7.5   The student repeats the experiment twice more, but uses strontium and barium instead of calcium.
Predict which metal produced 80 cm^3 of gas in the shortest time. Justify your answer.

....

....
(2 marks)

8   The industrial production of aluminium chloride ($M_r = 133.5$) involves
heating aluminium metal with chlorine at a temperature of 750 °C.

The equation for the reaction is:

$$2Al + 3Cl_2 \rightarrow 2AlCl_3$$

8.1   Write the full electron configuration of aluminium.

....
(1 mark)

8.2 Give the oxidation state of aluminium and chlorine in aluminium chloride.

Aluminium oxidation state: .... Chlorine oxidation state: ....

(1 mark)

8.3 The melting points of aluminium and chlorine are 660 °C and −101 °C respectively.
Explain the difference in the melting points of these two substances in terms of their structure and bonding.

....

....

....

....

(4 marks)

8.4 In a reaction, 2.00 kg of aluminium is heated with excess chlorine. 7.14 kg of aluminium chloride is formed.
Calculate the percentage yield of this reaction.

percentage yield = ... %

(3 marks)

Above a certain temperature, gaseous aluminium chloride forms an equilibrium mixture of $AlCl_3$ and Al_2Cl_6:

$$2AlCl_3 \rightleftharpoons Al_2Cl_6$$

8.5 Write an expression for K_c for this reaction.

....

(1 mark)

Al_2Cl_6 contains two Cl-Al coordinate bonds, with each Al atom bonded to 4 Cl atoms.
There are no lone pairs around the Al atoms.

8.6 Predict the bond angle around each Al atom in Al_2Cl_6.

....

(1 mark)

8.7 Deduce the shape of a molecule of Al_2Cl_6.
Hence draw a 3D diagram showing the bonding and shape of an Al_2Cl_6 molecule.

(2 marks)

Being presented with an unfamiliar compound in the exam can be a bit daunting, but don't be alarmed. Try and work out whether it shares any similarities with a compound that you've studied before — you can use this as a guide to predict the properties of the new compound.

Score

38

Mixed Questions — 2

1   Hex-1-ene and 3-methyl-pent-2-ene are structural isomers that belong to the homologous series of alkenes.

1.1   State what is meant by the term structural isomers.

....

....
(1 mark)

1.2   3-methyl-pent-2-ene exists as a pair of stereoisomers.
Draw the E isomer of 3-methyl-pent-2-ene.

(1 mark)

During combustion, hydrocarbons such as hex-1-ene and 3-methyl-pent-2-ene are oxidised to produce carbon dioxide and water.

1.3   Write a balanced symbol equation for the complete combustion of 3-methyl-pent-2-ene.

....
(1 mark)

1.4   Describe and explain how the shapes and polarities of carbon dioxide and water determine their physical states at room temperature (25 °C).

....

....

....

....

....

....

....

....

....

....

....

....
(6 marks)

The enthalpies of combustion of hex-1-ene, carbon and hydrogen are shown in **Table 1**.

Table 1

Compound	$\Delta_c H$ / kJ mol^{-1}
$H_2C=CH(CH_2)_3CH_{3(l)}$	−4003.0
$C_{(s)}$	−393.5
$H_{2(g)}$	−285.8

1.5   Use the data in **Table 1** to calculate the enthalpy of formation of hex-1-ene.

enthalpy of formation = ...kJ mol^{-1}

(3 marks)

Hex-1-ene can also be oxidised in a hydration reaction. One of the products of the reaction is hexan-2-ol.

1.6   Draw a mechanism for the hydration of hex-1-ene to produced hexan-2-ol.
State reagents and conditions for the reaction.

(5 marks)

1.7   Explain why hexan-2-ol has a higher boiling point than hex-1-ene.

....

....

....

(2 marks)

2   The structure of the alkene chloroethene is shown in **Figure 1**.

Figure 1

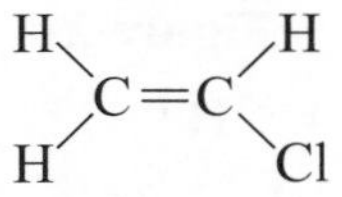

$$\begin{array}{c} H \\ \diagdown \\ H \end{array} C = C \begin{array}{c} H \\ \diagup \\ \diagdown \\ Cl \end{array}$$

2.1   Predict the shape and bond angle around each carbon atom in chloroethene.

Shape: ....

Bond angle:..

(2 marks)

2.2   Explain why chloroethene does **not** exhibit E/Z isomerism.

....

(1 mark)

Chloroethene can undergo an addition polymerisation reaction to form poly(chloroethene) (PVC).

2.3   Draw the structure of the repeating unit of PVC.

(1 mark)

2.4   Give **one** example of a use of PVC and state a property which makes it suitable for this use.

Use:..

Property: ....

(2 marks)

2.5   State how the addition of a plasticiser affects the properties of PVC.

....

(1 mark)

Chloroethene can also undergo an addition polymerisation reaction involving chlorine free radicals.
The initiation step in this reaction is:

$$Cl_2 \xrightarrow{\text{UV}} 2Cl\cdot$$

The first chain reaction in the propagation step forms a radical in a similar way to the formation of a carbocation during electrophilic addition. The second results in the formation of a trichlorobutane radical.

2.6   Write equations to represent the first two reactions in the propagation step.

It's fine if you only use molecular formulas here.

....

....

(2 marks)

2.7   Suggest how the amount of chlorine added to the mixture affects the length of the polymer chains in the final product.

....

....

(2 marks)

3   A scientist has a sample of a compound, **X** ($M_r = 88.0$).
The displayed formula of compound **X** is shown in **Figure 2**.

Figure 2

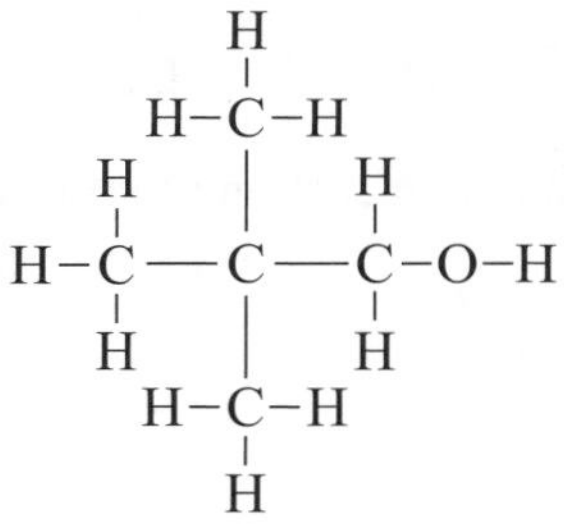

$$\begin{array}{ccc}
 & \text{H} & \\
 & | & \\
 & \text{H–C–H} & \\
\text{H} & | & \text{H} \\
| & | & | \\
\text{H–C} & \text{—C—} & \text{C–O–H} \\
| & | & | \\
\text{H} & | & \text{H} \\
 & \text{H–C–H} & \\
 & | & \\
 & \text{H} &
\end{array}$$

3.1   Name compound **X**.

....
(1 mark)

The scientist uses mass spectrometry to analyse a sample of compound **X**.

3.2   The mass spectrometer is fitted with an electron impact ionisation source.
Outline how ions are generated in electron impact ionisation.

....

....
(2 marks)

The ionisation of molecules during mass spectrometry can cause some of the bonds
within a molecule to break. This produces additional ions which are also detected
by the mass spectrometer. These ions are known as fragment ions.

3.3   A peak with m/z = 57 is present in the mass spectrum of compound **X**.
Suggest the displayed formula of the fragment ion that was responsible for this peak.

(1 mark)

3.4   Suggest why the ion you drew in question 3.3 is particularly stable.

....

....

....
(2 marks)

EXAM TIP

The last few questions in the exam paper are designed to be pretty challenging. They'll often
require you to <u>apply</u> your knowledge of chemistry to a situation or process that you might not
have studied before. Don't panic — the context might be different to what you're used to,
but you'll have studied the underlying chemistry principles that you need to answer the question.

Score

36

Mixed Questions — 3

For each of questions 1-4, give your answer by ticking the appropriate box.

1 Which of the following shows a valid rate equation?

  A Rate = $k[NO]_2[O_2]$ ☐ **B** Rate = $k[NO]^2[O_2]$ ☐

  C Rate = $k[NO]^2[O]_2$ ☐ **D** Rate = $k[2NO_2][O]$ ☐

(1 mark)

2 Which of the following statements about DNA is **not** correct?

  A The bases in DNA are attached to sugars in a sugar-phosphate backbone. ☐

  B Strands of DNA are made up of nucleotides joined by covalent bonds. ☐

  C The bases in DNA include adenine, cytosine and guanine. ☐

  D The strands in a DNA double helix are joined to each other by a sugar-phosphate backbone. ☐

(1 mark)

3 Phosphoric acid (H_3PO_4) is a triprotic acid. What mass of calcium hydroxide is required to neutralise 30 cm^3 of a solution of 1.2 mol dm^{-3} H_3PO_4?

  A 2.7 g ☐ **B** 2.5 g ☐

  C 4.0 g ☐ **D** 1.8 g ☐

(1 mark)

4 **Figure 1** shows the skeletal formulas of three organic compounds.

Figure 1

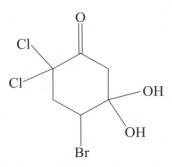 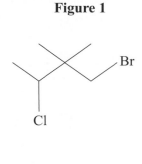 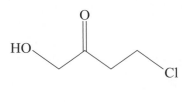

Which of the following is the **minimum** amount of information required to distinguish the compounds?

  A The number of peaks in the ^{13}C and ^1H NMR spectra. ☐

  B The number of peaks in the ^{13}C NMR spectrum only. ☐

  C The number of peaks in the ^1H NMR spectrum only. ☐

  D The IR spectrum in the range 1680-1750 cm^{-1} and the number of peaks in the ^{13}C and ^1H NMR spectra. ☐

(1 mark)

5 A scientist carried out a redox titration using acidified permanganate ions to determine the concentration of 150 cm³ of a solution of chloride ions.

Some information about the processes occurring during the redox reaction is shown in **Table 1**.

Table 1

Half-equation	E° / V
$Cl_{2(aq)} + 2e^- \rightleftharpoons 2Cl^-_{(aq)}$	+1.36
$MnO_4^-{}_{(aq)} + 8H^+{}_{(aq)} + 5e^- \rightleftharpoons Mn^{2+}{}_{(aq)} + 4H_2O_{(l)}$	+1.51

5.1 Give the oxidation state of Mn in MnO_4^-.

....
(1 mark)

5.2 Use the information in **Table 1** to construct a balanced ionic equation for the redox reaction.

....
(1 mark)

5.3 Calculate the EMF of the redox reaction.

EMF = ... V
(1 mark)

5.4 Explain how the information in **Table 1** shows that MnO_4^- is a suitable reagent for the oxidation of Cl^-.

....
(1 mark)

35.0 cm³ of the chloride solution was titrated against a 0.230 mol dm⁻³ solution of acidified MnO_4^- ions. 18.7 cm³ of the MnO_4^- solution was required for complete oxidation of the chloride ions.

5.5 Calculate the number of chloride ions in the scientist's 150 cm³ solution.
(Avogadro constant = 6.02×10^{23})

number of ions = ...
(4 marks)

5.6 Suggest and explain how both the rate and the EMF of the redox reaction would change if iodide ions were used in place of chloride ions.

....

....

....
(2 marks)

6 Urease is a protein found in soils. It is an enzyme that catalyses the hydrolysis of urea into carbon dioxide and ammonia. The reaction scheme for this process is shown in **Figure 2**.

Figure 2

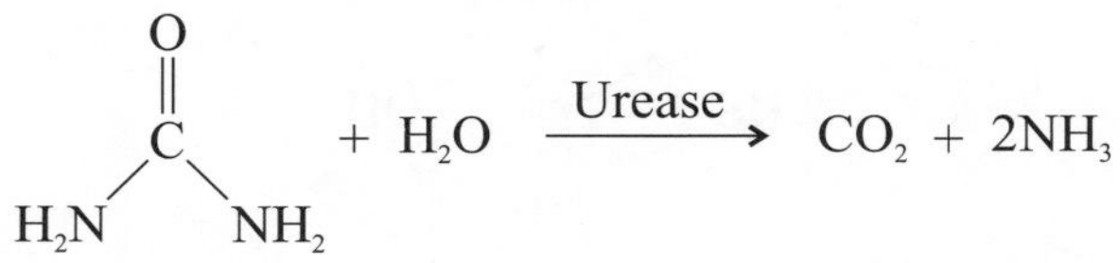

$H_2N-C(=O)-NH_2 + H_2O \xrightarrow{\text{Urease}} CO_2 + 2NH_3$

6.1 Suggest why soils that contain high concentrations of urease may have a relatively high pH.

....

....
(2 marks)

6.2 In the absence of urease, the hydrolysis of urea at 298 K has a rate constant of 1.46×10^{-7} s^{-1}. The Arrhenius constant for the reaction is 7.098×10^3 s^{-1}.

Use the Arrhenius equation ($k = Ae^{\frac{-E_a}{RT}}$) to calculate the activation energy of the hydrolysis of urea, in kJ mol^{-1}, at 298 K. (The gas constant, $R = 8.31$ J K^{-1} mol^{-1})

activation energy = ... kJ mol^{-1}
(2 marks)

The structure of the urease inhibitor phenyl phosphorodiamidate (PPDA) is shown in **Figure 3**.

Figure 3

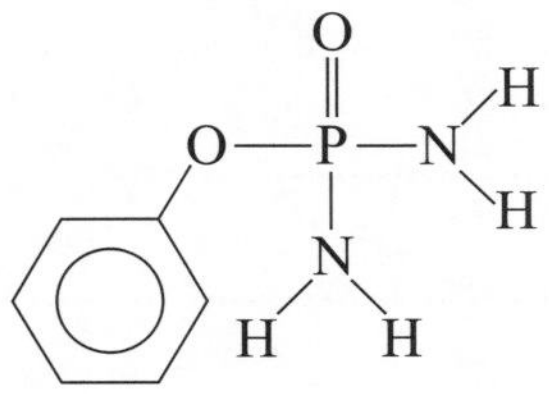

6.3 With reference to the structure shown in **Figure 3**, suggest how PPDA can inhibit the action of urease.

....

....
(2 marks)

6.4 Deduce how many atoms in the structure of PPDA can form a hydrogen bond.

....
(1 mark)

6.5 Under the basic conditions found in some soils, PPDA can be hydrolysed in a similar way to an ester. Suggest which bond in PPDA is broken during this hydrolysis.

....
(1 mark)

The primary structure of urease contains a high proportion of the amino acid cysteine.
The structure of cysteine is shown in **Figure 4**.

Figure 4

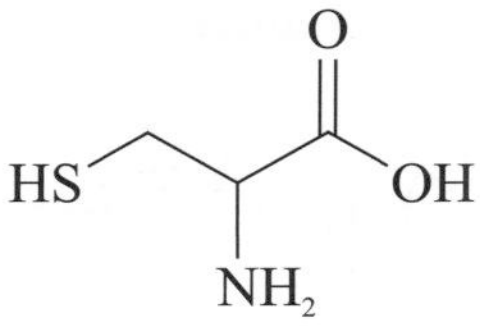

$$HS\text{-}CH\text{-}C(=O)\text{-}OH, \; NH_2$$

6.6 Cysteine contains a chiral centre. On **Figure 4**, label the chiral centre in cysteine using an asterisk (*).

(1 mark)

6.7 The tertiary structure of urease is stabilised by the formation of S-S bonds between cysteine residues.
Draw the skeletal formula of the compound formed when two cysteine molecules are joined by an S-S bond.

(1 mark)

The structure of two more amino acids, lysine and leucine, are shown in **Figure 5**.

Figure 5

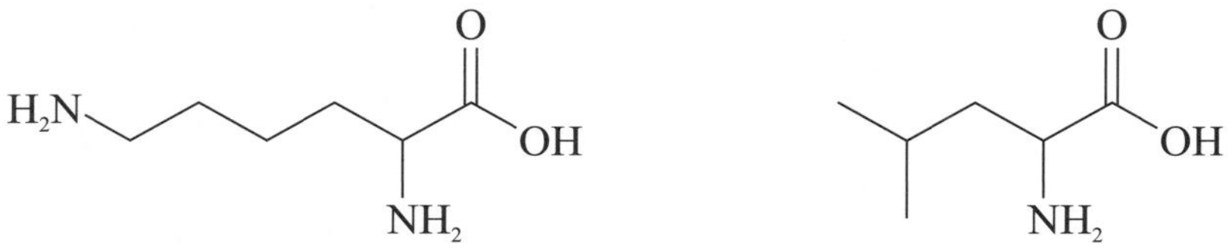

Lysine

Leucine

6.8 Suggest and explain which of the amino acids in **Figure 5** is more soluble in water.

....

....

....

(2 marks)

6.9 Two students analysed a sample of lysine using thin-layer chromatography.
The amino acid was found to have a different R_f value on each of the two students' chromatograms.
Suggest **two** possible reasons for this difference.

....

....

....

(2 marks)

EXAM TIP It's really important that you pay close attention to units when you're doing calculation questions in the exam. For example, if you've got a concentration in g dm⁻³ and a volume in cm³, you'll need to do a bit of maths to get them to be in the same units (e.g. g dm⁻³ and dm³).

Score

28

Mixed Questions — 4

1   Tris(ethane-1,2-diamine)cobalt(III) is a complex ion that exists as a pair of enantiomers.
The complex ion has the formula $[Co(en)_3]^{3+}$ (where en = ethane-1,2-diamine, $NH_2CH_2CH_2NH_2$).
One of the enantiomers of $[Co(en)_3]^{3+}$ is shown in **Figure 1**.

Figure 1

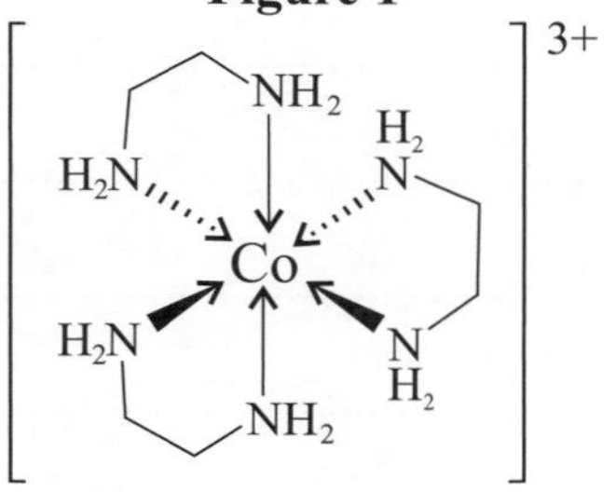

1.1   Draw the other enantiomer of $[Co(en)_3]^{3+}$.

(1 mark)

1.2   Deduce the oxidation state of Co in $[Co(en)_3]^{3+}$.

....
(1 mark)

1.3   State the co-ordination number of Co in $[Co(en)_3]^{3+}$.

....
(1 mark)

1.4   Explain why the entropy change for the ligand substitution reaction of $[Co(en)_3]^{3+}$
with H_2O does not lead to a favourable change in the Gibbs free-energy.

....

....
(2 marks)

Ethane-1,2-diamine can be used as a starting point for the synthesis of the multidentate ligand EDTA.
The skeletal formula of EDTA is shown in **Figure 2**.

Figure 2

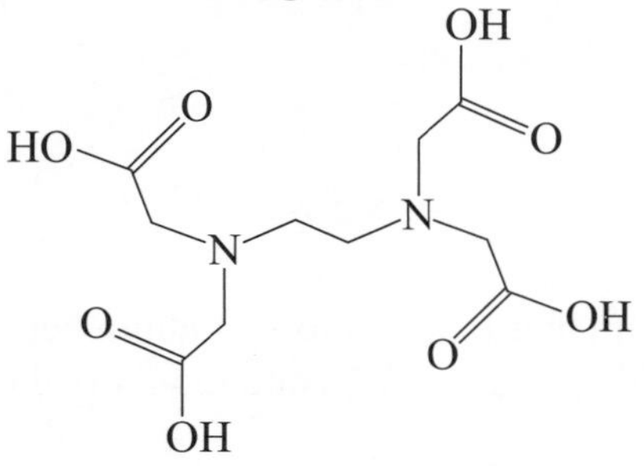

1.5   State what is meant by the term multidentate ligand.

....
(1 mark)

1.6 Suggest the name of a compound that could be reacted with ethane-1,2-diamine to produce EDTA.

....
(1 mark)

A scientist is attempting to dissolve a sample of EDTA in a solution with a pH of 7.
She finds that the sample of EDTA has a low solubility in the solution.

1.7 Suggest a reagent that could be used to increase the solubility of the EDTA sample. Explain your answer.

....

....

....

....

....
(4 marks)

2 The structures of three aromatic compounds are shown in **Figure 3**.

Figure 3

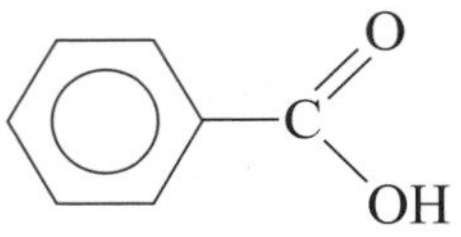

Benzoic acid 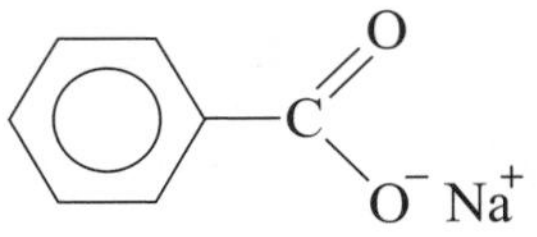   Sodium benzoate 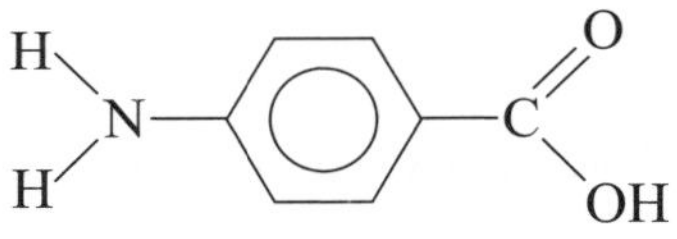   4-aminobenzoic acid

Benzoic acid is a weak acid.
A scientist makes up 750 cm³ of a solution of benzoic acid (C_6H_5COOH) with a concentration of 0.025 mol dm⁻³. The acid dissociation constant, K_a, for benzoic acid is 6.3×10^{-5} mol dm⁻³.

2.1 Calculate the pH of the solution of benzoic acid.

pH = ...
(4 marks)

Benzoic acid can react with sodium hydroxide to form sodium benzoate. The scientist slowly adds small amounts of solid sodium hydroxide to the solution and monitors the pH change during the reaction.

2.2 Write an ionic equation for the reaction that occurs between benzoic acid and sodium hydroxide.

....
(1 mark)

2.3 The scientist keeps adding more sodium hydroxide until it is in excess.
He finds that the pH of the resulting solution is 12.2.
Use this information to calculate the mass of sodium hydroxide that was added to the benzoic acid solution over the course of the experiment. (The ionic product of water, $K_w = 1.00 \times 10^{-14}$)

mass = ... g

(7 marks)

2.4 4-aminobenzoic acid can be synthesised from benzoic acid in a two-step process.
Suggest reagents and conditions for each step in the synthesis.

Step 1: ....

....

Step 2: ....

....

(5 marks)

2.5 State the number of peaks that you would expect to be produced
in the ^{1}H and ^{13}C NMR spectra of 4-aminobenzoic acid.

Number of peaks in ^{1}H spectrum: ....

Number of peaks in ^{13}C spectrum: ....

(2 marks)

2.6 Under certain conditions, 4-aminobenzoic acid undergoes a polymerisation reaction to form a polyamide.
Draw the repeating unit of the polyamide formed from 4-aminobenzoic acid.

(1 mark)

EXAM TIP

Some of the trickier questions in the exam may require you to bring together knowledge from different areas of chemistry, so take your time to read each question part carefully so you understand what it's asking. You don't want to go into autopilot and start writing about acids and bases, when the question is actually testing your knowledge of amino acids, for example.

Score

31

Answers

Unit 1: Section 1 — Atomic Structure

Pages 3-5: Atomic Structure — 1

1   C *[1 mark]*

2   C *[1 mark]*

All copper atoms have 29 protons in their nuclei, so copper-64 must have 64 − 29 = 35 neutrons.

3   C *[1 mark]*

Remember, chromium behaves a bit oddly in that it donates one of its 4s electrons to the 3d sub-shell. This gives it an exactly half-full 3d sub-shell ($3d^5$), which is a more stable arrangement.

4   B *[1 mark]*

m is the mass of the missing isotope.

$$\frac{(21 \times 0.3) + (20 \times 90.5) + (m \times 9.2)}{100} = 20.187$$

1816.3 + 9.2m = 2018.7

9.2m = 202.4

m = 22

5   C *[1 mark]*

Phosphorus has electron configuration $1s^2\, 2s^2\, 2p^6\, 3s^2\, 3p^3$. Electrons fill orbitals in a sub-shell singly before they start sharing, so each of the 3p orbitals contain just one unpaired electron.

6.1   Isotopes are atoms of the same element with different numbers of neutrons *[1 mark]*.

6.2 $^{17}_{8}\text{O}$ *[1 mark]*

There are 8 unshaded particles in the nucleus shown in Figure 1, which must be the protons since the atomic number of oxygen is 8. This means the 9 shaded particles are the neutrons.

6.3   The three isotopes have different masses *[1 mark]*. In a mass spectrometer they all have the same kinetic energy and so lighter isotopes will move at higher speeds *[1 mark]*.

6.4 $1s^2\, 2s^2\, 2p^4$

6.5   In oxygen, the outer electron is being removed from an (2p) orbital containing two electrons, whereas in nitrogen the outer electron is being removed from a (2p) orbital containing only 1 electron *[1 mark]*. The repulsion between the two electrons in the orbital makes the outer electron easier to remove from oxygen than from nitrogen, so less energy is needed to do so *[1 mark]*.

6.6   E.g. The model is easy to draw and understand *[1 mark]* and fits well with most observations of e.g. bonding or ionisation energy trends *[1 mark]*.

7.1 $1s^2\, 2s^2\, 2p^6\, 3s^2\, 3p^6\, 4s^2$ *[1 mark]*

7.2   Argon *[1 mark]*

7.3   The second electron is harder to remove because it is being removed from a positive ion/there are now a greater number of protons than of electrons so each outer shell electron receives a greater positive pull from the nucleus *[1 mark]*. There is less repulsion from other electrons so it is held more strongly by the nucleus *[1 mark]*.

7.4   Jumps between the 2nd and 3rd and the 10th and 11th ionisation energies indicate the presence of discrete shells/energy levels *[1 mark]*, as it takes significantly more energy to remove electrons held in shells/energy levels closer to the nucleus *[1 mark]*. The jump after the 2nd electron is removed indicates two electrons in the outermost shell/energy level *[1 mark]*. The jump after the 10th electron is removed indicates 8 electrons in the next shell/energy level *[1 mark]*.

Pages 6-8: Atomic Structure — 2

1.1   How to grade your answer:

     Level 0:   There is no relevant information. *[No marks]*

     Level 1:   Two stages are explained, but incompletely or with errors OR only one stage is explained, but correctly and in full. Answer does not have a logical structure. *[1-2 marks]*

     Level 2:   All stages are explained, but incompletely or with errors OR two stages are explained, but completely and in full. Explanation of stage 3 follows on from stage 1. *[3-4 marks]*

     Level 3:   All stages are explained correctly and in full. Explanation of stage 1 is followed by stage 2 and then stage 3. *[5-6 marks]*

You only need to talk about one method of ionisation (electrospray or electron impact) to explain stage 1 in full.

     Indicative content:

     Stage 1

     A sample is ionised to form 1+ ions.

     Two commonly used methods for ionisation are electrospray and electron impact.

     In electrospray ionisation the sample is dissolved and forced through a small nozzle at high pressure. A high voltage is applied, causing each sample particle to gain an H^+ ion.

     In electron impact ionisation, the sample is vaporised and high energy electrons are fired at it. This knocks one electron off each sample particle, so they become 1+ ions. The ions are accelerated in an electric field so they all have the same kinetic energy.

     The ions are allowed to drift a fixed distance through a region with no electric field, until they hit the detector.

     Stage 2

     The spectrometer measures the time the ions take to cover the fixed distance to the detector.

     Heavier particles will take longer to cover the fixed distance than lighter ones.

     Stage 3

     When ions hit the detector, an electric current is generated. This current may be measured to determine the number of ions arriving at the detector. The more ions that hit the detector, the larger the current.

     The spectrometer will register the number of ions detected at each mass to charge ratio over a range (spectrum) of values. This allows the mass spectrum to be produced and shows the relative abundances of the isotopes present.

1.2 $$A_r = \frac{(84 \times 0.560) + (86 \times 9.86) + (87 \times 7.02) + (88 \times 82.6)}{100}$$

     $= 87.7454$

     $= \mathbf{87.7}$ **(3 s.f.)**

     [3 marks for correct answer given to 3 s.f. or 2 marks for correct answer not given to 3 s.f., otherwise 1 mark for correct method for calculating A_r.]

1.3   Strontium *[1 mark]*

1.4 $t = d\sqrt{\dfrac{m}{2KE}}$

$\dfrac{t}{d} = \sqrt{\dfrac{m}{2KE}}$

$\left(\dfrac{t}{d}\right)^2 = \dfrac{m}{2KE}$

$m = 2KE\left(\dfrac{t}{d}\right)^2$

$m = 2 \times (2.000 \times 10^{-16}) \times \left(\dfrac{1.338 \times 10^{-5}}{0.7000}\right)^2$

$= 1.461423... \times 10^{-25}$ kg

$= \mathbf{1.461 \times 10^{-25}}$ **kg (4 s.f.)**

[3 marks for correct answer given to 4 s.f. or 2 marks for correct answer not given to 4 s.f., otherwise 1 mark for correctly rearranging equation.]

1.5   A molecular ion is formed in the mass spectrometer when one electron is removed from the molecule *[1 mark]*. The mass/charge ratio of the molecular ion peak in the spectrum then gives the relative mass of the molecule *[1 mark]*.

2.1   The 6th electron is taken from an inner shell/a shell closer to the nucleus *[1 mark]*. It also experiences less shielding by other electrons *[1 mark]*, and so the pull of the nucleus is greater/much more energy is required to remove the electron *[1 mark]*.

2.2 $X^{5+}_{(g)} \rightarrow X^{6+}_{(g)} + e^-$ *[1 mark]*

2.3   Phosphorus *[1 mark]*

*There is a large difference between the fifth and sixth ionisation energies of element **X**, which indicates that it has 5 electrons in its outermost shell, and so must be in Group 5 of the Periodic Table. The question tells you it's in Period 3, and so element **X** can only be phosphorus.*

3.1   First ionisation energy is the energy needed to remove 1 electron from each atom in 1 mole of gaseous atoms to form 1 mole of gaseous 1+ ions *[1 mark]*.

3.2   The overall shape of the graph would be similar *[1 mark]* because of similar sub-shell structure across the periods *[1 mark]*. But the line for Period 2 would be higher *[1 mark]*, because the outer electrons are closer to the nucleus and also less shielded from it, and so take more energy to remove *[1 mark]*.

Unit 1: Section 2 — Amount of Substance

Pages 9-12: Amount of Substance — 1

1   **B** *[1 mark]*

For every mole of PCl_5 molecules, there are 5 moles of Cl atoms. So the number of chlorine atoms is $5 \times 6.02 \times 10^{23} = 3.01 \times 10^{24}$.

2   **B** *[1 mark]*

3   **C** *[1 mark]*

The number of moles of $BaSO_4$ is $3.16 \div 233.4 = 0.0135$ moles. The balanced equation shows that one mole of $CuSO_4$ reacts to form one mole of $BaSO_4$. So you need $0.0135 \div 0.650 = 0.0208$ dm^3 $= 20.8$ cm^3 of $CuSO_4$ solution to form 3.16 g of $BaSO_4$.

4   **C** *[1 mark]*

Work out the mass of oxygen atoms that reacted: $4.26 - 1.86 = 2.40$ g. Then work out the number of moles of each element: moles of $P = 1.86 \div 31.0 = 0.06$ moles moles of $O = 2.4 \div 16 = 0.15$ moles. Then find the simplest whole number ratio of moles: $0.06 \div 0.06 = 1$, $0.15 \div 0.06 = 2.5$. So the ratio of P to O atoms is $1:2.5$, which is the same as $2:5$. So the empirical formula is P_2O_5.

5.1 $2H^+_{(aq)} + 2OH^-_{(aq)} \rightarrow 2H_2O_{(l)}$ / $H^+_{(aq)} + OH^-_{(aq)} \rightarrow H_2O_{(l)}$ *[1 mark]*

5.2   Volume of acid *[1 mark]*.

5.3

	Titre			
	Rough	1	2	3
Initial reading / cm³	11.10	28.50	11.25	27.60
Final reading / cm³	28.50	45.15	27.60	44.30
Volume of HCl added / cm³	17.40	16.65	16.35	16.70

[2 marks for all four answers correct to 4 significant figures, otherwise 1 mark for three answers correct to 4 significant figures.]

5.4   mean titre $= (16.65 + 16.70) \div 2 = 16.675 = \mathbf{16.68}$ **cm³**

[2 marks for correct answer, otherwise 1 mark for including only concordant results in the calculation.]

Concordant results are ones that are very similar to each other (usually within 0.10 cm³) — the result for titre 2 is quite a bit lower than for titres 1 and 3, so it isn't concordant and shouldn't be included when calculating the mean titre.

5.5   Moles of HCl $= 0.100 \times 0.01668 = 1.668 \times 10^{-3}$ mol
There are 2 moles of HCl for each mole of $Ca(OH)_2$, so moles of $Ca(OH)_2$ in 25 cm³ of diluted solution $= 1.668 \times 10^{-3} \div 2 = 8.34 \times 10^{-4}$ mol
Moles of $Ca(OH)_2$ in original sample $= (8.34 \times 10^{-4} \div 25.0) \times 250 = 8.34 \times 10^{-3}$ mol
Concentration of $Ca(OH)_2 = 8.34 \times 10^{-3} \div 0.0250$
$= \mathbf{0.334}$ **mol dm⁻³**

[4 marks for correct answer, otherwise 1 mark for correct number of moles of HCl, 1 mark for correct number of moles of $Ca(OH)_2$ in 25 cm³ of diluted solution, 1 mark for correct number of moles of $Ca(OH)_2$ in original sample (allow error carried forward from question 5.4 throughout).]

Be careful with units in calculations like this. The volumes you're given are in cm³, but the concentrations are in mol dm⁻³. So you need to convert the volume of the $Ca(OH)_2$ solution into dm³ before calculating its concentration. That's why you divide by 0.0250 in the last step rather than by 25.0.

6.1   Divide by the A_r of each element:
C: $40.9 \div 12.0 = 3.4083...$
H: $4.5 \div 1.0 = 4.5$
O: $54.6 \div 16.0 = 3.4125$
Divide through by the smallest number:
C: $3.4083... \div 3.4083... = 1.00$
H: $4.5 \div 3.4083... = 1.32...$
O: $3.4125 \div 3.4083... = 1.00...$
Simplest whole-number ratio of C:H:O = 3:4:3
Empirical formula $= \mathbf{C_3H_4O_3}$

[2 marks for correct answer, otherwise 1 mark for dividing by the A_r of each element.]

6.2   Empirical mass $= (3 \times 12.0) + (4 \times 1.0) + (3 \times 16.0) = 88.0$
Number of empirical units $= 176.0 \div 88.0 = 2$
Molecular formula $= 2 \times (C_3H_4O_3) = \mathbf{C_6H_8O_6}$ *[1 mark]*

6.3   Mass of ascorbic acid in grams $= 300 \div 1000 = 0.300$ g
Moles of ascorbic acid $= 0.300 \div 176.0$
$= 0.0017045...$
$= \mathbf{0.00170}$ **mol** *[1 mark]*

7.1 $p = (nRT) \div V$
$= ((2.50 \div 58.0) \times 8.31 \times (10.0 + 273)) \div (750 \times 10^{-6})$
$= 135157$ Pa $= 135.157$ kPa $= \mathbf{135}$ **kPa**

[4 marks for correct answer, otherwise 1 mark for correct working of moles of C_4H_{10}, 1 mark for correctly rearranging the ideal gas equation, 1 mark for substituting correct values into the equation.]

Again, be careful with your units here. Volume needs to be in m³, so you need to divide by 750×10^{-6} m³ rather than the 750 cm³ given in the question. Temperature needs to be in K, so you need to add 273 on to the given value of 10 °C. And the value for pressure that you'll get is in Pa, but you need to give an answer in kPa, so convert that by dividing by 1000.

7.2 Moles of O_2 = 3.84 ÷ (2 × 16.0) = 0.120
Moles of C_4H_{10} = 0.120 ÷ 6.5 = 0.0184...
Mass of C_4H_{10} = 0.0185... × 58.0 = 1.07... = **1.07 g**
[3 marks for correct answer, otherwise 1 mark for correct number of moles of O_2, 1 mark for correct number of moles of C_4H_{10}.]

7.3 C_8H_{18} + 12.5O_2 → 8CO_2 + 9H_2O *[1 mark]*

8.1 Any two from: e.g. rinse the weighing boat into the flask after transferring the solid/re-weigh the weighing boat after transferring the solid to determine the precise mass of solid added to the flask. / Add a small amount of distilled water to the volumetric flask first and swirl until all the solid has dissolved/dissolve the solid in a beaker of water before transferring to the volumetric flask. / Use a funnel to add the solid/solution to the volumetric flask. *[2 marks — 1 mark for each correct answer.]*

8.2 E.g. Moles of $NaHCO_3$ = 0.30 × (250 ÷ 1000) = 0.075 mol
M_r($NaHCO_3$) = 23.0 + 1.0 + 12.0 + (3 × 16.0) = 84
Mass of $NaHCO_3$ = 0.075 × 84
= **6.3 g**
[2 marks for correct answer, otherwise 1 mark for correct working.]
You could also have worked this out by finding the mass of $NaHCO_3$ required to make a 1 dm³ of 0.30 mol dm⁻³ solution, and dividing it by 4 to find the mass needed to make a 0.250 mol dm⁻³ solution.

8.3 Moles of $NaHCO_3$ = 0.075 × (100 ÷ 250) = 0.030 mol
Concentration of $NaHCO_3$ = 0.030 ÷ (250 ÷ 1000)
= **0.12 mol dm⁻³**
[2 marks for correct answer, otherwise 1 mark for correct number of moles of $NaHCO_3$.]

8.4 Error 1: the mean titre would be lower than it should be *[1 mark]*. Error 2: the mean titre would be higher than it should be *[1 mark]*.

Pages 13-16: Amount of Substance — 2

1.1 Moles of PbS = 4.50 × 10⁶ ÷ 239.3 = 18804.84... mol
Moles of O_2 = 18804.84... × (3 ÷ 2) = 28207.27... mol
Mass of O_2 = 28207.27... × (2 × 16.0) = 902632.67... g
= 902.632... kg
= **903 kg**
[3 marks for correct answer, otherwise 1 mark for correct number of moles of PbS, 1 mark for correct number of moles of O_2.]

1.2 E.g. 2 moles of PbS react to give 2 moles of PbO in step 1.
2 moles of PbO reacts to give 2 moles of Pb in step 2.
So 2 moles of PbS reacts to give 2 moles of Pb.
Moles of Pb = 18804.84... mol
Mass of Pb = 207.2 × 18804.84... = 3896364.39... g
= 3896.364... kg
= **3900 kg**
[2 marks for correct answer, otherwise 1 mark for correct working.]
You could also have worked this out by finding the mass of lead in 4.5 tonnes of PbS — (4.50 × 10⁶) × (207.2 ÷ 239.3) = 3896364.39... g.

1.3 2FeS$_2$ + 5.5O_2 → Fe$_2$O$_3$ + 4SO$_2$ *[1 mark]*

1.4 Atom economy of reaction A = (A_r(Ti) ÷ M_r(reactants)) × 100
= 47.9 ÷ ((47.9 + (4 × 35.5)) + (2 × 24.3)) × 100 = **20.1%**
Atom economy of reaction B = (A_r(Ti) ÷ M_r(reactants)) × 100
= 47.9 ÷ ((47.9 + (4 × 35.5)) + (4 × 23.0)) × 100 = **17.0%**
[2 marks — 1 mark for each correct atom economy.]

2 $n = (pV) ÷ (RT)$
= ((101 × 10³) × (29.4 × 10⁻⁶)) ÷ (8.31 × 298)
= 1.19... × 10⁻³ mol of H_2 produced
1 mole of H_2 is produced from 1 mole of X,
so moles of X = 1.19... × 10⁻³ mol.
M_r (X) = mass ÷ moles = 0.0784 ÷ (1.19... × 10⁻³) = 65.4
Metal X is zinc.
[4 marks for correct answer, otherwise 1 mark for correctly rearranging the ideal gas equation, 1 mark for correct number of moles of H_2, 1 mark for correct M_r of X.]

3.1 Percentage of oxygen = 100 − (40.0 + 14.3) = 45.7%
Divide by the A_r of each element:
N: 40.0 ÷ 14.0 = 2.85...
H: 14.3 ÷ 1.0 = 14.3
O: 45.7÷ 16.0 = 2.85...
Divide through by the smallest number:
N: 2.85... ÷ 2.85... = 1.00
H: 14.3 ÷ 2.85... = 5.00
O: 2.85... ÷ 2.85... = 1.00
Empirical formula = NH_5O
[3 marks — 1 mark for correct percentage of oxygen, 1 mark for dividing by the A_r of each element, 1 mark for dividing through by the smallest number.]

3.2 $V = (nRT) ÷ p$
= (0.0820 × 8.31 × 298) ÷ (101 × 10³)
= 2.010... × 10⁻³ m³
= 2.01... dm³ = **2.01 dm³**
[3 marks for correct answer, otherwise 1 mark for correctly rearranging the ideal gas equation, 1 mark for substituting correct values into the equation.]

3.3 0.0820 × 6.02 × 10²³ = **4.94 × 10²²** *[1 mark]*

4.1 $n = (pV) ÷ (RT)$
= ((101 × 10³) × (280 × 10⁻⁶)) ÷ (8.31 × (22 + 273))
= 0.0115... mol of CO_2 produced
1 mole of CO_2 is produced from 1 mole of $CaCO_3$,
so moles of $CaCO_3$ = 0.0115... mol
Mass of $CaCO_3$ = 0.0115... × (40.1 + 12 + (3 × 16.0))
= 1.15... g
Percentage of $CaCO_3$ in sample = (1.15... ÷ 1.75) × 100
= **66.0%**
[5 marks for correct answer, otherwise 1 mark for correctly rearranging the ideal gas equation, 1 mark for correct number of moles of CO_2, 1 mark for correct number of moles of $CaCO_3$, 1 mark for correct mass of $CaCO_3$.]

4.2 E.g. moles of CuO = (3.60 ÷ (63.5 + 16.0)) = 0.0452... mol
1 mole of CuO is produced from 1 mole of $CuCO_3$,
so moles of $CuCO_3$ that reacted = 0.0452... mol.
Total moles of $CuCO_3$ that were heated =
0.0452 × (100 ÷ 92.4) = 0.0490...
Mass of $CuCO_3$ that was heated =
0.0490... × (63.5 + 12.0 + (3 × 16.0)) = 6.0524... = **6.05 g**
[4 marks for correct answer, otherwise 1 mark for correct number of moles of CuO, 1 mark for correct number of moles of $CuCO_3$, 1 mark for correct total number of moles of $CuCO_3$ that were heated.]
You could also work this out by finding the theoretical mass of CuO that would have formed had all of the $CuCO_3$ reacted, converting this to moles and then using this figure to find the moles (and mass) of $CuCO_3$ that was heated.

4.3 Atom economy = (M_r(CuO) ÷ M_r(reactants)) × 100
= [(63.5 + 16.0) ÷ (63.5 + 12.0 + (3 × 16.0))] × 100
= **64.4%** *[1 mark]*

4.4 Environmental reason: any one of, e.g.: reactions with high atom economies produce less waste so are less polluting / make more efficient use of raw materials so are more sustainable. *[1 mark]*.
Economic reason: any one of, e.g.: reactions with high atom economies require less money to be spent on separating the desired product from the waste products / require less money to be spent on treating/disposing of waste *[1 mark]*.

5 How to grade your answer:
Level 0: There is no relevant information. *[No marks]*
Level 1: One stage is covered well OR two stages are covered but they are incomplete and not always accurate. The answer is not in a logical order. *[1 to 2 marks]*
Level 2: Two stages are covered well OR all 3 stages are covered but they are incomplete and not always accurate. The answer is mostly in a logical order. *[3 to 4 marks]*

Level 3:   All 3 stages are covered and are complete and accurate. The answer is coherent and is in a logical order. *[5 to 6 marks]*

Indicative content:

Stage 1: Carrying out a titration

Use a pipette to add a set volume of one of the acids to a conical flask.

Add a few drops of an appropriate indicator to the flask.

Fill a burette with the standard solution of sodium hydroxide. Use a funnel to carefully pour the sodium hydroxide into the burette. Do this below eye level to avoid any acid splashing on to your face or eyes.

Do a rough titration to get an idea where the end point is. Add the alkali to the acid using a burette, giving the flask a regular swirl.

Then do an accurate titration. Run the alkali in to within 2 cm^3 of the end point. When you get to this stage, add it dropwise.

Repeat the titration several times.

Repeat these steps for the other acid.

Stage 2: Collecting and processing results

Take an initial reading to see exactly how much alkali is in the burette before adding any to the flask.

Work out the amount of alkali used to neutralise the acid by subtracting the initial reading from the final reading, after the alkali has been added to the flask.

Use the results from each repeat to calculate the mean volume of alkali required to neutralise each acid.

Leave out any anomalous results when calculating the mean.

Stage 3: Identifying the acids

The equations for the two reactions are:

$H_2SO_4 + 2NaOH \rightarrow Na_2SO_4 + 2H_2O$

$HCl + NaOH \rightarrow NaCl + H_2O$

H_2SO_4 reacts with NaOH in a 1:2 molar ratio and HCl reacts with NaOH in a 1:1 molar ratio.

So, the acid that required twice as much NaOH to neutralise is H_2SO_4.

Unit 1: Section 3 — Bonding

Pages 17-19: Bonding — 1

1   B *[1 mark]*
C_2H_4 contains a double covalent bond between the two carbon atoms. H_2O and CH_4 have only single covalent bonds, and HCN contains a triple covalent bond and a single covalent bond.

2   A *[1 mark]*
Caesium is in Group 1 of the Periodic Table, so it forms 1+ ions. Selenium is in Group 6 of the Periodic Table, so it forms 2− ions. Two caesium ions are needed to balance out the charge on one selenium ion.

3   B *[1 mark]*

4   D *[1 mark]*
F_2 doesn't contain any polar bonds, but CBr_4, CO_2 and PF_3 all do. In CBr_4 and CO_2, the polar bonds are arranged symmetrically:

*So neither CBr_4 nor CO_2 has an overall dipole.
But in PF_3 (which is trigonal pyramidal), thanks to the polar bonds, the bottom of the molecule is slightly negative and the top is slightly positive:*

So PF_3 does have an overall dipole.

5   C *[1 mark]*
PF_5 has 5 electron pairs around the central phosphorus atom, with no lone pairs — so it must be trigonal bipyramidal.

6.1

Name	Formula	Formulas of ions present	
Iron(III) sulfate	$Fe_2(SO_4)_3$	**Fe^{3+}**	**SO_4^{2-}**
Aluminium nitrate	$Al(NO_3)_3$	**Al^{3+}**	**NO_3^-**
Chromium (III) hydroxide	**$Cr(OH)_3$**	Cr^{3+}	OH^-
Ammonium carbonate	**$(NH_4)_2CO_3$**	NH_4^+	CO_3^{2-}

[1 mark for each row correct]

6.2

A coordinate bond is a covalent bond in which both electrons in the shared pair come from the same atom *[1 mark]*.

6.3

[1 mark]

You still get the mark here if you've shown the positive charge on the N atom itself (rather than on the whole ion).

7.1   (giant) ionic (lattice) *[1 mark]*
The key idea here is that it's ionic — if you said that, you get the mark.

7.2   It takes a lot of energy to overcome the strong electrostatic attractions between the positive and negative ions *[1 mark]*.

7.3   Chloride ions have a single negative charge *[1 mark]*. As the chloride has the formula XCl_2, X must be an element that forms 2+ ions *[1 mark]*.

7.4   Melting or dissolving the substance allows the ions to move and carry a charge *[1 mark]*.

8.1   Diagram: e.g.

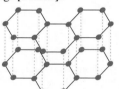

[1 mark]

The carbon atoms are arranged in sheets of hexagons, with each carbon atom covalently bonded to three other carbon atoms *[1 mark]*. The fourth outer electron of each carbon atom is delocalised *[1 mark]*. The sheets of carbon atoms are held together by Van der Waals forces *[1 mark]*.

It's fine to use any valid alternative name for 'Van der Waals forces' (e.g. 'induced dipole-dipole forces', 'London forces' or 'dispersion forces').

8.2   Covalent bonds and Van der Waals forces *[1 mark]*.
That's covalent bonds between the atoms in the I_2 molecules, and Van der Waals forces between the molecules.

8.3   To melt graphite you have to break the strong covalent bonds holding the carbon atoms together *[1 mark]*, which needs a lot of energy *[1 mark]*.

8.4   Graphite — conducts electricity, because it contains delocalised/free electrons *[1 mark]*.
Iodine — does not conduct electricity, because it does not contain any free electrons or ions *[1 mark]*.

Pages 20-22: Bonding — 2

1.1

Liquid Formula	Deflection/cm	Polarity
H_2O	4	Polar
Br_2	0	**Non-polar**
CCl_4	0	Non-polar
$CHCl_3$	3	**Polar**

[1 mark for both rows correct]

1.2 Any three from: e.g. the flow rate of the liquid / the position of the charged rod / the charge on the rod / the height of the burette / the volume of liquid in the burette / the position of the ruler *[1 mark for each sensible suggestion]*.

1.3 How to grade your answer:
Level 0: There is no relevant information *[No marks]*.
Level 1: There is a good explanation of why one of the molecules given has the observed polarity, or an incomplete explanation of why two of the molecules given have the observed polarities. *[1 to 2 marks]*
Level 2: There is a good explanation of why two of the molecules given have the observed polarity, or an incomplete explanation of why all three of the molecules given have the observed polarities. *[3 to 4 marks]*
Level 3: There is a complete and accurate explanation of why all three of the molecules given have the observed polarities. The answer is coherent. *[5 to 6 marks]*

Indicative content:
Br_2
The Br–Br bond in Br_2 is non-polar, as both atoms have the same electronegativity.
So the molecule has no overall dipole.
Diagram to show molecule: Br — Br
CCl_4
All of the C–Cl bonds in CCl_4 are polar, because chlorine is more electronegative than carbon.
But the polar bonds in CCl_4 are arranged symmetrically. This means that the charges cancel out, so the molecule has no permanent dipole and is non-polar.
Diagram to show symmetry:

$$Cl^{\delta^-}$$
$$C^{\delta^+}$$
$$\delta^-Cl \quad Cl^{\delta^-}$$
$$Cl^{\delta^-}$$

$CHCl_3$
All of the C–Cl bonds in $CHCl_3$ are polar.
Carbon and hydrogen have similar electronegativities/are much less electronegative than chlorine.
The negative charge is all pulled towards the chlorine atoms, making them slightly negative.
So the carbon and hydrogen atoms become slightly positive, creating a permanent dipole.
Diagram to show dipole:

$$H^{\delta^+}$$
$$C^{\delta^+}$$
$$\delta^-Cl \quad Cl^{\delta^-}$$
$$Cl^{\delta^-}$$

2.1 tetrahedral *[1 mark]*
2.2 109.5° *[1 mark]*
2.3 Silicon dioxide — giant covalent/macromolecular *[1 mark]*
Ice — molecular *[1 mark]*
2.4 E.g.

$$H^{\delta^+} \quad \delta^+ \quad {}^{\delta^-}_{\times\times}O_{\times\times}$$
$$H^{\delta^+} \quad H^{\delta^+}$$
$$\delta^- {}_{\times\times}O_{\times\times}$$
$$\delta^+ H$$

[2 marks — 1 mark for correctly showing the lone pairs and partial charges on the atoms, 1 mark for a dashed line showing a δ⁺ hydrogen on one water molecule being attracted to an oxygen lone pair on another water molecule.]

2.5 To melt SiO_2 many strong covalent bonds have to be broken, so its melting point is high *[1 mark]*. To melt ice you only need to break the hydrogen bonds holding the molecules together *[1 mark]*. These are much weaker than covalent bonds so less energy is needed to break them *[1 mark]*.

2.6 As the ice is heated, the molecules gain energy and vibrate more *[1 mark]*. At the melting point they have enough energy to break some of the hydrogen bonds between them *[1 mark]*, so they can break away from the lattice and move about randomly *[1 mark]*.

2.7 The regular lattice structure of ice contains more hydrogen bonds than liquid water *[1 mark]*. This regular structure holds the molecules further apart on average than the molecules in water/creates empty spaces between the molecules, making ice less dense than water *[1 mark]*.

Pages 23-24: Bonding — 3

1.1 SF_2:

Diagram with bond angle between 97° and 107° *[1 mark]*.
Name of shape: bent/non-linear *[1 mark]*
SF_6:

$$F$$
$$F \quad F$$
$$S \quad \text{all bond angles } 90°$$
$$F \quad F$$
$$F$$
[1 mark]

Name of shape: octahedral *[1 mark]*

1.2 Sulfur is a Group 6 element, so it has 6 electrons in its outer shell *[1 mark]*. It's bonded to two fluorine atoms, so it also has two bonding electrons *[1 mark]*. This gives a total of two bonding pairs and two lone pairs, giving SF_2 a bent shape (since the lone pairs repel each other more than the bonding pairs) *[1 mark]*.

1.3 Sulfur is less electronegative than fluorine, so the S–F bond is polar *[1 mark]*. In SF_6, the polar bonds are arranged symmetrically/the charge is evenly distributed across the molecule, so the molecule is non-polar *[1 mark]*. In SF_2, the fluorine atoms pull the shared electrons/negative charge in the same direction *[1 mark]*, creating an uneven distribution of charge across the molecule/making the fluorine atoms slightly negative and the sulfur atom slightly positive *[1 mark]*.

1.4 SF_2 is a smaller molecule than SF_6, so it will have weaker Van der Waals forces *[1 mark]*. But SF_2 also has a permanent dipole (while SF_6 is non-polar), so it will have permanent dipole-dipole interactions *[1 mark]*. Which fluoride has the higher melting point will depend on whether the strength of the SF_2 dipole is greater than the strength of the Van der Waals forces in SF_6 *[1 mark]*.

2.1 There is a trend of increasing boiling point from PH_3 to SbH_3. This is because the Van der Waals forces increase as the number of electrons in/size of the group 5 atoms increases *[1 mark]*.

2.2 Compared to the other Group 5 hydrides, the boiling point of NH_3 is higher than expected *[1 mark]*. Nitrogen is very electronegative *[1 mark]*, so hydrogen bonds can form between NH_3 molecules *[1 mark]*. Hydrogen bonds are stronger than Van der Waals forces, so more energy is needed to break them *[1 mark]*.

Unit 1: Section 4 — Energetics

Pages 25-27: Energetics — 1

1 B *[1 mark]*
Remember that the symbol ⊖ means under standard conditions — that's 100 kPa pressure and a stated temperature (often 298 K).

2 C *[1 mark]*
Endothermic reactions absorb energy, with ΔH being positive.
Exothermic reactions give out energy, with ΔH being negative.

3   D *[1 mark]*

Bonds broken: 1 C=C bond, 1 H–Cl bond

Bonds made: 1 C–C bond, 1 C–H bond, 1 C–Cl bond

ΔH = *bonds broken – bonds made*

    = $(612 + 432) - (347 + 413 + 346) = -62$ *kJ mol⁻¹*

4   B *[1 mark]*

500 cm³ of solution has a mass of 500 g, so m = 500 g.

$\Delta T = 3.5\,°C = 3.5\,K.$

$q = mc\Delta T = 500\,g \times 4.18\,JK^{-1}g^{-1} \times 3.5\,K = 7315\,J = 7.315\,kJ$

Moles of NaOH = 0.5 × 0.25 = 0.125 mol

The reaction was exothermic, because the temperature rose. So:

Molar enthalpy change of reaction = $\dfrac{q}{n} = \dfrac{-7.315}{0.125} = -59$ *kJ mol⁻¹ (2 s.f.)*

5.1 $\Delta_r H^{\ominus} = \Sigma\,\Delta_f H^{\ominus}$ products $- \Sigma\,\Delta_f H^{\ominus}$ reactants

       $\Delta_r H^{\ominus} = (-467 + 0) - (+64.8 + 0)$

            $= -531.8$ kJ mol⁻¹ = **–532 kJ mol⁻¹ (3 s.f.)**

    [4 marks for correct answer given to 3 s.f. or 3 marks for correct answer not given to 3 s.f., otherwise 1 mark for stating the formula and 1 mark for correctly substituting the enthalpies of formation into the formula.]

It's fine if you drew a Hess's law diagram to work out what calculation you needed to do here, instead of just stating the formula.

5.2

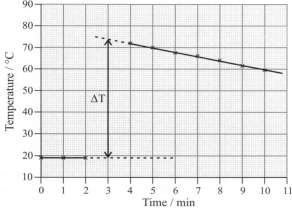

    Maximum temperature change = 55°C

    [5 marks — 1 mark for a sensible scale and labelled axes, 1 mark for correct plotting of all points (to within half a square), 1 mark for both lines of best fit correct, 1 mark for reading the lines of best fit at 3 minutes, 1 mark for maximum temperature change in the range 54 °C - 56 °C.]

5.3   The temperature of the mixture increased when the reaction started *[1 mark]*, so heat energy must have been given out to the surroundings *[1 mark]*.

5.4   20 cm³ of solution has a mass of 20 g, so m = 20 g

       $\Delta T = 55\,°C = 55\,K$

       $q = mc\Delta T = 20 \times 4.18 \times 55 = 4598\,J = 4.958\,kJ$

       Moles of $CuSO_4 = 0.50 \times (20 \div 1000) = 0.010$ mol

       $\Delta_r H = \dfrac{-4.598}{0.010} = -459.8 =$ **–460 kJ mol⁻¹ (2 s.f.)**

    [4 marks for correct answer given to 2 s.f. or 3 marks for correct answer not given to 2 s.f., otherwise 1 mark for correctly substituting the values into q = mcΔT and 1 mark for correct units.]

You still get full marks if you calculated $\Delta_r H$ using a different value for ΔT taken from your graph in question 5.3, even if your ΔT was incorrect. You'd also still get the marks if you gave a correct answer in J mol⁻¹.

5.5   Reason: Heat was lost from the system to the surroundings *[1 mark]*.

       Change: Insulate the system more/use a polystyrene beaker/ put a lid on the beaker *[1 mark]*.

5.6   To make sure heat was evenly distributed throughout the reaction mixture *[1 mark]*.

5.7   E.g. the student should make sure that the copper sulfate solution is disposed of correctly/not poured down the drain. / The student should wear gloves to protect their hands *[1 mark for any sensible suggestion]*.

Pages 28-30: Energetics — 2

1.1   Bonds broken: 2 C–C bonds, 8 C–H bonds, 5 O=O bonds

       Energy absorbed = $(2 \times 347) + (8 \times 413) + (5 \times 498)$

                 = 6488 kJ mol⁻¹

       Bonds made: 6 C=O bonds, 8 O–H bonds

       Energy released = $(6 \times 805) + (8 \times 464)$

               = 8542 kJ mol⁻¹

       Enthalpy of reaction = energy absorbed – energy released

                 = 6488 – 8542 = **–2054 kJ mol⁻¹**

    [3 marks for correct answer, otherwise 1 mark for calculating enthalpy of bonds broken and 1 mark for calculating enthalpy of bonds made.]

1.2 $\Delta_c H = \Sigma\,\Delta_f H$ products $- \Sigma\,\Delta_f H$ reactants

       $= ((3 \times -393.5) + (4 \times -241.8)) - (-104.5)$

       $= -2147.7 + 104.5 =$ **–2043.2 kJ mol⁻¹**

    [3 marks for correct answer, otherwise 1 mark for stating the formula and 1 mark for correctly substituting the enthalpies of formation into the formula.]

Again, you still get the mark if you drew a Hess's law diagram here, instead of just stating the formula.

1.3   Mean bond enthalpies are average values over a range of compounds *[1 mark]*. The enthalpies of formation given are for the exact compounds in this reaction *[1 mark]*.

1.4   50.0 cm³ of solution has a mass of 50.0 g, so m = 50.0 g

       $\Delta T = 74.0\,°C - 21.5\,°C = 52.5\,°C = 52.5\,K$

       $q = mc\Delta T = 50.0 \times 4.18 \times 52.5 = 10972.5\,J = 10.9725\,kJ$

       Mass of propan-2-ol burned = 75.2 – 74.8 = 0.4 g

       M_r of propan-2-ol = $(12.0 \times 3) + (16.0 \times 1) + (1.0 \times 8)$

                  = 60.0 g mol⁻¹

       moles of propan-2-ol burnt = $\dfrac{0.4}{60.0} = 0.00666...$ mol

       $\Delta_c H = \dfrac{-10.9725}{0.00666...} = 1645.875 =$ **1650 kJ mol⁻¹ (3 s.f.)**

    [6 marks for correct answer, otherwise 1 mark for finding the temperature change, 1 mark for correctly substituting the values into q = mcΔT, 1 mark for calculating q, 1 mark for finding the mass of propan-2-ol burned and 1 mark for finding the number of moles of propan-2-ol burned.]

2.1 $\Delta_r H^{\ominus} = \Sigma\,\Delta_f H^{\ominus}$ products $- \Sigma\,\Delta_f H^{\ominus}$ reactants

       So $\Sigma\,\Delta_f H^{\ominus}$ products $= \Delta_r H^{\ominus} + \Sigma\,\Delta_f H^{\ominus}$ reactants

                $= 20.00 + (-277.1 + -191.5)$

                = **–448.6 kJ mol⁻¹**

    [3 marks for correct answer, otherwise 1 mark for stating the formula and 1 mark for correctly substituting the enthalpies of reaction and formation into the formula.]

Once again, you'd get the mark if you drew a Hess's law diagram here instead of stating the formula.

2.2   Bonds broken: 1 C=O and 1 O–H

       Bonds made: 2 C–O and 1 O–H

       $\Delta_r H = (736 + (O–H)) - ((2 \times C–O) + (O–H))$

            $= 736 + O–H - (2 \times C–O) - O–H$

       $20.00 = 736 - (2 \times C–O)$

       $2 \times C–O = 716$

       C–O = 716 ÷ 2 = **358 kJ mol⁻¹ (3 s.f.)**

    [3 marks for correct answer, otherwise 1 mark stating what bonds are broken and what bonds are made and 1 mark for correctly substituting the values and unknowns into the formula for the enthalpy change of the reaction.]

2.3   The two C–O bonds in Compound R have slightly different enthalpies *[1 mark]*, because the enthalpy of a bond is affected by the environment it is in/what other atoms it is bonded to *[1 mark]*.

Unit 1: Section 5 — Kinetics, Equilibria and Redox Reactions

Pages 31-34: Kinetics, Equilibria and Redox Reactions — 1

1   A *[1 mark]*

The reaction is exothermic, so decreasing the temperature will improve the product yield, and there are more moles of gas on the reactant side than the product side, so increasing the pressure will increase the product yield.

2   D *[1 mark]*

$Rate = \dfrac{amount\ of\ reactant\ used\ (g)}{time\ (s)} = \dfrac{10.47 - 10.32}{60} = 0.0025\ g\ s^{-1}$

3   C *[1 mark]*

4   C *[1 mark]*

The overall oxidation state is zero. The sulfate ion has an oxidation state of −2 and the oxygen has an oxidation state of −2, so the oxidation state of vanadium is O − (−2) − (−2) = +4

5.1   A reducing agent is a substance that donates electrons in a reaction *[1 mark]*.

5.2 $K \rightarrow K^+ + e^-$ *[1 mark]*

It's fine if your half-equation is a multiple of this, e.g. $2K \rightarrow 2K^+ + 2e^-$.

5.3   −1 *[1 mark]*

Combined oxygen almost always has an oxidation state of −2, except in peroxides (like this one), fluorides, and elemental O_2.

5.4   Increasing the pressure will increase the rate of reaction *[1 mark]*. At higher pressure, there will be more oxygen molecules in a given volume/the molecules will be pushed closer together *[1 mark]*, so collisions between the oxygen molecules and the potassium metal are more likely *[1 mark]*. More collisions means more successful collisions and a higher rate of reaction *[1 mark]*.

5.5

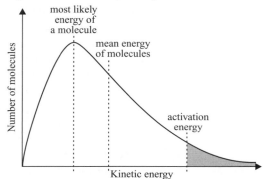

[1 mark for shading correct area.]

5.6   Adding a catalyst will increase the number of molecules able to react *[1 mark]*. Adding a catalyst provides a different reaction route with lower activation energy *[1 mark]*, meaning that more molecules will have sufficient energy to react *[1 mark]*.

6.1   A reaction where all of the reactants and products are in the same physical state/phase *[1 mark]*.

6.2 $K_c = \dfrac{[CH_3OH]}{[CO][H_2]^2}$ *[1 mark]*

6.3   There are 3 moles of gas on the reactant side and only 1 mole of gas on the product side *[1 mark]*. Increasing the pressure will shift the equilibrium to the right/towards the products (to lower the pressure again) *[1 mark]*, which will increase the yield of methanol *[1 mark]*.

6.4   E.g. high pressures are expensive to produce. / Specialist equipment is required to create and maintain high pressures *[1 mark]*.

6.5   At a higher temperature the molecules have more energy, so more molecules will have enough energy to react/ energy above the activation energy *[1 mark]*. At a higher temperature, the molecules move more quickly, so collisions will be more frequent *[1 mark]*.

6.6   The reaction is exothermic *[1 mark]*, so increasing the temperature would shift the equilibrium to the left/in the endothermic direction (to try to decrease the temperature) *[1 mark]*. This would decrease the yield of methanol *[1 mark]*. Using a catalyst is a better option because it increases the rate of reaction without affecting the position of equilibrium/yield of methanol *[1 mark]*.

6.7   Using a catalyst will have no effect on the value of K_c *[1 mark]*

7.1 $Ag^+ + e^- \rightarrow Ag$ *[1 mark]*

7.2 $Cu \rightarrow Cu^{2+} + 2e^-$ *[1 mark]*

7.3 $Cu + 2Ag^+ \rightarrow Cu^{2+} + 2Ag$ *[1 mark]*

7.4   The time taken for the reaction mixture to change colour would decrease *[1 mark]*. Increasing the concentration of the solution means that there are more silver ions in a given volume *[1 mark]*, so the frequency of collisions between the reacting particles increases *[1 mark]*. Therefore the rate of the reaction would increase *[1 mark]*.

Pages 35-37: Kinetics, Equilibria and Redox Reactions — 2

1.1   E.g.

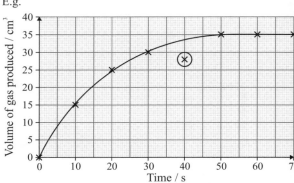

[3 marks for correctly plotted graph with appropriate trend line, otherwise 1 mark for correctly labelled axes and 1 mark for correctly plotted data points.]

1.2   Point circled as on graph above *[1 mark]*.
E.g. the students might have measured or recorded the volume incorrectly. / The students might have read the volume at the wrong time *[1 mark]*.

1.3   50 s *[1 mark for an answer in range 47 s-52 s]*
The volume of gas produced didn't increase after this time. / The line on the graph flattened out at this time *[1 mark]*.

1.4   As the temperature increases, the initial rate of reaction increases *[1 mark]*.

1.5   The initial rate of reaction at each temperature would be higher *[1 mark]*.

1.6   E.g. use a gas syringe/collect the gas over water in an upturned measuring cylinder *[1 mark]*.
Any two from: e.g. the apparatus must not let any gas escape. / The apparatus must be large enough to collect all the gas produced. / The apparatus needs to have the right level of sensitivity. *[2 marks — 1 mark for each sensible factor.]*

2.1   If a reaction at equilibrium is subjected to a change in concentration, pressure or temperature, the position of equilibrium will move to counteract the change *[1 mark]*.

2.2   Any two from: e.g. the forward and reverse reactions must be proceeding at the same rate. / The concentrations of the reactants and products must remain constant / The reaction must take place in a closed system. *[2 marks — 1 mark for each correct condition.]*

2.3 $K_c = \dfrac{[CO_2][H_2]}{[CO][H_2O]} = \dfrac{0.12 \times 0.17}{0.031 \times 0.048} = 13.7096...$

$K_c = \mathbf{14\ (2\ s.f.)}$

[3 marks for correct answer given to 2 s.f. or 2 marks for correct answer not given to 2 s.f., otherwise 1 mark for writing a correct expression for K_c.]

2.4 Temperature X is higher *[1 mark]*. A higher K_c at temperature Y means that more product was formed/the equilibrium was shifted to the right *[1 mark]*.
As the reaction is exothermic, this would be caused by a lower temperature *[1 mark]*.

Pages 38-40: Kinetics, Equilibria and Redox Reactions — 3

1.1 In the first half-equation, oxygen atoms/water molecules are oxidised (lose electrons) *[1 mark]*. In the second half-equation, hydrogen ions are reduced (gain electrons) *[1 mark]*. As reduction and oxidation occur simultaneously, the reaction can be described as a redox reaction *[1 mark]*.

1.2 $2H_2O \rightarrow O_2 + 2H_2$ *[1 mark]*

The key thing here is spotting that you need to double the second half-equation, so that the electrons and the H$^+$ ions cancel out.

1.3 The activation energy is the minimum amount of energy that particles need in order to react *[1 mark]*.

1.4 The catalyst offers an alternative reaction pathway that has a lower activation energy *[1 mark]*.

1.5 Catalysts are chemically unchanged at the end of the reaction/are not used up during the reaction *[1 mark]*.

1.6 Overall oxidation state of $Bi_2O_3 = 0$
Oxidation state of oxygen $= -2$
Oxidation state of bismuth $= 0 - ((-2 \times 3) \div 2) = $ **+3**
[2 marks for correct answer, otherwise 1 mark for correctly stating the oxidation state of oxygen.]

2.1 E.g. the molecules may not have sufficient energy to react. / The molecules may not collide in the correct orientation *[1 mark]*.

2.2 The oxidation state of carbon changes from +2 (in CO) to +4 (in CO_2) so it must be oxidised *[1 mark]*.

2.3 A catalyst is a substance that increases the rate of a reaction *[1 mark]*, without being changed in chemical composition or amount *[1 mark]*.

2.4 E.g.

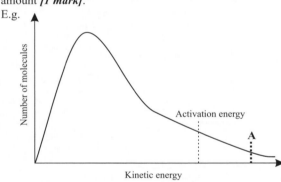

[1 mark for a line drawn anywhere to the right of the existing activation energy line.]

2.5 E.g.

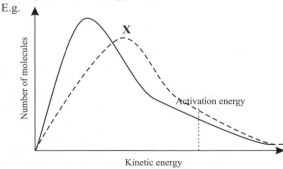

[2 marks — 1 mark for peak to right of existing peak, 1 mark for peak lower than existing peak.]

2.6 Heating up the catalytic converter quickly means that the gas molecules inside it will have more energy *[1 mark]*. As a result, more of the molecules will have enough energy to react/energy above the activation energy *[1 mark]*. The molecules will also move more quickly, leading to more frequent collisions *[1 mark]*. So the rate of reaction will be faster *[1 mark]* and more carbon monoxide will be converted to carbon dioxide before being released in the exhaust emissions *[1 mark]*.

3.1 $K_c = \dfrac{[NO]^2}{[N_2][H_2]}$

$2.00 \times 10^2 = \dfrac{[NO]^2}{0.0250 \times 0.0125} = \dfrac{[NO]^2}{3.125 \times 10^{-4}}$

$[NO]^2 = (2.00 \times 10^2) \times (3.125 \times 10^{-4}) = 0.0625$

$[NO] = \sqrt{0.0625} = $ **0.250 mol dm^{-3} (3 s.f.)**
[3 marks for correct answer or 2 marks for correct answer not given to 3 s.f., otherwise 1 mark for writing a correct expression for K_c.]

3.2 Increasing the pressure has no effect on the position of equilibrium *[1 mark]*, because there are the same number of moles of gas on both sides of the reaction *[1 mark]*.

Pages 41-42: Kinetics, Equilibria and Redox Reactions — 4

1.1 In this reaction, two moles of reactant give four moles of product/there are more moles of products than of reactants *[1 mark]*. Increasing the pressure would shift the equilibrium in favour of the reactants, reducing the yield of acetylene *[1 mark]*.

1.2 How to grade your answer:
Level 0: There is no relevant information. *[No marks]*
Level 1: One factor from rate, yield and cost is covered well OR two factors are covered but they are incomplete and not always accurate. The answer is not in a logical order *[1 to 2 marks]*.
Level 2: Two factors from rate, yield and cost are covered well OR all three factors are covered but they are incomplete and not always accurate. The answer is mostly in a logical order *[3 to 4 marks]*.
Level 3: All three factors are covered and are complete and accurate. The answer is coherent and is in a logical order. *[5 to 6 marks]*

Indicative content:
Rate of reaction
Using a high temperature will increase the rate of reaction. This is because the particles have more kinetic energy, so they will collide more frequently and more of the collisions will be successful.
A higher rate of reaction means that the product (acetylene) can be produced more quickly.
Yield (equilibrium position)
The forward reaction is endothermic.
Using a high temperature will shift the equilibrium in favour of the product.
This will increase the yield of acetylene.
Cost
A high temperature is beneficial in terms of yield and rate of reaction.
However, higher temperature require a lot of energy to produce and maintain. This can be expensive.
High temperatures may also require specialised equipment.
Therefore a compromise temperature must be chosen that is as high as possible (to give a good rate and yield) without costing too much to produce and maintain.

1.3 $K_c = \dfrac{[H_2]^3[C_2H_2]}{[CH_4]^2}$ *[1 mark]*

1.4 From the equation, 1 mole of acetylene is produced from 2 moles of methane, so 0.372 moles of acetylene must be produced from $2 \times 0.372 = 0.744$ moles of methane. Therefore there must be $1.00 - 0.744 = 0.256$ moles of methane left at equilibrium

3 moles of hydrogen are produced for every 1 mole of acetylene so $0.372 \times 3 = 1.116$ moles of hydrogen were present at equilibrium.

Equilibrium concentrations:

$$[C_2H_2] = \frac{0.372}{3.00} = 0.124 \text{ mol dm}^{-3}$$

$$[H_2] = \frac{1.116}{3.00} = 0.372 \text{ mol dm}^{-3}$$

$$[CH_4] = \frac{0.256}{3.00} = 0.0853... \text{ mol dm}^{-3}$$

$$K_c = \frac{0.372^3 \times 0.124}{(0.0853...)^2} = 0.8766...$$

Units of $K_c = \dfrac{(\text{mol dm}^{-3})^{\cancel{3}} \times \text{mol dm}^{-3}}{(\cancel{\text{mol dm}^{-3}})^{\cancel{2}}}$

$= \text{mol dm}^{-3} \times \text{mol dm}^{-3} = \text{mol}^2 \text{ dm}^{-6}$

$K_c = \textbf{0.877 mol}^2 \textbf{ dm}^{-6}$ **(3 s.f.)**

[7 marks for correct answer, otherwise 1 mark for number of moles of methane at equilibrium correct, 1 mark for number of moles of hydrogen at equilibrium correct, 1 mark for each equilibrium concentration correct, and 1 mark for correct units.]

1.5 The value of K_c would decrease because the reaction is endothermic *[1 mark]*, so decreasing the temperature would shift the equilibrium to the left/towards the reactants *[1 mark]*.

1.6 The value of K_c would not change *[1 mark]*.

Unit 1: Section 6 — Thermodynamics

Pages 43-46: Thermodynamics — 1

1 C *[1 mark]*

Remember, when you're thinking about the enthalpy change of atomisation of an <u>element</u> it's the quantity of gaseous atoms <u>formed</u> you need to worry about — it must be <u>1 mole</u>.

2 D *[1 mark]*

$\Delta G = \Delta H - T\Delta S$, *so if ΔS is positive and T is high enough, $T\Delta S$ will be greater than ΔH and ΔG will be negative, making the reaction feasible.*

3 B *[1 mark]*

The actual sizes of the hydration enthalpies and the lattice dissociation enthalpy individually aren't important — it's their total value that determines whether a compound is soluble or not. For a soluble substance, this total needs to be less than or very close to zero, to give an exothermic enthalpy of solution.

4 A *[1 mark]*

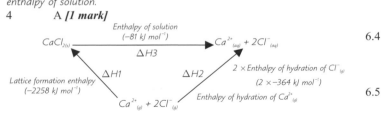

$\Delta H2 = \Delta H1 + \Delta H3$
$= -2258 + -81$
$= -2339 \text{ kJ mol}^{-1}$

Enthalpy of hydration of $Ca^{2+}_{(g)} = \Delta H2 - 2 \times$ Enthalpy of hydration of $Cl^-_{(g)}$
$= -2339 - 2 \times -364$
$= -1611 \text{ kJ mol}^{-1}$

5.1

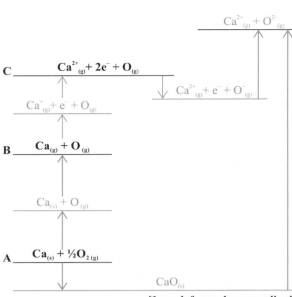

[1 mark for each correct line]

5.2 Enthalpy of atomisation of oxygen = Enthalpy of formation of calcium oxide + Lattice dissociation enthalpy of calcium oxide − Second electron affinity of oxygen − First electron affinity of oxygen − Second ionisation energy of calcium − First ionisation energy of calcium − Enthalpy of atomisation of calcium = $-635 + 3513 - (+844) - (-142) - (+1150) - (+590) - (+193)$

$= \textbf{+243 kJ mol}^{-1}$

[3 marks for correct answer, otherwise 1 mark for correct expression for enthalpy of atomisation of oxygen, 1 mark for substituting in correct values]

6.1 The enthalpy change when 1 mole of a solute is dissolved *[1 mark]* in enough solvent that no further enthalpy change occurs on further dilution *[1 mark]*.

6.2 $MgCl_{2(s)} \rightarrow Mg^{2+}_{(aq)} + 2Cl^-_{(aq)}$ *[1 mark]*

OR

$MgCl_{2(s)} \rightarrow MgCl_{2(aq)}$ *[1 mark]*

6.3

Enthalpy of solution
$MgCl_{2(s)} \xrightarrow{\Delta H3} Mg^{2+}_{(aq)} + 2Cl^-_{(aq)}$

Lattice dissociation enthalpy $\Delta H1$ (+2526 kJ mol⁻¹)

$\Delta H2$

$2 \times$ Enthalpy of hydration of $Cl^-_{(g)}$ (2×-364 kJ mol⁻¹)

$Mg^{2+}_{(g)} + 2Cl^-_{(g)}$

Enthalpy of hydration of $Mg^{2+}_{(g)}$ (-1920 kJ mol⁻¹)

$\Delta H3 = \Delta H1 + \Delta H2$
$= +2526 + (2 \times (-364) + (-1920))$
$= \textbf{−122 kJ mol}^{-1}$

[2 marks for correct answer, otherwise 1 mark for correct cycle or equation]

6.4 Dissolving gives free ions in solution, so increases disorder *[1 mark]*. So there is an increase in entropy/ΔS is positive *[1 mark]*. This means that the reaction can be feasible/ΔG can be negative even when ΔH is positive *[1 mark]*.

6.5 Magnesium ions are smaller than sodium ions and have a higher charge *[1 mark]*. Therefore the chloride ions are more strongly attracted to the magnesium ions/the ionic bonding is stronger in magnesium chloride *[1 mark]*.

7.1 Negative, since there are 3 moles of reactants and only 2 moles of product *[1 mark]*. Fewer molecules means fewer possible arrangements of molecules, and so lower entropy *[1 mark]*.

7.2 $\Delta S = S_{\text{products}} - S_{\text{reactants}}$
$= (2 \times 240.0) - (2 \times 210.8 + 205.3)$
$= \textbf{−146.9 J K}^{-1} \textbf{ mol}^{-1}$

[2 marks for correct answer, otherwise 1 mark for correct equation for ΔS]

7.3 For a reaction to be feasible, ΔG must be less than or equal to zero *[1 mark]*. This only happens below a certain temperature as though the reaction is exothermic/has negative ΔH, entropy decreases/ΔS is negative *[1 mark]*.

OR

$T = \dfrac{\Delta H}{\Delta S} = \dfrac{-114\ 000}{-146.9} = 776$ K (3 s.f.) *[1 mark]*

The reaction is only feasible at temperatures of 776 K or lower, as at these temperatures ΔG is zero or lower *[1 mark]*.

7.4 Molecules in a liquid are less free to move around than molecules in a gas *[1 mark]*, so there is less disorder/are fewer ways of arranging the molecules and the entropy decreases *[1 mark]*.

Pages 47-50: Thermodynamics — 2

1.1 The enthalpy change when 1 mole of gaseous 1– ions *[1 mark]* is formed from 1 mole of gaseous atoms *[1 mark]*.

1.2 The incoming electron and the protons in the nucleus are attracted to each other *[1 mark]*, causing energy to be released *[1 mark]*.

1.3 Stage 1: Construction of Born-Haber cycle
E.g.

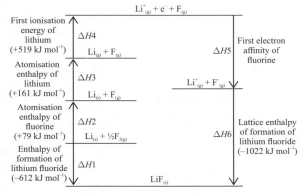

Enthalpy changes shown in a correct order *[1 mark]*
Species shown correctly on each line *[1 mark]*
Arrows all shown correctly *[1 mark]*
Stage 2: Calculation for electron affinity established
$\Delta H5 = -\Delta H4 - \Delta H3 - \Delta H2 + \Delta H1 - \Delta H6$ *[1 mark]*
Stage 3: Calculation completed
$\Delta H5 = -(+519) - (+161) - (+79) + (-612) - (-1022)$
[1 mark]

$= -349$ kJ mol^{-1} *[1 mark]*

1.4 The bond dissociation enthalpy is the energy required to break the covalent bonds in 1 mole of gaseous molecules *[1 mark]*. This forms 2 moles of gaseous fluorine atoms, $F_{2(g)} \rightarrow 2F_{(g)}$ *[1 mark]*. The atomisation energy is the energy required to form 1 mole of gaseous atoms, $\frac{1}{2}F_{2(g)} \rightarrow F_{(g)}$ *[1 mark]*, so the bond dissociation energy is equal to twice the atomisation energy of fluorine *[1 mark]*.

2.1 Carbon is a solid and oxygen is a gas *[1 mark]*. Solids have a more ordered structure/gases are more disordered *[1 mark]*.

2.2 $\Delta_r H = \Delta_f H(CO_2) = -394$ kJ mol^{-1} *[1 mark]*

2.3 $\Delta S = S(CO_2) - (S(C) + S(O_2))$
$= 214.0 - (5.70 + 205.3)$
$= 3.00$ J K^{-1} mol^{-1}
$\Delta G = \Delta H - T\Delta S$
$= -394\ 000 - (298 \times 3.00)$
$= -394\ 894$
$= -395\ 000$ J mol^{-1} (3 s.f.)
[4 marks for correct answer, otherwise 1 mark for correct equation for ΔS, 1 mark for correct ΔS, 1 mark for correct answer not to 3 s.f.]

3.1 Stage 1: Calculating ΔH
$\Delta_r H = -\Delta_f H(Al_2O_3) + 3 \times \Delta_f H(CO)$ *[1 mark]*
$= -(-1676) + (3 \times -110.5)$
$= +1344.5$ kJ mol^{-1} *[1 mark]*
Stage 2: Calculating ΔS
$\Delta S = (3 \times S(CO) + 2 \times S(Al)) - (3 \times S(C) + S(Al_2O_3))$ *[1 mark]*
$= (3 \times 198 + 2 \times 28.3) - (3 \times 5.70 + 50.9)$
$= +582.6$ J K^{-1} mol^{-1} *[1 mark]*
Stage 3: Calculating ΔG
$277\ °C = 550$ K
$\Delta G = \Delta H - T\Delta S$
$= 1\ 344\ 500 - (550 \times 582.6)$ *[1 mark]*
$= 1\ 024\ 070$ J mol^{-1}
$= 1\ 020\ 000$ J mol^{-1} (3 s.f.) *[1 mark]*

3.2 ΔG is positive, therefore the reaction is not feasible at this temperature *[1 mark]*.

3.3 $\Delta G = 0$ therefore $T = \dfrac{\Delta H}{\Delta S}$
$T = \dfrac{1\ 344\ 500}{582.6} = 2307.758... = 2310$ K (3 s.f.)
[2 marks for correct answer, otherwise 1 mark for correct equation for T]

You can still get both marks in Q3.3 if your values from Q3.1 are incorrect, as long as you use the values you got in Q3.1 and your calculation is correct.

3.4 E.g. temperatures that high are too expensive/the activation energy is too high even though the reaction is feasible at high temperatures/the reaction proceeds too slowly *[1 mark]*.

4.1 How to grade your answer:
Level 0: There is no relevant information. *[No marks]*
Level 1: One stage is covered well or two stages are covered but they are incomplete and may not be entirely accurate. The answer is not in a logical order. *[1 to 2 marks]*
Level 2: Two stages are covered well or all three stages are covered, but they are incomplete or may not be entirely accurate. The answer is mostly in a logical order. *[3 to 4 marks]*
Level 3: All three stages are covered and are complete and accurate. The answer is coherent and written in a logical order. *[5 to 6 marks]*
Indicative content:
Stage 1: Comparison of data
The experimental value is greater than theoretical value in both cases.
Magnesium iodide shows a much greater difference between the theoretical and experimental values.
Stage 2: Explanation of difference between theoretical and experimental values
Theoretical values calculated using purely ionic model.
Experimental values calculated from Born-Haber cycles.
Additional covalent bonding as well as ionic bonding causes the greater experimental value.
Purely ionic model assumes ions are perfect spheres and have their charge evenly distributed around them.
Positive and negative ions cannot be exactly spherical.
Positive ions polarise negative ions by attracting electron density towards themselves.
Stage 3: Explanation for greater difference in MgI_2 values than in NaCl values
Values show that sodium chloride is almost a perfect ionic compound.
Greater experimental value for magnesium iodide indicates more covalent character.
The more polarisation in the bonding, the more covalent character.
The magnesium ion is smaller and more highly charged than the sodium ion, so draws electrons towards it more strongly.
Iodide ion is more easily polarised than the chloride ion due to its large size.
Sodium ion does not polarise the chloride ion to any great extent, so bonding is almost purely ionic.

4.2 Lattice dissociation enthalpy and lattice formation enthalpy both have the same numerical value because they are both measures of the ionic bond strength of a compound *[1 mark]*. But they have opposite signs because they represent opposite processes *[1 mark]*. The (endothermic) lattice dissociation enthalpy is the amount of energy needed to break all the bonds in the lattice to give its gaseous ions *[1 mark]*. The (exothermic) lattice formation enthalpy is the amount of energy given out when bonds are made between all the gaseous ions to produce the lattice *[1 mark]*.

Unit 1: Section 7 — Rate Equations and K_p

Pages 51-52: Rate Equations and K_p — 1

1 **B** *[1 mark]*
Tripling [A] makes the rate $3^2 = 9$ times faster. Tripling [B] makes the rate 3 times faster. So the overall rate of reaction would be $9 \times 3 = 27$ times faster.

2 **B** *[1 mark]*
[X] must decrease with time as it is used up in the reaction. The gradient of graph 2 stays the same as [X] decreases, showing the rate doesn't change with concentration of X i.e. the reaction is order 0 with respect to X.

3 **D** *[1 mark]*
$N_2O_{4(g)} \rightleftharpoons 2NO_{2(g)}$

$K_p = \dfrac{(p_{NO_2})^2}{p_{N_2O_4}}$

$(p_{NO_2})^2 = K_p \times p_{N_2O_4}$
$\quad = (6.03 \times 10^3) \times (1.78 \times 10^3)$
$\quad = 1.07334 \times 10^7$

$p_{NO_2} = \sqrt{1.07334 \times 10^7}$
$\quad = 3.28 \times 10^3 \text{ atm (3 s.f.)}$

4 **C** *[1 mark]*
$k = Ae^{\frac{-E_a}{RT}}$

$\ln k = \ln A - \dfrac{E_a}{RT}$

$\dfrac{E_a}{RT} = \ln A - \ln k$

$T = \dfrac{E_a}{R(\ln A - \ln k)}$

$T = \dfrac{254\,400}{8.31\,(\ln(4.00 \times 10^{14}) - \ln(1.37 \times 10^{-4}))}$
$\quad = 720 \text{ K (3 s.f.)}$

5.1 E.g.

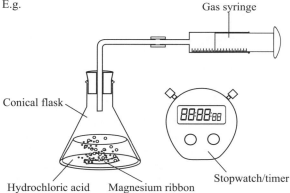

Gas syringe

Conical flask

Hydrochloric acid   Magnesium ribbon

Stopwatch/timer

[3 marks — 1 mark for magnesium ribbon and hydrochloric acid in conical flask, 1 mark for showing a suitable method of collecting and measuring all of the gas produced, 1 mark for timing device.]
You would also get the marks if you showed the gas being collected in a measuring cylinder over water instead of in a gas syringe.

5.2 E.g.

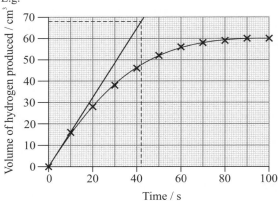

Change in $y = 68 - 0 = 68 \text{ cm}^3$
Change in $x = 42 - 0 = 42 \text{ s}$
Gradient $= 68 \div 42 = 1.619... \text{ cm}^3 \text{ s}^{-1}$
Rate $= 1.6 \text{ cm}^3 \text{ s}^{-1}$ (2 s.f.)
[4 marks for correct answer in the range 1.5-1.7, otherwise 1 mark for tangent, 1 mark for calculating change in y and x, 1 mark for correct units.]

5.3 The rate of reaction decreases *[1 mark]* as the concentration/ amount of the hydrochloric acid decreases as it is used up/ reacts with the magnesium *[1 mark]*.

Pages 53-55: Rate Equations and K_p — 2

1.1

Concentration of $Na_2S_2O_{3(aq)}$ / mol dm^{-3}	Time taken / s	Rate of reaction / $\times 10^{-3}$ s^{-1}
0	0	0
0.200	404	**2.48**
0.400	199	**5.03**
0.600	137	**7.30**
0.800	103	**9.71**

[2 marks for all 4 values correct, otherwise 1 mark for 2 values correct.]

1.2

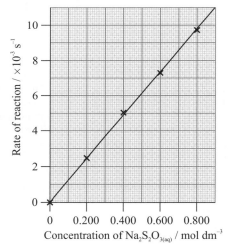

[3 marks — 1 mark for appropriate axes and scales, 1 mark for all points correctly plotted, 1 mark for appropriate straight line of best fit.]

1.3 The graph is a straight line through the origin *[1 mark]*. This suggests that the reaction is first order with respect to sodium thiosulfate *[1 mark]*.

1.4 Rate $= k[Na_2S_2O_3]$ *[1 mark]*

2.1 $K_p = \dfrac{(p_{NH_3})^2}{p_{N_2} \times (p_{H_2})^3}$ *[1 mark]*

2.2 Total moles of gas = $15 + 30 + 22 = 67$

Partial pressure = mole fraction × p_{total}

$$p_{N_2} = \frac{15}{67} \times 200 = 44.776... \text{ atm}$$

$$p_{H_2} = \frac{30}{67} \times 200 = 89.552... \text{ atm}$$

$$p_{NH_3} = \frac{22}{67} \times 200 = 65.671... \text{ atm}$$

$$K_p = \frac{65.671...^2}{44.776... \times 89.552...^3} = 1.3411... \times 10^{-4}$$

Units of $K_p = \frac{\text{atm}^2}{\text{atm} \times \text{atm}^3} = \text{atm}^{-2}$

$K_p = 1.34 \times 10^{-4} \text{ atm}^{-2}$ (3 s.f.)

[6 marks for correct answer given to 3 s.f. or 5 marks for correct answer not given to 3 s.f., otherwise 1 mark for correct total moles of gas, 1 mark for correct calculation of partial pressures, 1 mark for substituting into expression for K_p, 1 mark for units.]

2.3 How to grade your answer:

Level 0:   There is no relevant information. *[No marks]*

Level 1:   One stage is covered well OR two stages are covered but they are incomplete and not always accurate. The answer is not in a logical order. *[1 to 2 marks]*

Level 2:   Two stages are covered well OR all 3 stages are covered but they are incomplete and not always accurate. The answer is mostly in a logical order. *[3 to 4 marks]*

Level 3:   All 3 stages are covered and are complete and accurate. The answer is coherent and is in a logical order. *[5 to 6 marks]*

Indicative content:

Stage 1: Increasing the pressure

Increasing the total pressure increases the partial pressures of all the gases in the system.

There are fewer moles of products/on the right than of reactants/on the left.

So equilibrium shifts towards the products/to the right to oppose the increase in pressure.

This causes the partial pressure of ammonia to increase, but because the partial pressures of hydrogen and nitrogen have also increased, K_p stays the same.

Stage 2: Increasing the temperature

Negative ΔH means the forward reaction is exothermic.

So the equilibrium shifts towards the reactants/to the left (in the endothermic direction) to absorb excess heat.

Less product is formed.

The partial pressure of ammonia decreases and the partial pressures of nitrogen and hydrogen increase, so K_p decreases.

Stage 3: Adding a catalyst

The catalyst affects the rates of the forward and back reactions equally so there is no change in the equilibrium position.

The ratio of products to reactants remains the same and so there is no change in K_p.

2.4

$$K_p = \frac{(p_{SO_3})^2}{p_{O_2} \times (p_{SO_2})^2}$$

$$(p_{SO_2})^2 = \frac{(p_{SO_3})^2}{p_{O_2} \times K_p}$$

$$= \frac{96^2}{40 \times 0.056} = 4114.285...$$

$$p_{SO_2} = \sqrt{4114.285...} = 64 \text{ kPa (2 s.f.)}$$

[3 marks for correct answer, otherwise 1 mark for correct expression for K_p, 1 mark for rearranging K_p.]

2.5 Total pressure = $64 + 40 + 96 = 200$ kPa (2 s.f.) *[1 mark]*

Pages 56-58: Rate Equations and K_p — 3

1.1 When [E] increases by a factor of 1.5 and [F] stays constant, the rate also increases by a factor of 1.5. So the reaction is first order with respect to E *[1 mark]*. When [F] increases by a factor of 1.5 and [E] stays constant the rate also increases by a factor of 1.5. So the reaction is first order with respect to F *[1 mark]*.

1.2 Rate = k[E][F] *[1 mark]*

1.3 Second order *[1 mark]*.

1.4 $k = \dfrac{\text{Rate}}{[E][F]}$

$$k = \frac{8.00 \times 10^{-4}}{0.0800 \times 0.0600} = 0.166...$$

Units of $k = \dfrac{\text{mol dm}^{-3} \text{ s}^{-1}}{\text{mol dm}^{-3} \times \text{mol dm}^{-3}} = \text{mol}^{-1} \text{ dm}^3 \text{ s}^{-1}$

$k = 0.167 \text{ mol}^{-1} \text{ dm}^3 \text{ s}^{-1}$ (3 s.f.)

[4 marks for correct answer given to 3 s.f. or 3 marks for correct answer not given to 3 s.f., otherwise 1 mark for rearranging the rate equation, 1 mark for correct units.]

1.5 Rate = $0.167 \times (0.200 \times 0.500)$

$= 0.0167 \text{ mol dm}^{-3} \text{ s}^{-1}$ *[1 mark]*

2.1 E.g.

Expt.	Vol 1.0 mol dm^{-3} CH$_3$COCH$_3$ / cm^3	Vol 0.004 mol dm^{-3} I$_2$ / cm^3	Vol 1.0 mol dm^{-3} HCl / cm^3	Vol H$_2$O / cm^3	Time / s
1	10	4	10	26	210
2	20	4	10	16	105

[1 mark for changing volume of CH$_3$COCH$_3$ and keeping volumes of I$_2$ and HCl the same, 1 mark for adding water to give a total volume of 50 cm^3, 1 mark for correct time in relation to volume of CH$_3$COCH$_3$ given.]

Other answers you could have given include halving the volume of propanone to 5 cm^3 and doubling the reaction time to 420 s, or tripling the volume to 30 cm^3 and dividing the reaction time by 3 to give 70 s.

2.2 Rate = k[CH$_3$COCH$_3$][HCl] *[1 mark]*

2.3 E.g. $k = \dfrac{\text{Rate}}{[CH_3COCH_3][HCl]}$

$[CH_3COCH_3] = \dfrac{10}{50} \times 1 \text{ mol dm}^{-3} = 0.2 \text{ mol dm}^{-3}$

$[HCl] = [CH_3COCH_3] = 0.2 \text{ mol dm}^{-3}$

$$k = \frac{1.5 \times 10^{-6}}{0.2 \times 0.2} = 3.75 \times 10^{-5}$$

Units of $k = \dfrac{\text{mol dm}^{-3} \text{ s}^{-1}}{\text{mol dm}^{-3} \times \text{mol dm}^{-3}} = \text{mol}^{-1} \text{ dm}^3 \text{ s}^{-1}$

$k = 3.8 \times 10^{-5} \text{ mol}^{-1} \text{ dm}^3 \text{ s}^{-1}$ (2 s.f.)

[5 marks for correct answer given to 2 s.f. or 4 marks for correct answer not given to 2 s.f., otherwise 1 mark for rearranging the rate equation, 1 mark for calculating concentrations, 1 mark for correct units.]

2.4 The rate equation contains propanone and HCl and the proposed step involves propanone and H$^+$ ions from HCl *[1 mark]*. The equation shows that the reaction is first order with respect to propanone and HCl *[1 mark]*, and only one molecule of each appears in this rate-determining step *[1 mark]*.

3.1 Plot a graph of ln$k$ on the y-axis against $\dfrac{1}{T}$ on the x-axis *[1 mark]*. Draw a straight line of best fit through the data points *[1 mark]*. Calculate the gradient of the straight line *[1 mark]*. The gradient of the line is $\dfrac{-E_a}{R}$ *[1 mark]*. So the activation energy for the reaction can be calculated by multiplying the value of the gradient by $-R$ *[1 mark]*.

3.2 An increase in temperature increases the energies of the reactant particles *[1 mark]*. This means that they move faster and are more likely to collide *[1 mark]*, and that they are more likely to have an energy equal to or greater than the activation energy *[1 mark]*. This causes an increase in the rate of reaction so the value of the rate constant must increase too *[1 mark]*.

3.3
$$\ln k = \frac{-E_a}{RT} + \ln A$$
$$\ln A = \ln k + \frac{E_a}{RT}$$
$$\ln A = \ln(1.54 \times 10^{-6}) + \frac{44\,900}{8.31 \times 298}$$
$$= 4.7475...$$
$$A = e^{4.7475...} = 115.3044...$$
$$= \textbf{115 mol}^{-1}\,\textbf{dm}^3\,\textbf{s}^{-1}\,\textbf{(3.s.f.)}$$
[2 marks for correct answer, otherwise 1 mark for correctly rearranging the equation to find A.]

You could also do this question by first rearranging the equation into the form $A = ke^{\frac{E_a}{RT}}$.

Unit 1: Section 8 — Electrode Potentials and Cells

Pages 59-60: Electrode Potentials and Cells — 1

1 A *[1 mark]*

Under standard conditions, any solutions must have a concentration of 1 mol dm⁻³.

2 C *[1 mark]*

The oxidising agent must be on the right of the cell diagram, in the half-cell where reduction occurs. In that half-cell, Fe^{3+} is reduced to Fe^{2+}, so Fe^{3+} must be the oxidising agent.

3 C *[1 mark]*

Al is the only substance with a more negative $E^{\ominus}$ than hydrogen, and so the only one which will be oxidised in a reaction with hydrogen ions.

4 D *[1 mark]*

$EMF = E^{\ominus}_{reduced} - E^{\ominus}_{oxidised} = -0.41 - (-0.76) = +0.35\,V$

5.1 Pt | H₂ | OH⁻, H₂O || O₂ | H₂O, OH⁻ | Pt
[2 marks for correct answer including Pt electrodes or 1 mark for correct answer omitting Pt electrodes, otherwise 1 mark for each half-cell correct]

You could also draw the cell like this: Pt | H_2 | H_2O || O_2 | OH^- | Pt, showing only the species that are oxidised or reduced.

5.2
$$EMF = E^{\ominus}_{reduced} - E^{\ominus}_{oxidised}$$
$$= +40 - (-0.83)$$
$$= \textbf{+1.23 V} \textit{ [1 mark]}$$

5.3 Hydrogen and oxygen can be continuously supplied *[1 mark]*.

5.4 $KOH_{(aq)}$ *[1 mark]*

5.5 Advantage: Any one from: e.g. no CO₂ emissions from cell/ no toxic waste products, just water/more efficient *[1 mark]*. Disadvantage: Any one from: e.g. hydrogen is highly flammable/hydrogen is difficult to store/infrastructure does not yet exist *[1 mark]*.

Pages 61-63: Electrode Potentials and Cells — 2

1.1

Half-cells	Reaction equation
A and C	$Zn_{(s)} + 2H^+_{(aq)} \rightarrow Zn^{2+}_{(aq)} + H_{2(g)}$
B and D	$Fe_{(s)} + Cu^{2+}_{(aq)} \rightarrow Fe^{2+}_{(aq)} + Cu_{(s)}$
E and F	$2Fe^{3+}_{(aq)} + 2I^-_{(aq)} \rightarrow 2Fe^{2+}_{(aq)} + I_{2(aq)}$
B and G	$5Fe_{(s)} + 2MnO_4^-{}_{(aq)} + 16H^+_{(aq)}$ $\rightarrow 5Fe^{2+}_{(aq)} + 2Mn^{2+}_{(aq)} + 8H_2O_{(l)}$

[1 mark for each line correct]

1.2 A and C: $Zn_{(s)} | Zn^{2+}_{(aq)} || H^+_{(aq)} | H_{2(g)} | Pt$
[1 mark for each half-cell correct]
B and D: $Fe_{(s)} | Fe^{2+}_{(aq)} || Cu^{2+}_{(aq)} | Cu_{(s)}$
[1 mark for each half-cell correct]
E and F: $Pt | I^-_{(aq)}, I_{2(aq)} || Fe^{3+}_{(aq)}, Fe^{2+}_{(aq)} | Pt$
[2 marks for correct answer including Pt electrodes or 1 mark for correct answer omitting Pt electrodes, otherwise 1 mark for each half-cell correct]

1.3
$$EMF = E^{\ominus}_{reduced} - E^{\ominus}_{oxidised}$$
$$= +1.51 - (-0.44)$$
$$= \textbf{+1.95 V} \textit{ [1 mark]}$$

1.4
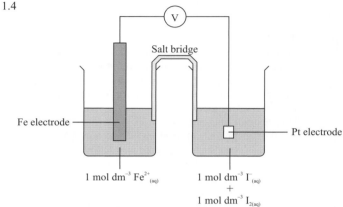

Temperature: 298 K / 25 °C
[6 marks — 1 mark for each correctly labelled electrode in solution, 1 mark for salt bridge, 1 mark for voltmeter, 1 mark for correct 1 mol dm⁻³ solutions, 1 mark for correct temperature.]

The size that you've drawn your platinum electrode doesn't matter. As long as you've labelled it correctly, you'll get the mark.

1.5
$$\text{Percentage uncertainty} = \frac{\text{uncertainty}}{\text{reading}} \times 100$$
$$= \frac{0.005}{0.98} \times 100$$
$$= 0.51020...$$
$$= \textbf{0.5\% (1 s.f.)} \textit{ [1 mark]}$$

2.1
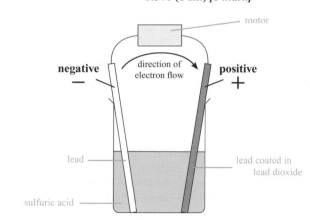

[1 mark for correctly labelled electrodes, 1 mark for arrow correctly showing electron flow]

2.2 Discharge: $Pb + PbO_2 + 2SO_4^{2-} + 4H^+ \rightarrow 2PbSO_4 + 2H_2O$
[1 mark]
Recharge: $2PbSO_4 + 2H_2O \rightarrow Pb + PbO_2 + 2SO_4^{2-} + 4H^+$
[1 mark]

2.3 An electric current is supplied to the cell *[1 mark]* connected so that electrons move from the PbO_2 electrode to the Pb electrode/to drive the reaction in the opposite direction (to when the cell is discharging) *[1 mark]*.

At the PbO_2 electrode the following reaction occurs:
$PbSO_4 + 2H_2O \rightarrow PbO_2 + SO_4^{2-} + 4H^+ + 2e^-$ *[1 mark]*.

At the Pb electrode the following reaction occurs:
$PbSO_4 + 2e^- \rightarrow Pb + SO_4^{2-}$ *[1 mark]*.

When the electric current is supplied, the charges on the electrodes swap over, which makes the electrons flow in the opposite direction to when the cell is discharging.

2.4 $Li^+ + e^- \rightarrow Li$ *[1 mark]*
$Li^+[CoO_2]^- \rightarrow Li^+ + CoO_2 + e^-$ *[1 mark]*

2.5 E.g. the battery gets hotter than 298 K/may not be under standard conditions *[1 mark]*.

3.1 $H_2O_2 + 2H^+ + 2e^- \rightleftharpoons 2H_2O$ *[1 mark]*

3.2 $H_2O_2 \rightleftharpoons O_2 + 2H^+ + 2e^-$ *[1 mark]*

3.3 $2H_2O_2 \rightleftharpoons O_2 + 2H_2O$ *[1 mark]*

3.4 $EMF = E^{\circ}_{reduced} - E^{\circ}_{oxidised}$
$E^{\circ}_{reduced} = EMF + E^{\circ}_{oxidised}$
$= +1.09 + 0.68$
$= +1.77\ V$

[2 marks for correct answer, otherwise 1 mark for correctly rearranging equation]

Unit 1: Section 9 — Acids, Bases and pH

Pages 64-66: Acids, Bases and pH — 1

1 A *[1 mark]*
Monoprotic acids release one proton when they dissociate. Sulfuric and ethanedioic acids are both diprotic acids, and whilst ethanoic acid is monoprotic, it's weak.

2 B *[1 mark]*
$pH = -log_{10}[H^+]$
$= -log_{10}(0.050)$
$= 1.301...$
$= 1.3\ (2\ s.f.)$

3 C *[1 mark]*

4 A *[1 mark]*
$pK_a = -log_{10}K_a$
$= -log_{10}(2.24 \times 10^{-5})$
$= 4.649...$
$= 4.65\ (3\ s.f.)$

5 C *[1 mark]*
$K_w = [H^+][OH^-]$
$[H^+] = \dfrac{K_w}{[OH^-]}$
$[Ca(OH)_2] = 0.0200$ mol dm^{-3} and calcium hydroxide is a dibasic strong base, so $[OH^-] = 2 \times 0.0200$ mol dm^{-3} = 0.0400 mol dm^{-3}.
$[H^+] = \dfrac{1.00 \times 10^{-14}}{0.0400}$
$= 2.50 \times 10^{-13}$ mol dm^{-3}
$pH = -log_{10}(2.50 \times 10^{-13})$
$= 12.602...$
$= 12.6\ (3\ s.f.)$

6.1 proton acceptor *[1 mark]*

6.2 Strong acids dissociate/ionise fully in water *[1 mark]*. Weak acids only partially dissociate/ionise in water (to set up an equilibrium) *[1 mark]*.

6.3 $HCl + H_2O \rightarrow H_3O^+ + Cl^-$ / $HCl \rightarrow H^+ + Cl^-$ *[1 mark]*

6.4 $pH = -log_{10}[H^+]$
H_2SO_4 is a diprotic acid so $[H^+]$ is given by multiplying $[H_2SO_4]$ by 2.
$[H^+] = 2 \times 0.0500$ mol dm^{-3}
$= 0.100$ mol dm^{-3}
$pH = -log_{10}(0.100)$
$= 1.00\ (3\ s.f.)$

[2 marks for correct answer, otherwise 1 mark for calculating [H⁺]]

6.5 $[H^+] = 10^{-pH}$
$= 10^{-1.75}$
$= 1.778... \times 10^{-2}$ mol dm^{-3}
$[H^+] = 2 \times [H_2SO_4]$
$[H_2SO_4] = [H^+] \div 2$
$= (1.778... \times 10^{-2}) \div 2$
$= 8.891... \times 10^{-3}$ mol dm^{-3}
$= 8.89 \times 10^{-3}$ mol dm^{-3} **(3 s.f.)**

[2 marks for correct answer, otherwise 1 mark for calculating [H⁺]]

7.1 Number of moles of NaOH = mass ÷ molar mass
$= 1.20$ g ÷ 40.0 g mol^{-1}
$= 0.0300$ mol
Concentration = number of moles ÷ volume
$[NaOH] = 0.0300$ mol ÷ $\dfrac{200}{1000}$ dm^3
$= 0.150$ mol dm^{-3}

[2 marks for correct answer, otherwise 1 mark for calculating number of moles]

7.2 Average titre $= \dfrac{23.45\ cm^3 + 23.40\ cm^3 + 23.45\ cm^3}{3}$
$= 23.4333...\ cm^3$
Number of moles of NaOH reacting
$=$ concentration × volume
$= 0.150$ mol dm$^{-3} \times \dfrac{23.4333...}{1000}$ dm^3
$= 3.515 \times 10^{-3}$ mol
The reaction equation is:
$H_2CO_3 + 2NaOH \rightarrow Na_2CO_3 + 2H_2O$
From the equation there is a 1:2 ratio so the number of moles of H_2CO_3 is half the number of moles of NaOH
Number of moles of $H_2CO_3 = (3.515 \times 10^{-3})$ mol ÷ 2
$= 1.7575 \times 10^{-3}$ mol
Concentration = number of moles ÷ volume
$= 1.7575 \times 10^{-3}$ mol ÷ $\dfrac{25.0}{1000}$ dm^3
$= 0.0703$ mol dm^{-3}
$= 0.0703$ mol dm^{-3} **(3 s.f.)**

[5 marks for correct answer, otherwise 1 mark for calculating average titre value, 1 mark for balanced symbol equation, 1 mark for calculating number of moles of NaOH, 1 mark for calculating number of moles of H₂CO₃]

You still get full marks if you followed the correct method but used the wrong value for the concentration of NaOH from your answer to question 7.1.

7.3 Percentage uncertainty $= \dfrac{uncertainty}{measurement} \times 100$
$= \dfrac{0.15}{23.4333...} \times 100$
$= 0.64011...$
$= 0.64\ \%\ (2\ s.f.)$

[2 marks for correct answer given to 2 s.f. or 1 mark for correct answer not given to 2 s.f.]

Again, if you've carried out the correct calculation but using an incorrect average titre value, you still get the marks.

7.4 E.g. Use a greater volume of carbonic acid, so that the mean titre of sodium hydroxide required is also greater *[1 mark]*.

Pages 67-69: Acids, Bases and pH — 2

1.1 $CH_3CH_2COOH + H_2O \rightleftharpoons CH_3CH_2COO^- + H_3O^+$ /
$CH_3CH_2COOH \rightleftharpoons CH_3CH_2COO^- + H^+$ *[1 mark]*

1.2 $K_a = \dfrac{[H^+][CH_3CH_2COO^-]}{[CH_3CH_2COOH]}$ / $K_a = \dfrac{[H^+]^2}{[CH_3CH_2COOH]}$
[1 mark]

172

1.3 M_r of $CH_3CH_2COOH = (12.0 \times 3) + (1.0 \times 6) + (16.0 \times 2)$
$$= 74.0$$

number of moles = mass ÷ molar mass

number of moles of $CH_3CH_2COOH = 12.0 \div 74.0$
$$= 0.16216... \text{ mol}$$

$[CH_3CH_2COOH]$ = number of moles ÷ volume
$$= 0.16216... \text{ mol} \div \frac{150}{1000} \text{ dm}^3$$
$$= 1.081081... \text{ mol dm}^{-3}$$

As propanoic acid is a weak acid it can be assumed that $[H^+] = [CH_3CH_2COO^-]$.

Therefore it is possible to use the expression:

$$K_a = \frac{[H^+]^2}{[CH_3CH_2COOH]}$$

$[H^+]^2 = K_a \times [CH_3CH_2COOH]$

$[H^+] = \sqrt{K_a \times [CH_3CH_2COOH]}$
$$= \sqrt{1.34 \times 10^{-5} \text{ mol dm}^{-3} \times 1.081081... \text{ mol dm}^{-3}}$$
$$= 3.8061... \times 10^{-3} \text{ mol dm}^{-3}$$

$pH = -\log_{10}[H^+]$
$$= -\log_{10}(3.8061... \times 10^{-3})$$
$$= 2.4195...$$
$$= \mathbf{2.42 \text{ (3 s.f.)}}$$

[5 marks for correct answer, otherwise 1 mark for calculating moles of propanoic acid, 1 mark for calculating concentration of propanoic acid, 1 mark for rearranging K_a expression to find $[H^+]$, 1 mark for calculating $[H^+]$]

2.1 $K_w = [H^+][OH^-]$ *[1 mark]*

2.2 The equilibrium shifting to the right means that the concentrations of H^+ and OH^- ions increase *[1 mark]* and so the value of K_w increases too *[1 mark]*.

2.3 $[H^+] = \dfrac{K_w}{[OH^-]}$

$[H^+] = \dfrac{1.00 \times 10^{-14} \text{ mol}^2 \text{ dm}^{-6}}{0.800 \text{ mol dm}^{-3}}$
$$= 1.25 \times 10^{-14} \text{ mol dm}^{-3}$$

$pH = -\log_{10}[H^+]$

$pH = -\log_{10}(1.25 \times 10^{-14} \text{ mol dm}^{-3})$
$$= 13.903...$$
$$= \mathbf{13.9 \text{ (3 s.f.)}}$$

[3 marks for correct answer, otherwise 1 mark for rearranging equation to find $[H^+]$, 1 mark for calculating $[H^+]$]

2.4 $[H^+] = 10^{-pH}$
$$= 10^{-12.19}$$
$$= 6.456... \times 10^{-13} \text{ mol dm}^{-3}$$

$K_w = [H^+][OH^-]$
$$= (6.456... \times 10^{-13} \text{ mol dm}^{-3}) \times (0.800 \text{ mol dm}^{-3})$$
$$= 5.165... \times 10^{-13} \text{ mol}^2 \text{ dm}^{-6}$$
$$= \mathbf{5.17 \times 10^{-13} \text{ mol}^2 \text{ dm}^{-6} \text{ (3 s.f.)}}$$

[2 marks for correct answer, otherwise 1 mark for calculating $[H^+]$]

3.1 E.g. pH meter may lose accuracy during storage/to avoid systematic error/make sure readings taken are accurate *[1 mark]*.

3.2 How to grade your answer:

Level 0:   There is no relevant information. *[No marks]*

Level 1:   One stage is covered well OR two stages are covered but they are incomplete and not always accurate. The answer is not in a logical order. *[1 to 2 marks]*

Level 2:   Two stages are covered well OR all 3 stages are covered but they are incomplete and not always accurate (details of apparatus used may be missing). The answer is mostly in a logical order. *[3 to 4 marks]*

Level 3:   All 3 stages are covered and are complete and accurate, with all apparatus correctly selected. The answer is coherent and is in a logical order. *[5 to 6 marks]*

Indicative content:

Stage 1: Measuring the initial volume and pH of the butanoic acid

The 25 cm³ butanoic acid should have been measured out into a beaker/conical flask using a 25 cm³ pipette/a graduated pipette/a burette.

The initial pH of the butanoic acid solution should be measured and recorded using a calibrated pH meter before the addition of potassium hydroxide.

Rinse the calibrated pH meter with deionised/distilled water and clamp it into position so that its bulb is sitting in the butanoic acid solution.

Stage 2: Monitoring the pH whilst adding the potassium hydroxide

Gradually add equal (e.g. 2 cm³) portions of the 1.0×10^{-5} mol dm⁻³ potassium hydroxide solution to the butanoic acid using a burette.

Stir the mixture gently after every addition using a stirring rod/by swirling the conical flask.

Use the calibrated pH meter to measure and record the pH of the solution after the addition of each portion of potassium hydroxide solution.

Stage 3: Adding the potassium hydroxide solution to excess and measuring final pH

Continue adding the potassium hydroxide solution until all 50 cm³ has been added.

Measure and record the final pH of the solution.

Rinse the pH meter with deionised/distilled water.

3.3 E.g.

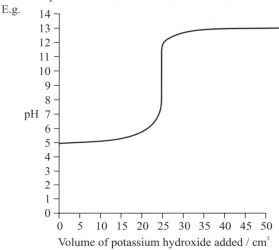

Volume of potassium hydroxide added / cm³

[3 marks — 1 mark for curve starting at pH value between 4 and 6, 1 mark for vertical line between pH 8 and around pH 12 at a volume of about 25 cm³, 1 mark for curve ending at pH value around 13]

Pages 70-72: Acids, Bases and pH — 3

1.1 $CH_3CH_2COONa \rightarrow Na^+ + CH_3CH_2COO^-$ *[1 mark]*

1.2   concentration = number of moles ÷ volume

$[CH_3CH_2COOH] = 5.0 \times 10^{-4} \text{ mol} \div \dfrac{50}{1000} \text{ dm}^3$

$= 0.010 \text{ mol dm}^{-3}$

$[CH_3CH_2COONa] = 5.0 \times 10^{-3} \text{ mol} \div \dfrac{50}{1000} \text{ dm}^3$

$= 0.10 \text{ mol dm}^{-3}$

$K_a = \dfrac{[H^+][CH_3CH_2COO^-]}{[CH_3CH_2COOH]}$

$[H^+] = \dfrac{K_a \times [CH_3CH_2COOH]}{[CH_3CH_2COO^-]}$

$= \dfrac{(1.34 \times 10^{-5} \text{ mol dm}^{-3}) \times 0.010 \text{ mol dm}^{-3}}{0.10 \text{ mol dm}^{-3}}$

$= 1.34 \times 10^{-6} \text{ mol dm}^{-3}$

$pH = -\log_{10}[H^+]$

$= -\log_{10}(1.34 \times 10^{-6})$

$= 5.8728...$

$= \textbf{5.9 (2 s.f.)}$

[6 marks for correct answer, otherwise 1 mark for calculating [CH_3CH_2COOH], 1 mark for calculating [CH_3CH_2COONa], 1 mark for K_a expression, 1 mark for rearranging K_a expression to find [H^+], 1 mark for calculating [H^+]]

1.3   The pH of the solution does not change/only changes slightly *[1 mark]*. Adding a small amount of acid increases the concentration of H^+ ions in the solution *[1 mark]*. The equilibrium of the buffer solution shifts to the left as the extra H^+ ions combine with the $CH_3CH_2COO^-$ ions to produce CH_3CH_2COOH, so there is no overall increase in the concentration of H^+ ions *[1 mark]*.

1.4   Any two from: E.g. shampoo/biological washing powder/ blood *[2 marks — 1 mark for each correct application]*

2.1   E.g. The equivalence point of a titration is shown on the pH curve as the vertical portion of the curve *[1 mark]*. An indicator can be used if the pH range over which it acts falls within the pH range covered by this vertical portion of the curve *[1 mark]*.

2.2   Indicator: methyl orange

Colour change: red to yellow

[1 mark]

2.3   E.g. In a weak acid/weak base titration there is no sharp pH change at the equivalence point so any colour change would only occur very gradually, making it very difficult to accurately identify the equivalence point *[1 mark]*.

2.4 $CH_3CH_2CH_2COOH + NaOH \rightarrow CH_3CH_2CH_2COONa + H_2O$

OR

$CH_3CH_2CH_2COOH + OH^- \rightarrow CH_3CH_2CH_2COO^- + H_2O$

[1 mark]

2.5   From the reaction equation. there is a 1:1 ratio of acid reacting with base, so 25.0 cm^3 of 0.0500 mol dm^{-3} NaOH neutralises 25.0 cm^3 of 0.0500 mol dm^{-3} butanoic acid.

So initial moles of acid $= 0.0500 \times \dfrac{25.0}{1000} = 0.00125$ mol

So moles of acid at half-neutralisation point

$= 0.00125 \div 2 = 6.25 \times 10^{-4}$ mol

Volume of reaction mixture at half-neutralisation point

$= 25.0 + 12.5 = 37.5 \text{ cm}^3$

So concentration of acid at half-neutralisation point

$= (6.25 \times 10^{-4}) \div \dfrac{37.5}{1000}$

$= 0.01666...$ mol dm^{-3}

$= 0.0167$ mol dm^{-3} (3 s.f.)

At the half-neutralisation point, moles of salt produced = moles of acid reacted = moles of acid remaining

So concentration of salt = concentration of acid

$= 0.0167$ mol dm^{-3} (3 s.f.)

[6 marks for correct answers given to 3 s.f. or 5 marks for correct answers not given to 3 s.f., otherwise 1 mark for calculating initial moles of acid, 1 mark for calculating moles of acid at half-neutralisation point, 1 mark for calculating volume at half-neutralisation point, 1 mark for calculating concentration of acid at half-neutralisation point]

2.6 $K_a = \dfrac{[H^+][CH_3CH_2CH_2COO^-]}{[CH_3CH_2CH_2COOH]}$ *[1 mark]*

2.7 $[H^+] = 10^{-pH}$

$= 10^{-4.80}$

$= 1.5848... \times 10^{-5}$ mol dm^{-3}

$K_a = \dfrac{(1.5848... \times 10^{-5}) \times 0.01666...}{0.01666...}$

$= \textbf{1.58} \times \textbf{10}^{-5} \textbf{ mol dm}^{-3}$ (3 s.f.)

[2 marks – 1 mark for correct calculation of [H^+], 1 mark for correct use of expression to calculate K_a]

Unit 2: Section 1 — Inorganic Chemistry

Pages 73-76: Inorganic Chemistry — 1

1   A *[1 mark]*

2   C *[1 mark]*

3   C *[1 mark]*

4   B *[1 mark]*

5   C *[1 mark]*

In general, the first ionisation energies of the elements increase as you move across a period, so Group 2 elements have higher first ionisation energies than Group 1 elements in the same period. The drop in first ionisation energy from Group 2 to Group 3 occurs because the outer electron of a Group 2 element is in an s-orbital, whilst the outer electron of a Group 3 element is in a p-orbital. The p-orbital is slightly further from the nucleus than the s-orbital, so it's slightly easier to remove the outer electron from a Group 3 element than a Group 2 element in the same period.

6.1   Al, Si, P, S, Cl, Ar *[1 mark]*

6.2 $1s^2\ 2s^2\ 2p^6\ 3s^2\ 3p^3$ *[1 mark]*

6.3   The number of protons in the nucleus increases across Period 3, so the positive charge of the nucleus increases *[1 mark]*. This causes the electrons to be pulled closer to the nucleus, which makes the atomic radius smaller *[1 mark]*. The extra electrons that the elements gain across Period 3 are added to the outer energy level, so don't provide any extra shielding *[1 mark]*.

7.1   E.g. the outermost electron of a Group 2 atom is in an s sub-shell *[1 mark]*.

7.2   Group 2 metals react more vigorously with water as you descend the group *[1 mark]*. This is because the ionisation energy decreases/the outer electrons are more easily lost as you descend the group *[1 mark]*.

7.3   Similarity: e.g. fizzing/effervesce/bubbles of gas given off *[1 mark]*.

Difference: e.g. the reaction of barium would be more vigorous *[1 mark]*.

7.4 Group 2 metals react with water to produce metal hydroxides *[1 mark]*. Strontium hydroxide is more soluble than calcium hydroxide, so it will produce more hydroxide ions in solution and have a higher pH than the calcium hydroxide solution *[1 mark]*.

7.5 E.g. dip a nichrome wire loop in concentrated hydrochloric acid *[1 mark]*. Dip the loop into the strontium chloride solution *[1 mark]*. Hold the loop in the clear blue part of a Bunsen burner flame *[1 mark]* and observe the colour change in the flame *[1 mark]*. The flame would turn red if strontium ions are present *[1 mark]*.

It's fine if you described a different test here, e.g. observing whether precipitates form when you add NaOH and H_2SO_4 to samples of the solution. If you did, give yourself up to 4 marks for describing the steps of your method and up to 2 marks for describing the observations you would make, for a maximum of 5 marks altogether.

8.1 The student did not add dilute hydrochloric acid before adding the barium sulfate *[1 mark]*. Hydrochloric acid is added in order to react with any carbonate ions in solution *[1 mark]*. Sulfate and carbonate ions both produce a white precipitate with barium sulfate, so a white precipitate would have formed in both solutions *[1 mark]*.

8.2 Add dilute hydrochloric acid *[1 mark]*. The sodium carbonate solution will effervesce/fizz as carbon dioxide gas is formed *[1 mark]*. The gas will turn limewater cloudy *[1 mark]*.

8.3 Add dilute nitric acid *[1 mark]* followed by a few drops of silver nitrate solution *[1 mark]*. A cream precipitate will form if the solution contains sodium bromide *[1 mark]*. To confirm that the solution contains bromide ions and not iodide ions, add concentrated ammonia *[1 mark]*. Silver bromide will dissolve, but silver iodide would not *[1 mark]*.

9.1 The strength of the van der Waals forces between molecules of chlorine is weaker than between molecules of iodine *[1 mark]*. This is because the size/mass of the chlorine molecules is less than iodine molecules/chlorine molecules contain fewer electrons than iodine molecules *[1 mark]*.

Chlorine molecules are smaller than iodine molecules because they contain fewer electrons, so have fewer occupied shells and take up less space.

9.2 The reducing ability of the halides increases down the group, as the attraction between the nucleus and the outer electrons decreases *[1 mark]*. This is because the halide ions get larger/the electrons are further from the nucleus *[1 mark]*, and because the effect of shielding on the outer electrons increases down the group *[1 mark]*.

9.3 Chlorine is a stronger oxidising agent than bromine, whereas iodine is a weaker oxidising agent than bromine *[1 mark]*.

9.4 $Cl_2 + 2Br^- \rightarrow 2Cl^- + Br_2$ *[1 mark]*

9.5 $NaF + H_2SO_4 \rightarrow NaHSO_4 + HF$ *[1 mark]*

9.6

Hydrogen halide	Reaction products	
HBr	Br_2, SO_2, H_2O	
HI	I_2, SO_2, H_2O, H_2S	*[1 mark]*

9.7 $8HI + H_2SO_4 \rightarrow 4I_2 + 4H_2O + H_2S$ *[1 mark]*

Pages 77-79: Inorganic Chemistry — 2

1.1 Reagent: e.g. calcium sulfate/sulfuric acid *[1 mark for any soluble sulfate or solution containing sulfate ions.]*
Equation: $Ba^{2+}_{(aq)} + SO_4^{2-}_{(aq)} \rightarrow BaSO_{4(s)}$ *[1 mark]*

The barium ions would react with a source of sulfate ions to form a white precipitate of insoluble $BaSO_4$.

1.2 A precipitate (of $Mg(OH)_2$) would begin to form *[1 mark]*.

1.3 E.g. add the same number of moles of each hydroxide to a set volume of water *[1 mark]*. Test the pH of each solution using the pH meter *[1 mark]*. A more soluble hydroxide produces more hydroxide ions in solution, so the pH of the barium hydroxide solution should be higher than that of the calcium hydroxide solution *[1 mark]*.

1.4 E.g. a patient swallows a barium meal/suspension of barium sulfate *[1 mark]*. X-rays can not pass through barium sulfate/barium sulfate is opaque to X-rays *[1 mark]*. The insoluble barium sulfate coats the tissues in the oesophagus/stomach/intestines, which makes them show up on the X-ray diagram/radiograph *[1 mark]*.

1.5 Compound: calcium oxide/calcium carbonate *[1 mark]*
Equation: $CaO + SO_2 \rightarrow CaSO_3$/
$CaCO_3 + SO_2 \rightarrow CaSO_3 + CO_2$ *[1 mark]*

1.6 Antacid medicines: e.g. magnesium hydroxide *[1 mark]*
Neutralising acidic soils: e.g. calcium hydroxide *[1 mark]*
Extracting titanium from $TiCl_4$: magnesium *[1 mark]*

2.1 Reaction 2: $Cl_2 + 2NaOH \rightarrow NaClO + NaCl + H_2O$ *[1 mark]*
Reaction 3: $NaClO + H_2O \rightleftharpoons HClO + NaOH$ *[1 mark]*

2.2 $Cl_2 + H_2O \rightleftharpoons 2H^+ + Cl^- + ClO^-$ *[1 mark]*

2.3 Reactions 1 and 2 *[1 mark]*

2.4 When chlorine is added to water in the presence of sunlight, disproportionation can occur to form HCl and HClO *[1 mark]*. In the presence of sunlight, chlorine can also decompose water to form HCl and O_2 *[1 mark]*. There is only one reaction that happens sodium chlorate(I) is added to water, with the products being HClO and NaOH *[1 mark]*. When added to water, sodium chlorate(I) is a more efficient disinfectant than chlorine because a greater proportion of the Cl atoms in sodium chlorate(I) are converted to ClO^- *[1 mark]*.

2.5 Any two from: e.g. chlorine gas is very harmful if breathed in, so is difficult to store/transport safely. / Liquid chlorine causes severe chemical burns, so is difficult to store/transport safely. / Chlorine reacts with organic compounds in water to form chlorinated hydrocarbons, which can be carcinogenic/cause cancer. *[2 marks — 1 mark for each correct answer]*

3 How to grade your answer:
Level 0:   There is no relevant information. *[No marks]*
Level 1:   One stage is covered well OR two stages are covered but they are incomplete and not always accurate. The answer is not in a logical order. *[1 to 2 marks]*
Level 2:   Two stages are covered well OR all three stages are covered but they are incomplete and not always accurate. The answer is mostly in a logical order. *[3 to 4 marks]*
Level 3:   All three stages are covered and are complete and accurate. The answer is coherent and is in a logical order. *[5 to 6 marks]*

Indicative content:
Stage 1: Metallic substances
Sodium, magnesium and aluminium are metals.
Their melting points increase across the period because the metal-metal bonds get stronger.
The bonds get stronger because the metal ions have an increasing positive charge, an increasing number of delocalised electrons and a decreasing radius.
Stage 2: Silicon
Silicon is macromolecular.
It has a structure made of strong covalent bonds that link all its atoms together.
A lot of energy is needed to break these bonds, so silicon has a high melting point.

Stage 3: Molecular and monatomic substances

Phosphorus (P_4), sulfur (S_8) and chlorine (Cl_2) are all molecular substances.

Their melting points depend upon the strength of the van der Waals forces between the molecules.

Van der Waals forces are weak and easily overcome so these elements have low melting points.

More atoms in a molecule mean stronger van der Waals forces. Sulfur forms the biggest molecules, so it's got a higher melting point than phosphorus or chlorine.

Phosphorus is the next biggest, so it has a higher melting point than chlorine.

Argon has a very low melting point because it exists as individual atoms (it's monatomic). This results in very weak van der Waals forces.

Unit 2: Section 2 — More Inorganic Chemistry

Pages 80-82: More Inorganic Chemistry — 1

1 D *[1 mark]*

Na, Mg, P and S react readily with oxygen, whilst Al and Si react slowly.

2 B *[1 mark]*

Adding hydroxide ions causes the water ligands around the Fe^{3+} ions to become deprotonated. However, this only happens to three of the water ligands before the complex becomes uncharged and therefore insoluble, forming the precipitate $Fe(OH)_3(H_2O)_3$.

3 C *[1 mark]*

Cu has a full 3d subshell — $1s^2\ 2s^2\ 2p^6\ 3s^2\ 3p^6\ 3d^{10}\ 4s^1$ — it's more stable that way.

4 C *[1 mark]*

In VO_2^+, vanadium has an oxidation state of +5. It's reduced first to VO^{2+}, with an oxidation state of +4, which is blue in colour, then to V^{3+}, with an oxidation state of +3, which is green, and finally to V^{2+}, with an oxidation state of +2, which is violet. So that's three different ions with three different colours that are produced over the course of the reaction.

5.1 Cobalt has the electron configuration $1s^2\ 2s^2\ 2p^6\ 3s^2\ 3p^6\ 3d^7\ 4s^2$ *[1 mark]*, and so has a partially filled d-subshell both as an atom and when it forms stable ions *[1 mark]*. Zinc has the electron configuration $1s^2\ 2s^2\ 2p^6\ 3s^2\ 3p^6\ 3d^{10}\ 4s^2$ *[1 mark]* and only forms Zn^{2+} ions (by losing its 4s electrons), so has a full d-subshell as both an atom and an ion *[1 mark]*.

5.2 co-ordinate/dative (covalent) bonding *[1 mark]*

5.3 A ligand is an ion or molecule that donates a pair of electrons to a central transition metal ion to form a co-ordinate bond *[1 mark]*.

5.4

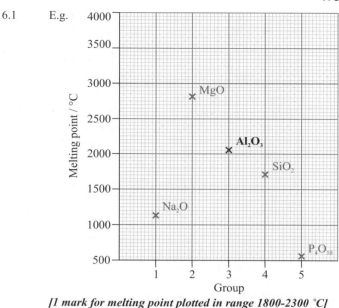

[2 marks — 1 mark for tetrahedral shape, 1 mark for bond angle]

5.5 $[CoCl_4]^{2-} + 6H_2O \rightleftharpoons [Co(H_2O)_6]^{2+} + 4Cl^-$ *[1 mark]*

You can write the equilibrium going in either direction for the mark.

5.6 Cl^- ions are larger than water molecules, so only four ligands can fit around the central cobalt ion, changing the co-ordination number *[1 mark]*. Water molecules are neutral, so have an oxidation state of 0, whereas Cl^- ions have an oxidation state of −1, so the total oxidation state must change *[1 mark]*.

5.7 e.g. ammonia/NH_3 *[1 mark]*

5.8 chelate effect/chelation *[1 mark]*

6.1 E.g.

[1 mark for melting point plotted in range 1800-2300 °C]

6.2 Mg forms 2+ ions, which have a greater charge than Na^+ ions *[1 mark]* and so bond more strongly to the O^{2-} ions *[1 mark]*.

6.3 SiO_2 has a macromolecular/giant covalent structure *[1 mark]*. For it to melt, lots of energy is needed to break the strong covalent bonds between atoms *[1 mark]*, and so its melting point is high. P_4O_{10} has a simple molecular/simple covalent structure *[1 mark]*, with its molecules held together by weak intermolecular forces that take little energy to break *[1 mark]*, so its melting point is much lower.

Pages 83-86: More Inorganic Chemistry — 2

1.1 Formula: $[Cu(H_2O)_6]^{2+}$ *[1 mark]*
Shape: octahedral *[1 mark]*

1.2 +1 *[1 mark]*

1.3 The copper metal acts as a reducing agent *[1 mark]*.

1.4 E.g. the colour of a complex depends on the frequencies of visible light it absorbs *[1 mark]*, which depends on the size of the energy gap (ΔE) between the higher and lower energy d orbitals *[1 mark]*. Different complexes have different oxidation states, co-ordination numbers and ligands, which all affect the size of their energy gap, and so their colour *[1 mark]*.

2.1 MgO has a giant ionic structure *[1 mark]*. There are strong ionic bonds/forces of electrostatic attraction between the ions *[1 mark]*, which take a lot of energy to break *[1 mark]*.

2.2 $MgO + H_2O \rightarrow Mg(OH)_2$ *[1 mark]*

2.3 $Mg(OH)_2$ is not very soluble in water *[1 mark]*, so the concentration of OH^- ions in solution is low *[1 mark]*.

2.4 $Mg_{(s)} + H_2O_{(g)} \rightarrow MgO_{(s)} + H_{2(g)}$ *[1 mark for correct reactants and products, 1 mark for correct state symbols]*

2.5 magnesium hydroxide/$Mg(OH)_2$ and hydrogen/H_2 *[1 mark]*

2.6 simple molecular/simple covalent *[1 mark]*

2.7 $SO_{2(g)} + H_2O_{(l)} \rightarrow H_2SO_{3(aq)}$ *[1 mark for correct equation including state symbols]*
$H_2SO_{3(aq)} \rightarrow 2H^+_{(aq)} + SO_3^{2-}_{(aq)}$ /
$H_2SO_{3(aq)} \rightarrow H^+_{(aq)} + HSO_3^-_{(aq)}$
[1 mark for a correct equation including state symbols]

2.8 Equation: $SO_2 + \frac{1}{2}O_2 \rightarrow SO_3$ *[1 mark]*
Catalyst: V_2O_5/vanadium(V) oxide *[1 mark]*

2.9 Equation: $P_4O_{10} + 12NaOH \rightarrow 4Na_3PO_4 + 6H_2O$ *[1 mark]*
Type of reaction: acid/base **OR** neutralisation *[1 mark]*

2.10 amphoteric *[1 mark]*

2.11 $Al_2O_3 + 3H_2SO_4 \rightarrow Al_2(SO_4)_3 + 3H_2O$ *[1 mark]*
$Al_2O_3 + 2NaOH + 3H_2O \rightarrow 2NaAl(OH)_4$ *[1 mark]*

3.1 $1s^2\ 2s^2\ 2p^6\ 3s^2\ 3p^6\ 3d^6$ *[1 mark]*

3.2 The solution containing $[Fe(H_2O)_6]^{3+}$ ions has a lower pH. Fe^{3+} ions have a greater charge to size ratio/charge density *[1 mark]* so are more polarising than Fe^{2+} ions/attract electrons from the O atoms of the co-ordinated water molecules more strongly *[1 mark]*. This polarisation weakens the O–H bond and so it is more likely that an H^+ ion will be released *[1 mark]*.

3.3 $[Fe(H_2O)_6]^{2+}$: A green precipitate will be formed *[1 mark]* with the formula $Fe(OH)_2(H_2O)_4$ *[1 mark]*.
$[Fe(H_2O)_6]^{3+}$: A brown precipitate will be formed *[1 mark]*, with the formula $Fe(OH)_3(H_2O)_3$ *[1 mark]*.

3.4 E.g. make sure the solution containing $[Fe(H_2O)_6]^{2+}$ ions is freshly made *[1 mark]* / Prepare/use the solution containing $[Fe(H_2O)_6]^{2+}$ ions in the absence of air *[1 mark]*.

3.5 $[Fe(H_2O)_6]^{3+} + 3C_2O_4^{2-} \rightarrow [Fe(C_2O_4)_3]^{3-} + 6H_2O$ *[1 mark]*

3.6 Two of the lone pairs on the ethanedioate ion form two co-ordinate bonds with a metal ion *[1 mark]*.

3.7 When monodentate ligands are substituted with bidentate ligands the number of particles in solution increases *[1 mark]*. This increases the entropy, so the forward reaction is much more likely to occur than the reverse reaction *[1 mark]*.

3.8 Oxygen forms a co-ordinate bond to the Fe^{2+} ion, forming oxyhaemoglobin *[1 mark]*. Where the oxygen is needed in the body, the oxygen molecule is exchanged for a water molecule which bonds to the Fe^{2+} and the haemoglobin returns to the lungs *[1 mark]*.

3.9 Carbon monoxide replaces oxygen and bonds co-ordinately to Fe^{2+} *[1 mark]*. It is a stronger ligand so does not readily exchange with oxygen or water ligands, disrupting the transport of oxygen around the body *[1 mark]*.

4 E.g.
Moles of $Cr_2O_7^{2-} = \dfrac{23.85}{1000} \times 0.0200$
$= 4.77 \times 10^{-4}$ mol
From reaction equation, Fe^{2+} and $Cr_2O_7^{2-}$ react in 6:1 ratio, so
Moles of Fe^{2+} in 25.0 cm³ $= 6 \times (4.77 \times 10^{-4})$
$= 0.002862$ mol
Moles of Fe^{2+} in 250 cm³ $= 0.02862$ mol
Mass of iron $= 0.02862 \times 55.8$
$= 1.596996$ g
Percentage of iron $= \dfrac{1.596996}{2.00} \times 100$
$= 79.8498$
$= \mathbf{79.8 \%}$ **(3 s.f.)**

[6 marks for correct answer given to 3 s.f. or 5 marks for correct answer not given to 3 s.f., otherwise 1 mark for calculating moles of $Cr_2O_7^{2-}$, 1 mark for calculating moles of Fe^{2+} in 25 cm³, 1 mark for calculating moles of Fe^{2+} in 250 cm³ or calculating mass of iron in 25 cm³, 1 mark for calculating mass of iron in 250 cm³.]

Page 87-88: More Inorganic Chemistry — 3

1.1 Add each sample base to a small amount of the Cu^{2+} solution in a test tube *[1 mark]*. A blue precipitate will form in the test tubes where NH_3 and NaOH have been added *[1 mark]*, and a green-blue precipitate will form in the test tube where Na_2CO_3 has been added, allowing Na_2CO_3 to be identified *[1 mark]*. Keep adding the other two bases to their test tubes until one precipitate dissolves to give a deep blue solution. The base that dissolves the precipitate is NH_3, the other base is NaOH *[1 mark]*.

1.2 Initially a white precipitate will be formed *[1 mark]*, that will dissolve to give a colourless solution once the NaOH is in excess *[1 mark]*.
The equation for the formation of the precipitate is:
$[Al(H_2O)_6]^{3+} + 3OH^- \rightarrow Al(H_2O)_3(OH)_3 + 3H_2O$ *[1 mark]*
and for the formation of the colourless solution is:
$Al(H_2O)_3(OH)_3 + OH^- \rightarrow [Al(OH)_4(H_2O)_2]^- + H_2O$ *[1 mark]*
You could write the full equations for these reactions instead, for example,
$Al(H_2O)_3(OH)_3 + NaOH \rightarrow Na[Al(OH)_4(H_2O)_2] + H_2O$

2.1 iron/Fe *[1 mark]*

2.2 Heterogeneous means the catalyst is in a different phase to the reactants *[1 mark]*.

2.3 Sites on the catalyst on which reactants may be adsorbed and where the reaction then takes place *[1 mark]*.

2.4 Impurities may bind to the catalyst's surface *[1 mark]* and stop the reactants from being adsorbed *[1 mark]*.

2.5 E.g. less product can be made in a certain amount of time/with a certain amount of energy. / The catalyst may need replacing/regenerating *[1 mark]*.

2.6 Both ions are negatively charged so repel one another, making it unlikely they will collide and react *[1 mark]*.

2.7 $S_2O_8^{2-} + 2Fe^{2+} \rightarrow 2Fe^{3+} + 2SO_4^{2-}$ *[1 mark]*
$2Fe^{3+} + 2I^- \rightarrow I_2 + 2Fe^{2+}$ *[1 mark]*

3 E.g. Moles of $X^{2+} = \dfrac{25.00}{1000} \times 0.160$
$= 0.004$ mol
Moles of $MnO_4^- = \dfrac{26.7}{1000} \times 0.0300$
$= 8.01 \times 10^{-4}$ mol
Moles of e^- accepted by $MnO_4^- = 5 \times (8.01 \times 10^{-4})$
$= 0.004005$
Moles of e^- per mole of $X = \dfrac{0.004005}{0.004}$
$= 1.00125$
$= 1$ (nearest whole number)
So $X^{2+} \rightarrow X^{3+} + e^-$
Oxidation state $= +3$
[5 marks for correct answer, otherwise 1 mark for calculating moles of X^{2+}, 1 mark for calculating moles of MnO_4^-, 1 mark for calculating moles of e^-, 1 mark for calculating moles of e^- per mole of X.]

Another way you could do this question is by working out the ratio of X^{2+} to MnO_4^- in the full reaction equation,
i.e. $(4.00 \times 10^{-3}) \div (8.01 \times 10^{-4}) \approx 5$, then writing out the full equation:
$5X^{2+} + MnO_4^- + 8H^+ \rightarrow 5X^{3+} + Mn^{2+} + 4H_2O$
You know from the half-equation given that each MnO_4^- needs $5e^-$, and so each X^{2+} must donate e^-, making the product X^{3+}, with an oxidation state of +3.

Pages 89-91: More Inorganic Chemistry — 4

1.1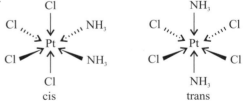
[1 mark]
You don't need to show the 3D structure here — if you've just shown normal arrows for the bonds that's fine too.

1.2 E.g.

cis   trans

[3 marks — 1 mark for cis isomer with NH_3 ligands adjacent, 1 mark for trans isomer with NH_3 ligands opposite one another, 1 mark for correct labelling.]

1.3 $Pt(NH_3)_2Cl_2 + NH_2CH_2CH_2NH_2 \rightarrow$
$Pt(NH_2CH_2CH_2NH_2)Cl_2 + 2NH_3$ *[1 mark]*

2.1 The solution absorbs wavelengths towards the red end of the visible spectrum *[1 mark]* and transmits or reflects wavelengths around the blue end of the visible spectrum *[1 mark]*.

2.2 colorimeter *[1 mark]*

2.3 Cu^{2+} has a more positive electrode potential, so it is more easily reduced and therefore less stable *[1 mark]*.

2.4 Different ligands affect the value of the redox potential *[1 mark]*. The standard electrode potential is measured in aqueous solution, so the ligands in that case are H_2O *[1 mark]*.

2.5 $$\Delta E = \frac{hc}{\lambda}$$
$$= \frac{(6.63 \times 10^{-34}) \times (3.00 \times 10^8)}{670 \times 10^{-9}}$$
$$= 2.9686... \times 10^{-19}$$
$$= \mathbf{2.97 \times 10^{-19} \ J \ (3 \ s.f.)}$$

[3 marks for correct answer given to 3 s.f. or 2 marks for correct answer not given to 3 s.f., otherwise 1 mark for correct equation for ΔE.]

2.6 linear *[1 mark]*

2.7 Ag^+ ions have a full d-subshell and so transitions between lower and higher energy d-orbitals are not possible *[1 mark]*. All frequencies of visible light are reflected or transmitted by the solution and so it appears colourless *[1 mark]*.

2.8 When Tollens' reagent is added to aldehydes, the silver ions are reduced to silver metal, producing a silver mirror *[1 mark]*. There is no visible change when it is added to ketones, because they cannot be oxidised by Tollens' reagent *[1 mark]*.

3.1 Moles of $MnO_4^- = \frac{19.10}{1000} \times 0.0200$
$$= 3.82 \times 10^{-4} \ mol$$

From reaction equation, $C_2O_4^{2-}$ and MnO_4^- react in 5:2 ratio, so

Moles of $C_2O_4^{2-}$ in 25.0 cm³ $= \frac{5}{2} \times (3.82 \times 10^{-4})$
$$= 9.55 \times 10^{-4} \ mol$$

Moles of $C_2O_4^{2-}$ in 250 cm³ $= 9.55 \times 10^{-3}$ mol

Relative formula mass of hydrated acid $= \dfrac{\text{mass of acid}}{\text{number of moles}}$
$$= \frac{1.20}{9.55 \times 10^{-3}}$$
$$= 125.654...$$

Formula mass of $C_2O_4H_2 = (2 \times 12.0) + (4 \times 16.0) + (2 \times 1.0)$
$$= 90.0$$

So formula mass of $x.H_2O = 125.654... - 90.0$
$$= 35.654...$$

Formula mass of $H_2O = (2 \times 1.0) + 16.0$
$$= 18.0$$

$\frac{35.654...}{18.0} = 1.9808... = 2$ (nearest whole number)

therefore $x = 2$

[6 marks for correct answer, otherwise 1 mark for calculating moles of MnO_4^-, 1 mark for calculating moles of $C_2O_4^{2-}$ in 25 cm³, 1 mark for calculating moles of $C_2O_4^{2-}$ in 250 cm³, 1 mark for calculating relative formula mass of acid, 1 mark for calculating formula mass of $x.H_2O$]

You could also work out x like this:

Mass of 9.55×10^{-3} moles of $C_2O_4H_2 = (9.55 \times 10^{-3}) \times 90.0$
$$= 0.8595$$

Mass of H_2O in $C_2O_4H_2.xH_2O = 1.20 - 0.8595 = 0.3405$ g
Moles of H_2O in 0.3405 g $= 0.3405 \div 18.0 = 0.0189...$
Ratio of H_2O to $C_2O_4H_2 = 0.0189... \div 9.55 \times 10^{-3} \approx 2$
If you've done the question this way and not by calculating the number of moles of $C_2O_4^{2-}$ in 250 cm³ and the formula mass of $x.H_2O$, you get 1 mark for calculating the masses of $C_2O_4H_2$ and H_2O present and 1 mark for calculating the number of moles of H_2O.

3.2 The rate of reaction is initially slow as the reacting ions are both negative and so repel one another *[1 mark]*. The rate increases as Mn^{2+} is produced as Mn^{2+} acts as a catalyst *[1 mark]*. It does this by first reacting with MnO_4^- to form Mn^{3+} ions, according to the equation:
$MnO_4^- + 4Mn^{2+} + 8H^+ \rightarrow 5Mn^{3+} + 4H_2O$ *[1 mark]*.
The Mn^{3+} ions then react with $C_2O_4^-$ ions to form carbon dioxide and re-form Mn^{2+}:
$2Mn^{3+} + C_2O_4^{2-} \rightarrow 2Mn^{2+} + 2CO_2$ *[1 mark]*

Unit 3: Section 1 — The Basics of Organic Chemistry

Pages 92-94: The Basics of Organic Chemistry — 1

1 B *[1 mark]*
The strength of the carbon–halogen bond determines the reactivity of a halogenoalkane. The bond strength decreases as you go down Group 7 — so the C–I bond breaks most easily, and 1-iodobutane will react faster than 1-chlorobutane or 1-bromobutane.

2 C *[1 mark]*
The general formula of the alkanes is C_nH_{2n+2}. So an alkane with 16 H atoms will have 7 C atoms, because $(7 \times 2) + 2 = 16$.

3 A *[1 mark]*
To figure this out, you need to use the Cahn-Ingold-Prelog priority rules. Alkene N has two F atoms attached to the first double bond carbon, so it doesn't have stereoisomers. Of the other three, alkene M is the only one that has the two higher priority groups on the same side of the double bond.

4 B *[1 mark]*
To show stereoisomerism, both of an alkene's double bond carbons must have two different groups attached to them. In 2-methylbut-2-ene, the first double bond carbon has two CH_3 groups attached to it.

5.1 A or B *[1 mark]*

5.2
[1 mark]

5.3 2,3-dimethylbut-2-ene *[1 mark]*

5.4 E.g.
[1 mark]
Any molecule with the formula C_6H_{12} that isn't an alkene is fine here.

6.1 Any two from: e.g. compounds in a homologous series have similar chemical properties. / Compounds in a homologous series have the same general formula. / Compounds in a homologous series have the same functional group. / Each successive member in a homologous series differs by a CH_2 group. *[2 marks — 1 mark for each correct answer.]*

6.2 E.g. saturated hydrocarbons contain only single bonds/contain no double or triple bonds *[1 mark]*.

6.3 The actual number atoms of each element present in a molecule *[1 mark]*.

6.4 $C_{17}H_{36} + 26O_2 \rightarrow 17CO_2 + 18H_2O$ *[1 mark]*

6.5 carbon/soot *[1 mark]*

6.6 $C_{17}H_{36} \rightarrow C_8H_{18} + C_4H_8 + C_5H_{10}$ *[1 mark]*

6.7 Slight pressure, high temperature and a zeolite catalyst. *[2 marks for all three conditions correct, otherwise 1 mark for any 2 conditions correct.]*

6.8 Any two from: e.g. using a catalyst speeds up the reaction, which saves time and money. / A catalyst allows the reaction to be carried out at low pressure, which means less expensive equipment is needed. / A catalyst allows the reaction to be carried out at a lower temperature, which reduces the amount of money that needs to be spent on energy. *[2 marks — 1 mark for each sensible reason.]*

Pages 95-96: The Basics of Organic Chemistry — 2

1.1
[1 mark]
For this one, it doesn't matter if you drew out all the bonds in the $-CH_2CH_3$ group (or if you showed it as C_2H_5). And you get the mark for drawing the Z-isomer (like this one) or the E-isomer (with the Cl atoms opposite each other).

1.2 Both of the double-bond carbons have two different atoms or groups attached to them *[1 mark]* and there is restricted rotation around the double bond *[1 mark]*.

1.3 Any one from: e.g.

1,3-dichlorobut-1-ene:

1,4-dichlorobut-1-ene:

1,3-dichlorobut-2-ene:

2,3-dichlorobut-2-ene:

1,4-dichlorobut-2-ene:

[2 marks — 1 mark for a correct structure, 1 mark for a name that matches the structure drawn.]

There are a few more possible answers for this question — you get the marks if you correctly drew and named any isomer of $C_4H_6Cl_2$ that has a double bond with different groups attached to both double-bond carbons.

1.4 E.g. 1,1-dichlorobut-1-ene / 2,3-dichlorobut-1-ene / 3,3-dichlorobut-1-ene / 3,4-dichlorobut-1-ene / 4,4-dichlorobut-1-ene *[1 mark]*.

You'd get a mark here for naming any alkene isomer of $C_4H_6Cl_2$ that has identical atoms or groups attached to either of the double-bond carbons.

2.1 $C_5H_{12} + 5\frac{1}{2}O_2 \rightarrow 5CO + 6H_2O$ *[1 mark]*
Any correct multiple of this equation would get the mark too,
e.g. $2C_5H_{12} + 11O_2 \rightarrow 10CO + 12H_2O$.

2.2 They are fitted with catalytic converters *[1 mark]*.

2.3 Sulfur impurities in the fuel/petrol/diesel *[1 mark]* react with oxygen when the fuel is burned in car engines *[1 mark]*.

2.4 Calcium carbonate is mixed with water to make an alkaline slurry *[1 mark]*. The alkaline slurry is sprayed onto the flue gases *[1 mark]*, which react with the alkaline slurry to form a salt *[1 mark]*.

3 How to grade your answer:
Level 0: There is no relevant information. *[No marks]*
Level 1: 1 stage is covered well. Or, 2 stages are covered but they are incomplete and not always accurate. The answer is not in a logical order. *[1 to 2 marks]*
Level 2: 2 stages are covered well. Or, all 3 stages are covered but they are incomplete and not always accurate. The answer is mostly in a logical order. *[3 to 4 marks]*
Level 3: All 3 stages are covered and are complete and accurate. The answer is coherent and is in a logical order. *[5 to 6 marks]*

Indicative content:
Stage 1: Fractional distillation
Crude oil is a mixture of hydrocarbons (mostly alkanes).
In fractional distillation, crude oil is heated until it vaporises.
The crude oil is then pumped into a fractionating column.
The largest hydrocarbons don't vaporise, because their boiling points are too high. They run to the bottom of the column and form a residue.
The crude oil vapour rises up through the trays.
There is a temperature gradient in the fractionating column — as you go up the column, it gets cooler.
Because the alkane molecules have different chain lengths, they have different boiling points, so each fraction condenses at a different temperature.
The fractions are drawn off at different levels in the column.
The hydrocarbons with the lowest boiling points don't condense and are drawn off as gases at the top of the column.
Stage 2: Cracking
Some of the heavier fractions taken from the column are then cracked.
Cracking is breaking up long-chain alkanes into smaller hydrocarbons.
Thermal cracking takes place at high temperature (up to 1000 °C) and high pressure (up to 70 atm).
It produces a lot of alkenes, including propene.
Stage 3: Equation showing production of propene
This is one way that decane could be cracked to produce propene: $C_{10}H_{22} \rightarrow C_7H_{16} + C_3H_6$

Pages 97-100: The Basics of Organic Chemistry — 3

1.1 E.g. 1-chloropropane contains a polar C–Cl bond *[1 mark]* but propane contains only non-polar C–H and C–C bonds *[1 mark]*.

1.2 E.g. an electron-pair donor *[1 mark]*.

1.3 Mechanism:

Equation:
$C_3H_7Cl + 2NH_3 \rightarrow C_3H_7NH_2 + NH_4Cl$
[6 marks — 1 mark for curly arrow from NH_3 lone pair to correct carbon atom, 1 mark for curly arrow from C–Cl bond to Cl atom, 1 mark for curly arrow from NH_3 lone pair to H atom, 1 mark for curly arrow from N^+–H bond to N^+, 1 mark for correct structure of product, 1 mark for correct reaction equation.]

1.4 E.g. propylamine is a nucleophile itself, so it can react with 1-chloropropane to form other amines *[1 mark]*.

1.5 The rate of reaction would be slower *[1 mark]*, because the C–F bond is stronger than the C–Cl bond, so it breaks less easily *[1 mark]*.

2.1 UV light/sunlight *[1 mark]*

2.2 Initiation *[1 mark]*: $Cl_2 \rightarrow 2Cl\bullet$ *[1 mark]*
Propagation *[1 mark]*: $CH_2Cl_2 + Cl\bullet \rightarrow CHCl_2\bullet + HCl$ *[1 mark]*
$CHCl_2\bullet + Cl_2 \rightarrow CHCl_3 + Cl\bullet$ *[1 mark]*
Termination *[1 mark]*: e.g. $CHCl_2\bullet + Cl\bullet \rightarrow CHCl_3$ *[1 mark]*

2.3 $CHCl_2\bullet + CHCl_2\bullet \rightarrow C_2H_2Cl_4$ *[1 mark]*

2.4 $Cl\cdot + O_3 \rightarrow O_2 + ClO\cdot$ *[1 mark]*
$ClO\cdot + O_3 \rightarrow 2O_2 + Cl\cdot$ *[1 mark]*
Overall equation: $2O_3 \rightarrow 3O_2$ *[1 mark]*
Chlorine radicals are described as a catalyst as they are regenerated at the end of the reaction *[1 mark]*.

3.1

[4 marks — 1 mark for curly arrow from the lone pair on the hydroxide ion to a suitable hydrogen, 1 mark for curly arrow from C–H bond to end C–C bond, 1 mark for curly arrow from C–Br bond to Br atom, 1 mark for correct structure of product.]

3.2   The OH^- acts as a base *[1 mark]*.
3.3   Ethanolic/anhydrous/dry/no water present *[1 mark]*.
3.4   Stereoisomers have the same structural formula *[1 mark]* but a different arrangement of their atoms in space *[1 mark]*.
3.5

[1 mark for either isomer.]
Remember, as long as the question doesn't ask for a specific type of formula, it's okay to use things like skeletal or displayed formulas when drawing molecules — you'd get the marks as long as the structure was correct.

3.6   Mechanism: nucleophilic substitution *[1 mark]*
Conditions: aqueous/water present *[1 mark]*
4.1   free radical substitution *[1 mark]*
4.2   fluoromethane *[1 mark]*
4.3   Ethanolic *[1 mark]* KOH/potassium cyanide *[1 mark]*, heat under reflux *[1 mark]*.
4.4

Name of mechanism: nucleophilic substitution
[3 marks — 1 mark for curly arrow from cyanide lone pair to carbon atom, 1 mark for curly arrow from C–F bond to halogen atom, 1 mark for naming the mechanism.]

5   Reagents and conditions:
Warm *[1 mark]* bromoethane *[1 mark]* and ethanolic *[1 mark]* ethylamine *[1 mark]*.
Mechanism:

[1 mark for curly arrow from $NH_2CH_2CH_3$ lone pair to correct carbon atom in CH_3CH_2Br, 1 mark for curly arrow from C–Br bond to Br atom, 1 mark for curly arrow from a second $NH_2CH_2CH_3$ lone pair to a correct H atom, 1 mark for curly arrow from N^+–H bond to N^+.]

Unit 3: Section 2 — Alkenes and Alcohols

Pages 101-102 : Alkenes and Alcohols — 1
1   C *[1 mark]*
If you heat an aldehyde with acidified potassium dichromate, you get a carboxylic acid, not an alcohol.
2   D *[1 mark]*
3   A *[1 mark]*
A is a primary alcohol, so you can oxidise it to an aldehyde. But it can't be dehydrated, because the carbon atom next to the one with the -OH group can't donate an H^+.
4   B
The H^+ and Br^- from HBr are added to the carbons either side of where the double bond is in the original molecule.
5.1   2-methylbut-2-ene *[1 mark]*
5.2   Structure of A:

[1 mark]
Name of A: 2-methylbutan-2-ol *[1 mark]*
Structure of B:

[1 mark]
Name of B: 2-methyl-but-1-ene *[1 mark]*
5.3   Major product: 2-chloro-2-methylbutane
Minor product: 2-chloro-3-methylbutane
[2 marks for both correct, otherwise 1 mark if 1 correct, or 1 mark for both names correct with incorrect identification of major/minor product.]
5.4   The mechanism for the reaction between isoamylene and hydrogen chloride involves the formation of a carbocation *[1 mark]*. There are two possible carbocations, one of which leads to the formation of the major product, and one which leads to the formation of the minor product *[1 mark]*. The carbocation leading to the major product is more likely to form because it is tertiary/more stable, so more of this product is formed *[1 mark]*.

Pages 103-105: Alkenes and Alcohols — 2
1.1   E.g. potassium dichromate (VI) / $K_2Cr_2O_7$ *[1 mark]*
1.2   The method shown is distillation *[1 mark]*. The aldehyde has a lower boiling point than the alcohol, so it evaporates off from the reaction mixture first and can be collected as soon as it is formed *[1 mark]*.
1.3   A: a water bath is used to heat the alcohol instead of a naked flame as alcohols are flammable/to heat the reaction mixture more evenly/gently *[1 mark]*.
B: anti-bumping granules are used to give a smooth and even boil / prevent the formation of large bubbles *[1 mark]*.
C: an ice bath used so that the (volatile) aldehyde does not evaporate *[1 mark]*.
1.4   Use reflux apparatus/vertical condenser *[1 mark]* and excess oxidising agent/acidified potassium dichromate *[1 mark]*. The vaporised substances cool and condense and return back to the reaction mixture *[1 mark]*. This ensures that the aldehyde is fully oxidised to a carboxylic acid *[1 mark]*.
1.5 $CH_3OH + 2[O] \rightarrow HCOOH + H_2O$ *[1 mark]*
1.6   It has an aldehyde group / CHO *[1 mark]*.
2.1   The formation of a long chain molecule *[1 mark]* by joining lots of small (alkene) molecules/monomers together *[1 mark]*.
2.2   The double bond opens up *[1 mark]* and the monomers join together to form a chain *[1 mark]*.

2.3 The molecules in HDPE are more closely packed than in LDPE because LDPE is branched, so van der Waals/intermolecular forces are stronger in HDPE *[1 mark]*. This means that HDPE is more rigid and LDPE is more flexible *[1 mark]*.

2.4 E.g. they are non-polar *[1 mark]* and saturated *[1 mark]*.

2.5

but-2-ene *[1 mark]*

You'd get the mark for the diagram here if you just wrote 'CH₃' instead of drawing out the two methyl groups in full.

2.6

[1 mark for each correct structure.]

2.7 Ratio = 3:1 *[1 mark]*

Pages 106-108: Alkenes and Alcohols — 3

1.1 The solution would be decolourised / turn from orange to colourless *[1 mark]*.

1.2 The double bond is a region of high electron density *[1 mark]*.

1.3

[1 mark for curly arrow from C=C to bromine atom, 1 mark for curly arrow from Br–Br bond to other bromine atom.]

1.4 Carbocation B is more likely to be formed. It is a tertiary carbocation, so it is more stable than A (a secondary carbocation) *[1 mark]*.

1.5

[2 marks — 1 mark for each]

1.6 Add water *[1 mark]* and warm/heat gently *[1 mark]*.

2.1 10 *[1 mark]*

2.2 Geraniol will change acidified potassium dichromate from orange to green, whereas linalool would give no visible change/reaction *[1 mark]*. This is because geraniol is a primary alcohol and is easily oxidised *[1 mark]*, whereas linalool is a tertiary alcohol and is not easily oxidised *[1 mark]*.

2.3 When an alcohol is dehydrated, the OH group and H atom are lost from adjacent carbon atoms *[1 mark]*. Geraniol would not give an additional double bond in the position shown on myrcene as its OH group is at the end of the molecule *[1 mark]*.

Any explanation or diagram shown that clearly indicates you know where the double bond will form in linalool / geraniol will gain the marks.

2.4

Name of mechanism: Elimination

[5 marks — 1 mark for arrow from lone pair on O to H⁺, 1 mark for arrow from C–O bond to O, 1 mark for arrow from C–H bond to C–C bond, 1 mark for showing C=C bond in product, 1 mark for correct name.]

3 How to grade your answer:

Level 0: There is no relevant information. *[No marks]*

Level 1: One stage is covered well OR two stages are covered but they are incomplete and not always accurate. The answer is not in a logical order. *[1 to 2 marks]*

Level 2: Two stages are covered well OR all 3 stages are covered but they are incomplete and not always accurate. The answer is mostly in a logical order. *[3 to 4 marks]*

Level 3: All 3 stages are covered and are complete and accurate. The answer is coherent and is in a logical order. *[5 to 6 marks]*

Indicative content:

Stage 1: Production

Glucose/sugar cane is fermented.

In fermentation, yeast works at a low temperature/30–40 °C, therefore a low energy input is required.

Fermentation uses cheap, low technology equipment.

Fractional distillation is required to separate the ethanol. This requires time and energy, which will increase costs.

Large areas of land are needed to grow sugar crops for fuel.

Fossil fuels may be burned to produce the energy required at different stages of production – e.g. in harvesting and transporting the crops.

Stage 2: Use

Plants takes in carbon dioxide from the atmosphere in photosynthesis. This is stored as glucose.

Burning ethanol releases carbon dioxide.

The same amount of carbon dioxide is released by the combination of fermentation and burning ethanol as was absorbed by photosynthesis.

Photosynthesis: $6CO_2 + 6H_2O \rightarrow C_6H_{12}O_6 + 6O_2$

Fermentation: $C_6H_{12}O_6 \rightarrow 2C_2H_5OH + 2CO_2$

Combustion: $2C_2H_5OH + 6O_2 \rightarrow 4CO_2 + 6H_2O$

There is no net release of carbon dioxide into the atmosphere from these reactions, so bioethanol is described as a carbon neutral fuel.

Car engines may have to be modified to use bioethanol as a fuel, which leads to additional costs.

Bioethanol is only added to petrol, so it is not a replacement.

Stage 3: Environmental and ethical issues of bioethanol

Glucose is a renewable source.

Bioethanol is sustainable, so it won't run out like crude oil.

Use of bioethanol will help to conserve supplies of crude oil.

Bioethanol cannot be described as completely carbon neutral because of the fossil fuels burned and carbon dioxide released during its production.

Using land to grow crops for bioethanol could prevent land being used to produce crops for food.

Unit 3: Section 3 — Organic Analysis

Pages 109-110: Organic Analysis — 1

1 C *[1 mark]*

Tollens' reagent can be used to test for aldehydes, such as propanal, CH₃CH₂CHO.

2 C *[1 mark]*

NH₂CH₂CH₂NH₂, CH₃CH₂CH₂OH and CH₃COOH all show up as having an Mᵣ of 60 in a low resolution mass spectrometer, whereas CH₃COCH₃ has an Mᵣ of 58.

3 A *[1 mark]*

Pentanal has molecular formula C₅H₁₀O.

So Mᵣ of pentanal = (5 × 12.0107) + (10 × 1.0079) + 15.9994

= 86.1319 g mol⁻¹

4   B *[1 mark]*
C=O groups cause peaks in the range 1680-1750 cm⁻¹, and O–H groups in alcohols cause peaks in the range 3230-3550 cm⁻¹.

5.1   Place a small amount of compound **A** in a test tube and add a spatula-full of solid sodium carbonate/a small amount of sodium carbonate solution *[1 mark]*. If compound **C** is a carboxylic acid, fizzing will be observed as it reacts with the sodium carbonate to produce carbon dioxide gas *[1 mark]* according to the equation
$$2RCOOH + Na_2CO_3 \rightarrow 2RCOONa + H_2O + CO_2 \text{ } [1 \text{ mark}]$$
Bubble any gas produced through limewater. Carbon dioxide gas will turn the limewater cloudy *[1 mark]*.

5.2   Many organic compounds are flammable so the use of a naked flame poses the risk of fire *[1 mark]*.

5.3   Compound **B** must be an aldehyde *[1 mark]*.

5.4   Tests with sodium carbonate and Fehling's solution showed compounds **C** and **D** cannot be carboxylic acids or aldehydes. Compound **C** must be an alkene *[1 mark]* because alkenes can decolourise bromine water *[1 mark]*. Compound **D** must be an alcohol *[1 mark]* as it reacts with the sodium metal to produce hydrogen but does not react with sodium carbonate (as a carboxylic acid would) *[1 mark]*.

Pages 111-113: Organic Analysis — 2

1.1 M_r of pentane $= (5 \times 12.0107) + (12 \times 1.0079)$
                       $= 72.1483$
     M_r of butanone $= (4 \times 12.0107) + (8 \times 1.0079) + 15.9994$
                             $= 72.1054$
     Compound **F** is butanone.
     [1 mark for calculating precise molecular masses, 1 mark for identifying butanone]

1.2   The peak at 1720 cm⁻¹ indicates a C=O bond is present in compound **G**, and the peak at 2950 cm⁻¹ indicates C–H bonds *[1 mark]*. These bonds are present in both aldehydes (such as butanal) and ketones (such as butanone) *[1 mark]*.

1.3   Add a small amount of Tollens' reagent to a small amount of compound **G** in a test tube *[1 mark]*. Heat the test tube in a water bath for several minutes *[1 mark]*. If compound **G** is butanal, a silver mirror/thin coating of silver will be formed on the walls of the test tube *[1 mark]*. If compound **G** is butanone, no visible change will occur in the tube *[1 mark]*.

2   How to grade your answer:
     Level 0:   There is no relevant information. *[No marks]*
     Level 1:   One stage is covered well OR two stages are covered but they are incomplete and not always accurate. The answer is not in a logical order. *[1 to 2 marks]*
     Level 2:   Two stages are covered well OR all 3 stages are covered but they are incomplete and not always accurate. The answer is mostly in a logical order. *[3 to 4 marks]*
     Level 3:   All 3 stages are covered and are complete and accurate. The answer is coherent and is in a logical order. *[5 to 6 marks]*
     Indicative content:
     Stage 1: Oxidation of alcohol
     Heat compound **H** with the oxidising agent acidified potassium dichromate (VI).
     If compound **H** is a primary or secondary alcohol, a colour change from orange to green will be observed.
     This means an oxidation product has been formed/oxidation has occurred.
     If compound **H** is a tertiary alcohol, there will be no visible change, as oxidation will not occur.

Stage 2: Test for aldehydes/ketones
An oxidation product formed in Stage 1 can be removed by distillation and tested to determine whether it is an aldehyde or a ketone.
Add a small amount of the oxidation product to a small amount of Tollens' reagent **OR** Fehling's solution.
Heat the contents of the test tube gently using a water bath for several minutes Record any changes which occur.
If compound **H** is a primary alcohol, then a silver mirror will be formed on the walls of the test tube when the oxidation product, an aldehyde, is heated with Tollens' reagent.
                        OR
If compound **H** is a primary alcohol then a red/orange-red precipitate will be formed when the oxidation product, an aldehyde, is heated with Fehling's solution.
If compound **H** is a secondary alcohol, there will be no visible change when the oxidation product, a ketone, is heated with either Tollens' reagent or Fehling's solution.
Stage 3: Conclusion
Butan-2-ol is the only secondary alcohol that compound **H** could be.
Therefore if compound **H** is butan-2-ol, a colour change from orange to green would be observed in Stage 1 as it is oxidised to a ketone.
No colour change would be observed in Stage 2.

3.1   The larger the amount of infrared it absorbs, the more a gas acts as a greenhouse gas *[1 mark]*. The infrared spectra show the amount of infrared radiation absorbed *[1 mark]*. The infrared spectra of water vapour, carbon dioxide and methane could be compared to see which gas absorbs the most infrared radiation and therefore which one has the greatest ability to act as a greenhouse gas *[1 mark]*.

3.2   E.g. the pattern of the fingerprint region is unique for every compound *[1 mark]*. The fingerprint region can be used to confirm the identity of the compound by comparing it to a database of fingerprint regions of known compounds *[1 mark]*.

3.3   Compound **I** is butanal *[1 mark]*. There is a peak at around 3000 cm⁻¹ for the C–H bonds found in all three compounds *[1 mark]*. There is a second peak at around 1750 cm⁻¹ for the C=O bond, which is only present in butanal *[1 mark]*. There are no peaks above 3000 cm⁻¹, which would be expected for the O–H or N–H bond if compound **I** were butanol or butylamine *[1 mark]*.

Unit 3: Section 4 — Isomerism and Carbonyl Compounds

Pages 114-117: Isomerism and Carbonyl Compounds — 1

1   C *[1 mark]*
The structure in Figure 1 has a carboxylic acid functional group, and Na_2CO_3 reacts with carboxylic acids to produce CO_2. Tollens' reagent only gives a positive result with aldehydes, and acidified $K_2Cr_2O_7$ is used to identify alcohols.

2   D *[1 mark]*
A reaction between an amine and an acid anhydride produces an N-substituted amide.

3   D *[1 mark]*

4   C *[1 mark]*
A racemic mixture is made up of two different optical isomers. For a molecule to have a chiral centre (and so exist as two different optical isomers), there must be four different groups attached to one of its carbon atoms. The only pair of reagents that produce a chiral product are ethanal and CN⁻.

5.1 $(CH_3CO)_2O + CH_3CH_2CH_2OH \rightarrow$
                    $CH_3COOCH_2CH_2CH_3 + CH_3COOH$ *[1 mark]*

5.2   propyl ethanoate *[1 mark]*

5.3   Name of mechanism: (nucleophilic) addition-elimination
[1 mark]
Mechanism:

$$CH_3-C\overset{O}{\underset{Cl}{\delta^+}}\delta \quad CH_3CH_2CH_2\overset{..}{O}H \longrightarrow CH_3-\overset{\overset{\overset{..}{O^-}}{|}}{\underset{\overset{|}{O^+}}{C}}-Cl \quad \underset{H \quad CH_2CH_2CH_3}{}$$

$$CH_3-\overset{O}{\underset{O-CH_2CH_2CH_3}{C}} \longleftarrow CH_3-\overset{O}{\underset{\overset{O^+}{|}}{C}} \quad \underset{H \quad CH_2CH_2CH_3}{} \quad Cl^-$$

+ HCl

[4 marks — 1 mark for curly arrow from lone pair on O to C of C=O, 1 mark for curly arrow from double C=O bond to O, 1 mark for correct intermediate structure including negative charge on top O and positive charge on bottom O, 1 mark for final 3 curly arrows and O lone pair correct on intermediate structure.]

It's also okay to show the final 3 curly arrows all on the same structure, instead of in two separate stages. And don't worry if you didn't include the δ⁺ and δ⁻ in your mechanism — you don't need them for the marks.

5.4   Any two from: e.g. acid anhydrides are less corrosive. / The reaction using an acid anhydride is less vigorous. / Harmful HCl fumes are not produced when an acid anhydride is used. / Acid anhydrides are cheaper than acyl chlorides.
[2 marks — 1 mark for each correct answer]

5.5 $(CH_3)_2CHCOOH + CH_3OH \rightleftharpoons (CH_3)_2CHCOOCH_3 + H_2O$
[2 marks — 1 mark for correct reactants and 1 mark for correct products]
You also get the marks if you wrote this equation as:
$CH_3CH(CH_3)COOH + CH_3OH \rightleftharpoons CH_3CH(CH_3)COOCH_3 + H_2O$

5.6   E.g. reflux allows all of the reactant vapours to be returned to the reaction mixture. / Reflux allows the temperature of the reaction to be increased without losing volatile solvents, reactants or products *[1 mark]*.

5.7   E.g. the reaction is reversible *[1 mark]*, therefore an equilibrium mixture is produced / some carboxylic acid is produced by the backwards reaction/hydrolysis of the ester *[1 mark]*.

5.8   The mixture has separated into an organic layer and an aqueous layer *[1 mark]*.
The two layers form because the ester produced is only slightly soluble in water.

6.1 $C_6H_5NH_3Cl + CH_3COONa \rightarrow C_6H_5NH_2 + CH_3COOH + NaCl$
[1 mark]

6.2   Any two from: e.g. work in a fume cupboard. / Wear gloves. / Dispose of reaction mixture in a dedicated container.
[2 marks — 1 mark for each sensible precaution]

6.3

(mechanism diagram showing nucleophilic addition-elimination with aniline and acid anhydride)

[4 marks — 1 mark for curly arrow from lone pair on N to C of C=O, 1 mark for curly arrow from double C=O bond to O, 1 mark for correct intermediate structure with negative charge on O and positive charge on N, 1 mark for final 3 curly arrows and O lone pair correct on intermediate structure.]

Again, you could show the final 3 curly arrows all on the same structure. Don't worry if you didn't include the δ⁺ and δ⁻ in your mechanism — you'd still get the marks even if you didn't show them.

6.4   E.g.

(diagram of Büchner funnel apparatus labelled: Büchner funnel, Filter paper, Rubber tubing, Büchner flask, To vacuum pump)

[2 marks — 1 mark for showing a Büchner/side-arm flask, 1 mark for showing a Büchner funnel with filter paper.]

6.5   Filter the mixture under reduced pressure *[1 mark]* to remove any liquid containing soluble impurities *[1 mark]*. Wash the crystals with ice-cold solvent *[1 mark]* to remove soluble impurities from their surfaces *[1 mark]* and leave to dry.

6.6   E.g. some of the sample may have been lost during crystallisation. / Loss of some of the sample may have occurred during transfer from glassware. / The reaction may not have gone to completion *[1 mark]*.

6.7   E.g. the sample was not dried properly/is still wet/contains water. / The sample contains unreacted reactants/other products *[1 mark]*.

6.8   Pack a small amount of the sample into a glass capillary tube and place it inside the heating element of melting point apparatus *[1 mark]*. Gradually increase the temperature and record the range of temperatures from where the solid begins to melt to where it has melted completely *[1 mark]*.

6.9   The melting point range would be lower than for a pure sample *[1 mark]*. The melting point range would be broader than for a pure sample *[1 mark]*.

Pages 118-120: Isomerism and Carbonyl Compounds — 2

1.1

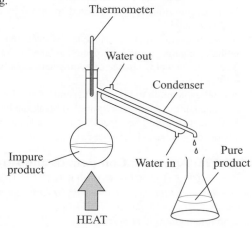

[1 mark]

1.2   E.g. use a large volume of water *[1 mark]*.

1.3   E.g.

Thermometer

Water out

Condenser

Impure product

Water in

Pure product

HEAT

[3 marks — 1 mark for showing impure product being heated in round-bottomed flask, 1 mark for showing thermometer, 1 mark for correctly showing condenser positioned over a suitable collecting vessel.]

1.4 $CH_3CH(OH)CH_2CH_2COONa$ *[1 mark]*.
It's fine if you've shown the charges here, i.e. $RCOO^-Na^+$.

1.5   e.g. dilute acid *[1 mark]*
You could also have given an example of a dilute acid, e.g. dilute HCl.

2.1   Reagent: methanol *[1 mark]*
Reaction conditions: a (KOH/NaOH/alkali) catalyst *[1 mark]*

2.2

$$H_3C-O-\overset{\overset{O}{\|}}{C}-(CH_2)_7-CH=CH-(CH_2)_5-CH_3$$

[1 mark]

$$H-\overset{\overset{H}{|}}{\underset{\underset{OH}{|}}{C}}-\overset{\overset{H}{|}}{\underset{\underset{OH}{|}}{C}}-\overset{\overset{H}{|}}{\underset{\underset{OH}{|}}{C}}-H$$

[1 mark]

You'd also get the marks if you drew full displayed formulas or skeletal formulas here.

2.3 $CH_3(CH_2)_5CH=CH(CH_2)_7COONa$ *[1 mark]*
Again, it's fine if you drew the charges on the carboxylate and sodium ions.

2.4   propane-1,2,3-triol *[1 mark]*
Remember, glycerol is just the common name of the molecule — the IUPAC name gives you information about the chain length, the functional groups present, and their positions.

3.1   E.g. a pair of optical isomers are molecules that are non-superimposable mirror images of one another *[1 mark]*.

3.2   E.g.

[1 mark for mirror images shown as 3D tetrahedral molecules with correct groups attached to central C atom.]

3.3   Name of mechanism: nucleophilic addition *[1 mark]*
Mechanism:

[4 marks — 1 mark for curly arrow from lone pair on H^- to C, 1 mark for curly arrow from double bond to O, 1 mark for correct intermediate structure including negative charge on O atom, 1 mark for curly arrow from lone pair on O^- to H^+.]

The H^- ions come from the reducing agent $NaBH_4$, and the H^+ ions come from H_2O.

3.4

[1 mark]

3.5

[1 mark]

OR

[1 mark]

4   How to grade your answer:
Level 0:   There is no relevant information. *[No marks]*
Level 1:   One stage is covered well OR two stages are covered but they are incomplete and not always accurate. The answer is not in a logical order. *[1 to 2 marks]*
Level 2:   Two stages are covered well OR all 3 stages are covered but they are incomplete and not always accurate. The answer is mostly in a logical order. *[3 to 4 marks]*
Level 3:   All 3 stages are covered and are complete and accurate. The answer is coherent and is in a logical order. *[5 to 6 marks]*.

Indicative content:
Stage 1: Chirality of propanone reaction product
Propanone is a symmetrical ketone.
The hydroxynitrile produced from propanone does not have a chiral carbon because none of its carbon atoms have four different groups attached.

Stage 2: Chirality of butanone reaction product
Butanone is an asymmetrical ketone.
The hydroxynitrile produced from butanone has a chiral carbon, because the addition of the CN⁻ group means that one of its carbon atoms has four different groups attached.
The C=O bond is planar.
So the cyanide ion can attack from above or below the plane of C=O.
Attack from above or below is equally likely, so a racemic mixture of the hydroxynitrile is produced from butanone.
A racemic mixture contains equal concentrations of both enantiomers/optical isomers.

Stage 3: Optical activity
The effect of the hydroxynitriles on plane-polarised light can be measured to determine their optical activity.
Chiral compounds rotate the plane of polarised light.
Separate samples of a pair of enantiomers rotate the plane of polarised light in opposite directions, but by the same angle.
A racemic mixture does not rotate the plane of polarised light. This is because the effect of equal concentrations of both enantiomers cancels out the overall rotation.
So the hydroxynitrile produced from butanone will not rotate the plane of polarised light because it is produced as a racemic mixture.
The hydroxynitrile produced from propanone will not rotate the plane of polarised light because it does not have a chiral carbon and so is not optically active.

Unit 3: Section 5 — Aromatic Compounds and Amines

Pages 121-122: Aromatic Compounds and Amines — 1

1   B *[1 mark]*
2   A *[1 mark]*
3   C *[1 mark]*
Although the lone pair on the nitrogen in phenylamine is less available than in aliphatic amines, it still reacts with halogenoalkanes in a similar way.
4   C *[1 mark]*
5.1   E.g. an electron-pair acceptor *[1 mark]*.
5.2   E.g. electrophilic addition reactions would destroy the stable delocalised ring of electrons *[1 mark]*.
5.3   How to grade your answer:
      Level 0:   There is no relevant information. *[No marks]*
      Level 1:   One stage is covered well OR two stages are covered but they are incomplete and not always accurate. The answer is not in a logical order. *[1 to 2 marks]*
      Level 2:   Two stages are covered well OR all 3 stages are covered but they are incomplete and not always accurate. The answer is mostly in a logical order. *[3 to 4 marks]*
      Level 3:   All 3 stages are covered and are complete and accurate. The answer is coherent and is in a logical order. *[5 to 6 marks]*
Indicative content:
Stage 1: Structure and bonding
Both benzene and cyclohexa-1,3,5-triene have a planar structure.
Cyclohexa-1,3,5-triene contains alternating single and double carbon-carbon bonds, so would contain bonds of different lengths as it contains two types of carbon-carbon bond.
In benzene, each carbon atom forms single covalent bonds to the carbons on either side of it and to one hydrogen atom.
Because of this, all carbon-carbon bonds lengths in benzene are the same.
The unpaired electron on each carbon atom is in a p-orbital that sticks out above and below the plane of the ring.
The p-orbitals on each carbon atom combine to form a ring of delocalised electrons.

Stage 2: Reactivity
Benzene is less reactive/more stable than you would expect cyclohexa-1,3,5-triene to be.
Benzene undergoes electrophilic substitution reactions.
Cyclohexa-1,3,5-triene would be expected to undergo electrophilic addition reactions.
Stage 3: Evidence for the structure of benzene
Cyclohexene has one double bond, so the enthalpy of hydrogenation of cyclohexa-1,3,5-triene would be expected to be three times that of cyclohexene.
When cyclohexene is hydrogenated, the enthalpy change is -120 kJ mol^{-1}.
So, when cyclohexa-1,3,5-triene is hydrogenated, the enthalpy change would be expected to be -360 kJ mol^{-1}.
The actual enthalpy change of hydrogenation of benzene is -208 kJ mol^{-1}.
As energy is put in to break bonds and released when bonds are made, more energy is required to break the bonds in benzene than would be expected to be needed to break the bonds in cyclohexa-1,3,5-triene.

Pages 123-125: Aromatic Compounds and Amines — 2

1.1 $C_6H_6 + CH_3CH_2COCl \rightarrow C_6H_5COCH_2CH_3 + HCl$ *[1 mark]*
You could also have used the molecular formula for each compound, i.e. $C_6H_6 + C_3H_5OCl \rightarrow C_8H_{10}CO + HCl$.
1.2   aluminium chloride *[1 mark]*
1.3

[5 marks — 1 mark for arrow from Cl lone pair to AlCl₃, 1 mark for curly arrow from benzene ring to C+, 1 mark for curly arrow from Al–Cl bond to correct hydrogen, 1 mark for curly arrow from C–H bond to positively charged ring, 1 mark for structure of product.]
1.4   1-phenylpropan-1-one *[1 mark]*
Normally, it would be incorrect to say "propan-1-one" — you'd use "propanal" instead. It's alright to use it here though, as the C–H bond in propanal has been replaced with a C–C bond to the phenyl group, so the compound is a ketone.

2.1

$$H-\overset{\overset{\displaystyle H}{|}}{\underset{\underset{\displaystyle H}{|}}{C}}-\overset{\overset{\displaystyle H}{|}}{\underset{\underset{\displaystyle H}{|}}{C}}-\overset{\overset{\displaystyle H}{|}}{\underset{\underset{\displaystyle H}{|}}{C}}-\overset{\overset{\displaystyle H}{|}}{\underset{\underset{\displaystyle H}{|}}{C}}-\ddot{N}\overset{\curvearrowright}{\underset{\displaystyle H}{}}\quad H-\overset{\overset{\displaystyle H}{|}}{\underset{\underset{\displaystyle H}{|}}{C}}\overset{\delta+}{}\overset{\delta-}{Br}$$

$$\downarrow$$

$$H-\overset{\overset{\displaystyle H}{|}}{\underset{\underset{\displaystyle H}{|}}{C}}-\overset{\overset{\displaystyle H}{|}}{\underset{\underset{\displaystyle H}{|}}{C}}-\overset{\overset{\displaystyle H}{|}}{\underset{\underset{\displaystyle H}{|}}{C}}-\overset{\overset{\displaystyle H}{|}}{\underset{\underset{\displaystyle H}{|}}{C}}-\overset{\overset{\displaystyle H}{|}}{N^+}-\overset{\overset{\displaystyle H}{|}}{\underset{\underset{\displaystyle H}{|}}{C}}-H \qquad :NH_2CH_2CH_2CH_2CH_3$$

$$\downarrow$$

$$H-\overset{\overset{\displaystyle H}{|}}{\underset{\underset{\displaystyle H}{|}}{C}}-\overset{\overset{\displaystyle H}{|}}{\underset{\underset{\displaystyle H}{|}}{C}}-\overset{\overset{\displaystyle H}{|}}{\underset{\underset{\displaystyle H}{|}}{C}}-\overset{\overset{\displaystyle H}{|}}{\underset{\underset{\displaystyle H}{|}}{C}}-\overset{\overset{\displaystyle H}{|}}{N}-\overset{\overset{\displaystyle H}{|}}{\underset{\underset{\displaystyle H}{|}}{C}}-H$$

Name of mechanism: nucleophilic substitution
[6 marks — 1 mark for curly arrow from
$CH_3CH_2CH_2CH_2NH_2$ lone pair to bromomethane carbon
atom, 1 mark for curly arrow from C–Br bond to Br atom,
1 mark for curly arrow from second $CH_3CH_2CH_2CH_2NH_2$
lone pair to correct H atom, 1 mark for curly arrow from
N^+–H bond to N^+, 1 mark for correct structure of product,
1 mark for correctly naming the mechanism.]

2.2 The secondary amine has a lone pair of electrons so can act as a nucleophile and react with other bromomethane molecules *[1 mark]*.

2.3 E.g. quaternary salts can be formed with a long hydrocarbon tail which binds to nonpolar substances/grease *[1 mark]*, and a cationic head that allows them to dissolve easily in water *[1 mark]*.

3.1 $HNO_3 + H_2SO_4 \rightarrow H_2NO_3^+ + HSO_4^-$
$H_2NO_3^+ \rightarrow NO_2^+ + H_2O$

[4 marks — 1 mark for correct equations to form NO_2^+,
1 mark for curly arrow from benzene ring to NO_2^+, 1 mark
for curly arrow from C–H bond to positively charged ring,
1 mark for structure of product.]

3.2 E.g. the methyl group pushes electron density into the delocalised benzene ring *[1 mark]*.

This is similar to the way in which the methyl group pushes electron density towards the amine group in methylamine — it makes the lone pair more nucleophilic.

3.3

[1 mark]

3.4 E.g. in explosives/precursor to amines *[1 mark]*.

4.1 The lone pair of electrons on the nitrogen atom can accept/ form a dative covalent/coordinate bond with a proton so the amine/amines can act as a base *[1 mark]*. Amines can act as nucleophiles as the lone pair of electron on the nitrogen atom can be donated *[1 mark]*.

4.2

$$H-\overset{\overset{\displaystyle H}{|}}{\underset{\underset{\displaystyle H}{|}}{C}}-\overset{\overset{\displaystyle H}{|}}{\underset{\underset{\displaystyle H}{|}}{C}}-\overset{\overset{\displaystyle H}{|}}{N}-\overset{\overset{\displaystyle O}{\|}}{C}-\overset{\overset{\displaystyle H}{|}}{\underset{\underset{\displaystyle H}{|}}{C}}-H$$

[1 mark]

4.3 The ethylamine solution would have a higher pH as it is a stronger base and therefore would accept more of the protons in solution *[1 mark]*. The alkyl group in ethylamine pushes electron density on to the amine group *[1 mark]*. This makes the lone pair more available to act as a base *[1 mark]*. The benzene ring in phenylamine draws in electron density from the amine group *[1 mark]*. This make the lone pair less available to act as a base *[1 mark]*.

4.4 Any one from: e.g. the benzene ring in chlorobenzene has an area of high electron density *[1 mark]*, which would repel the ammonia nucleophile *[1 mark]*. / The C–Cl bond in chlorobenzene is too strong/not polar enough *[1 mark]* for nucleophilic attack by ammonia to occur *[1 mark]*.

4.5 $CH_3CN + 4[H] \rightarrow CH_3CH_2NH_2$ *[1 mark]*
You could also have used the molecular formula for each compound, i.e. $C_2H_3N + 4[H] \rightarrow C_2H_7N$.

Unit 3: Section 6 — Polymers and Proteins

Pages 126-129: Polymers and Proteins — 1

1   A *[1 mark]*
2   D *[1 mark]*
3   D *[1 mark]*
At its isoelectric point, glycine can exist as a zwitterion, meaning that it contains both a positive and a negative charge.
4   C *[1 mark]*
Remember, you need to give the carbon atom with the carboxylic acid group attached the lowest possible number in the carbon chain.
5.1   polyesters *[1 mark]*
5.2   water/H_2O *[1 mark]*
5.3

$$-\overset{\overset{\displaystyle O}{\|}}{C}-\overset{\overset{\displaystyle H}{|}}{\underset{\underset{\displaystyle H}{|}}{C}}-\overset{\overset{\displaystyle H}{|}}{\underset{\underset{\displaystyle H}{|}}{C}}-\overset{\overset{\displaystyle O}{\|}}{C}-O-\overset{\overset{\displaystyle H}{|}}{\underset{\underset{\displaystyle H}{|}}{C}}-\overset{\overset{\displaystyle H}{|}}{\underset{\underset{\displaystyle H}{|}}{C}}-\overset{\overset{\displaystyle H}{|}}{\underset{\underset{\displaystyle H}{|}}{C}}-\overset{\overset{\displaystyle H}{|}}{\underset{\underset{\displaystyle H}{|}}{C}}-O-$$

[1 mark]

5.4 The C=O bond in polybutylene succinate is polar *[1 mark]*. This means that it is open to attack by nucleophiles/can be hydrolysed easily *[1 mark]*, so polybutylene succinate is biodegradable *[1 mark]*. Poly(ethene) is not biodegradable because it is inert/unreactive/non-polar *[1 mark]*.

5.5 Any three from: e.g. landfill requires larger areas of land than recycling. / Landfill is relatively cheap, whereas collecting, sorting and processing plastics for recycling is expensive. / Recycling saves raw materials, whereas landfill requires new plastic to be made from new raw materials. / Landfill is technically easy, but recycling is technically difficult. / Methane is released from landfill as waste decomposes, so recycling produces fewer greenhouse gas emissions.
[3 marks — 1 mark for each sensible comparison.]

6.1 E.g. α-amanitin might have a similar shape to the substrate of RNA-polymerase *[1 mark]*, and therefore would compete with the substrate for binding to the active site *[1 mark]*. Binding of α-amanitin would block the active site, preventing RNA-polymerase from catalysing the reaction *[1 mark]*.

6.2 A spot of the amino acid mixture is placed on a thin-layer chromatography plate *[1 mark]*. The bottom of the plate (but not the spot) is then dipped into a solvent *[1 mark]*. As the solvent moves up the plate, the amino acids dissolve and move with it *[1 mark]*. Different amino acids have different solubilities in the solvent/polarities/attractions to the stationary phase, and so move at different rates, separating out on the plate *[1 mark]*.

6.3 E.g. the amino acids could have been stained with ninhydrin solution *[1 mark]*. The amino acids could also have been viewed under UV light *[1 mark]*.

6.4   6 *[1 mark]*

6.5 $$R_f = \frac{\text{distance travelled by spot}}{\text{distance travelled by solvent}}$$

$$= \frac{4.0 \text{ cm}}{6.0 \text{ cm}}$$

= 0.67 (2 s.f.)

Amino acid **X** = tryptophan

[3 marks for correct answer, otherwise 1 mark for correctly measuring distances and 1 mark for a correctly calculated R_f value.]

6.6 2-amino-3-methylpentanoic acid *[1 mark]*

6.7 E.g.

[1 mark]

Pages 130-133: Polymers and Proteins — 2

1.1 The primary structure is the sequence of amino acids that makes up the polypeptide chain *[1 mark]*. The secondary structure is the shape of the polypeptide chain *[1 mark]*. The tertiary structure is the way the chain is coiled and folded into the overall three-dimensional shape of the protein *[1 mark]*.

1.2 **A:** β-pleated sheet *[1 mark]*
B: α-helix *[1 mark]*

1.3 The tertiary structure is stabilised by hydrogen bonds *[1 mark]*, which are formed between polar groups (e.g. –OH and –NH₂ groups) on the amino acids *[1 mark]*, and disulfide /sulfur-sulfur bonds *[1 mark]*, which are formed between the thiol/–SH groups of cysteine residues *[1 mark]*.

1.4 hydrolysis *[1 mark]*

1.5 Amino acid:

[1 mark]

Dipeptide:

[1 mark]

1.6 The high pH in the small intestine is likely to be above the isoelectric point of the amino acid *[1 mark]*, so the amino acid will have a net negative charge *[1 mark]*.

The amino acid has a net negative charge because the carboxyl group is deprotonated above the isoelectric point.

1.7 The active site is stereospecific/has a specific 3D shape *[1 mark]* because the amino acids that form the active site contain chiral centres *[1 mark]*. Therefore, a peptide formed from amino acids with the opposite chirality would not fit into the active site of the trypsin enzyme *[1 mark]*.

2.1 Adenine and thymine are both able to form 2 hydrogen bonds *[1 mark]*, while cytosine and guanine are both able to form 3 hydrogen bonds *[1 mark]*. As a result, adenine always bonds with thymine and guanine always bonds with cytosine, resulting in complementary DNA base pairing *[1 mark]*. In a cell, two DNA strands twist into a double helix *[1 mark]* so that the complementary base pairs are in the right alignment to form hydrogen bonds *[1 mark]*.

2.2 Adenine and thymine:

OR

Cytosine and guanine:

[3 marks — 1 mark for correct pairing of adenine with thymine OR cytosine with guanine, 1 mark for showing hydrogen bonds correctly, 1 mark for lone pairs and partial charges on all atoms involved in a hydrogen bond.]

2.3 Coordinate bonds *[1 mark]* are formed between the platinum ion of carboplatin and the guanine bases in the DNA of the cancer cells *[1 mark]* through displacement of the cyclobutane-1,1-dicarboxylic acid/cyclic ligand *[1 mark]*. This causes a kink in the DNA molecule, which prevents DNA replication, and as a result the cells cannot divide *[1 mark]*.

2.4 Carboplatin can bind to DNA and prevent replication of normal cells as well as cancer cells *[1 mark]*. As a result, healthy tissues can be damaged *[1 mark]*.

3.1

[1 mark]

[1 mark]

3.2 amide bond/amide link *[1 mark]*

3.3 water *[1 mark]*

3.4 The N–H and C=O groups in polymers like Kevlar® and Nomex® are polar *[1 mark]*. As a result, hydrogen bonds can form between the N–H and C=O groups *[1 mark]*, which take more energy to overcome than the van der Waals forces between addition polymer chains *[1 mark]*.

3.5 E.g. in Kevlar®, the chains are straight, whereas the chains in Nomex® are kinked *[1 mark]*. As a result, the Kevlar® chains can align so that the C=O and N–H groups are close together, whereas in Nomex® the C=O and N–H groups are further apart *[1 mark]*. This means that the intermolecular hydrogen bonds are stronger in Kevlar® than in Nomex® *[1 mark]*.

Unit 3: Section 7 — Further Synthesis and Analysis

Pages 134-137: Further Synthesis and Analysis — 1

1   **C** *[1 mark]*

The shortest possible reaction pathways for converting halogenoalkanes to carboxylic acids involve two steps. (For instance, you could convert a halogenoalkane to a primary alcohol, then oxidise it to get a carboxylic acid.)

2   **B** *[1 mark]*

B has 4 different carbon environments, so it will have 4 peaks in its ^{13}C NMR spectrum, whereas A has 7, C has 5, and D has 9.

3   **C** *[1 mark]*

Best to just draw all the structures out here so you can have a good look at where the hydrogens are.

4   **D** *[1 mark]*

An addition reaction converts the starting alkene into a bromoalkane. Then nucleophilic substitution of the bromine with a cyanide ion occurs, followed by reduction of the nitrile group to give a primary amine.

5   **A** *[1 mark]*

6.1   How to grade your answer:

Level 0:   There is no relevant information. *[No marks]*

Level 1:   One stage is covered well OR two stages are covered, but they are incomplete and not always accurate. The answer is not in a logical order. *[1 to 2 marks]*

Level 2:   Two stages are covered well OR all 3 stages are covered, but they are incomplete and not always accurate. The answer is mostly in a logical order. *[3 to 4 marks]*

Level 3:   All 3 stages are covered and the answer is complete and accurate. The answer is coherent and in a logical order. *[5 to 6 marks]*

Indicative content:

Stage 1: Stationary phase and mobile phase

In gas chromatography the mobile phase is an unreactive carrier gas (e.g. nitrogen).

The stationary phase is a solid/a solid coated with a viscous liquid that is packed into a tube.

Stage 2: Description of method for gas chromatography

The tube containing the stationary phase is coiled and built into an oven.

The sample is vaporised/heated.

The sample is injected into the tube and transported through it by the carrier gas.

Different components of the sample spend different amounts of time in the mobile and stationary phases, so they separate out as they travel through the tube.

At the end of the tube is a detector and recorder, which sense and record when substances are leaving the tube.

Stage 3: Use of data

Each component will take a different amount of time to reach the end of the tube — this is called its retention time.

You can identify components by comparing their retention times with known substances run under the same conditions.

Gas chromatography equipment can also be connected to a mass spectrometer for further analysis.

6.2   E.g. Work in a fume cupboard *[1 mark]* to prevent inhalation of the butanol solvent *[1 mark]*.

6.3   The solvent may evaporate once the plate is removed from the developing tank, so the solvent front is no longer visible *[1 mark]*.

6.4   The student shone UV light on the plate (and the spots showed up as dark patches) *[1 mark]*. The student had to draw around the spots to make them visible in normal light *[1 mark]*.

You don't get marks for mentioning ninhydrin or iodine here — they'd make the spots visible in normal light, so you wouldn't need to draw round them.

6.5   distance travelled by spot 2 = 2.1 cm
distance travelled by solvent = 5.5 cm

$$R_f \text{ value} = \frac{\text{distance travelled by spot}}{\text{distance travelled by solvent}}$$

$$= \frac{2.1 \text{ cm}}{5.5 \text{ cm}} = 0.38 \text{ (2.s.f.)}$$

This matches the data book R_f value for alanine.

Amino acid: alanine

[4 marks — 1 mark for both measurements correct, 1 mark for correct formula for R_f, 1 mark for correct R_f value, 1 mark for identifying alanine.]

6.6   If the conditions in the experiment are at all different to those used to obtain the data book values, the R_f values will be different *[1 mark]*. Using reference spots means that conditions for the known substances will be the same as for the sample *[1 mark]*.

The 'conditions' are things like the temperature and the make-up of the plate or solvent. Changing any of these even slightly will change the R_f value.

6.7   Using pure samples as reference spots relies upon knowing the composition of the mixture beforehand *[1 mark]*.

7.1   Any two from: e.g. choose reactions with a high atom economy. / Minimise the number of steps to give a higher percentage yield (as useful product is lost in each step) / Reduce the amount/number of solvents used.

[2 marks — 1 mark for each sensible suggestion]

7.2   **A**

[1 mark]

B

[1 mark]

You'd get the marks for drawing the correct skeletal formulas here too.

7.3   3-methylbut-1-ene *[1 mark]*

7.4   Heat under reflux *[1 mark]* with a solution of sodium hydroxide/potassium hydroxide *[1 mark]*

7.5   addition polymerisation *[1 mark]*

7.6   You could convert the bromoalkane to an alkene in one step *[1 mark]* by heating it under reflux *[1 mark]* with KOH/NaOH *[1 mark]* dissolved in ethanol *[1 mark]*.

Pages 138-140: Further Synthesis and Analysis — 2

1.1

[1 mark]

All 12 hydrogen atoms in TMS are in the same chemical environment *[1 mark]*, so TMS produces a single, intense peak (to the right of most other absorption peaks) *[1 mark]*.

1.2   E.g. CCl_4/$CDCl_3$/C_6D_6 *[1 mark]*. Chosen solvent does not contain any ^1H atoms that would produce additional peaks *[1 mark]*.

1.3   Compound **A**: 5 *[1 mark]*
Compound **C**: 3 *[1 mark]*

1.4   0.5-5.0 ppm *[1 mark]*

1.5

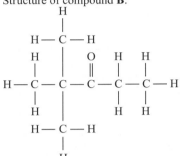

[1 mark]

1.6   Step 1: Ethanoyl chloride/CH_3COCl *[1 mark]* and aluminium chloride/$AlCl_3$ *[1 mark]*. Heat under reflux in a non-aqueous solvent/dry ether *[1 mark]*.
Step 2: $NaBH_4$ *[1 mark]* in water with methanol/in aqueous solution *[1 mark]*.

You could use another halogen carrier instead of $AlCl_3$ in Step 1.

1.7   reduction/nucleophilic addition *[1 mark]*

1.8   E.g. to limit environmental damage/the risk of accidents/ damage to the health of workers *[1 mark]*.

2.1   The spectrum has a triplet and a quartet, which must be caused by the CH_2CH_3 group of the ester *[1 mark]*.
The spectrum has a singlet, which must be caused by the CH_3 group in the ester that has no adjacent Hs *[1 mark]*.
The triplet is at $\delta \approx 1.1$ ppm, so it must be caused by the Hs in an RCH_3 group *[1 mark]*.
The singlet is at $\delta \approx 2.1$ ppm, so it must be caused by the Hs in an RC=OCH group *[1 mark]*.
The quartet is at $\delta \approx 4.1$ ppm, so it must be caused by the Hs in an RC=OOCH group *[1 mark]*.
The spectrum is produced by ester A, e.g. because the singlet is caused by the H atoms of the RC=OCH group, so the C of the ester group must be adjacent to only CH_3 *[1 mark]*.

You get the last mark here for explaining how you know from the shifts and splitting patterns which ester matches the spectrum. There are lots of things you could have said — you get the mark for any sensible explanation.

2.2

[1 mark]

2.3

Peak number	δ / ppm	
	A	**B**
1	15	10
2	23	28
3	60	52
4	**160 - 185**	**160 - 185**

[1 mark for both chemical shifts in correct range]
Peak 4 is caused by a C atom in an RC=O group in both ester **A** and ester **B** *[1 mark]*.

Pages 141-142: Further Synthesis and Analysis — 3

1.1   8 peaks *[1 mark]*

1.2   e.g. acidified potassium dichromate *[1 mark]*

1.3

$$O=C-CH-CH_2-CH_2-C-OH$$
with CH_3 CH_3 below and O double bonded above the final C

[1 mark]

You could also draw the skeletal or full displayed formula for the mark here.

1.4   7 peaks *[1 mark]*

1.5   e.g. acidified KCN/acidified NaCN/HCN *[1 mark]*

1.6   110-125 ppm *[1 mark]*

The $-C\equiv N$ group added to compound C to produce compound D produces a peak with a chemical shift in this range.

1.7   Compound B is a carbonyl compound which cannot be oxidised, which suggests that it is a ketone *[1 mark]*.
It has 3 peaks in its spectrum, indicating 3 different hydrogen environments *[1 mark]*.
The quartet is at $\delta = 2.4$ ppm, so it must be caused by Hs in an RC=OCH group, which are adjacent to 3 other Hs *[1 mark]*.
The triplet is at $\delta = 1.1$ ppm, so it must be caused by the Hs in an RCH_3 group, which are adjacent to 2 other Hs *[1 mark]*.
The quartet and triplet together suggest a CH_2CH_3 group *[1 mark]*.
The singlet with $\delta = 0.9$ ppm must be caused by Hs in an RCH_3 group with no adjacent Hs *[1 mark]*.
The integration ratio of 2 : 3: 9 suggests that the singlet represents three equivalent CH_3 groups (whilst the quartet and the triplet represent a CH_2 and a CH_3 respectively) *[1 mark]*.
Structure of compound **B**:

[1 mark]

Mixed Questions

Pages 143-146: Mixed Questions — 1

1   D *[1 mark]*

2   B *[1 mark]*

3   C *[1 mark]*

Hydrogen almost always has an oxidation state of −1 in metal hydrides.

4   D *[1 mark]*

5   C *[1 mark]*

When a halogenoalkane is heated with aqueous sodium hydroxide, the halogen is substituted for an −OH group.

6.1   Moles of NaOH = $1.20 \times (100 \div 1000) = 0.120$ mol
M_r(NaOH) = 23.0 + 16.0 + 1.0 = 40.0
Mass of NaOH = 0.120×40.0
$$= \textbf{4.80 g}$$
[2 marks for correct answer, otherwise 1 mark for correct number of moles of NaOH]

6.2   Moles of NaOH = $1.20 \times (30.0 \div 1000) = 0.0360$ mol
From the balanced symbol equation, 1 mole of HNO_3 reacts with 1 mole of NaOH. So 0.0360 mol of HNO_3 reacted *[1 mark]*.

6.3   Volume of solution = $50.0 + 30.0 = 80.0$ cm³
80.0 cm³ of solution has a mass of 80.0 g, so $m = 80.0$ g
$q = mc\Delta T = 80.0 \times 4.18 \times 6.05 = 2023.12$ J $= 2.02312$ kJ
Molar enthalpy change = $-2.02312 \div 0.0360 = -56.197...$
$$= \textbf{−56.2 kJ mol}^{-1}$$
[3 marks for correct answer, otherwise 1 mark for finding the volume of solution, 1 mark for calculating q.]

6.4   E.g. record the temperature at regular intervals for two minutes before the start of the reaction *[1 mark]*. Carry out the reaction and keep recording the temperature at regular intervals *[1 mark]*. Plot a graph with time on the x-axis and temperature on the y-axis *[1 mark]*. Draw lines of best fit through the points before the reaction started and through the points after it started *[1 mark]*. Extend both lines so they pass the time when the reaction started, and measure the distance between the two lines at the time the reaction started *[1 mark]*.

7.1 $Ca \rightarrow Ca^{2+} + 2e^-$ *[1 mark]*

7.2 +1 *[1 mark]*
Oxygen has an oxidation state of −2, and a molecule of water is neutral. Therefore, each hydrogen atom must have an oxidation state of +1.

7.3 If n is the number of moles of H_2 that occupy 100 cm³
Then $n = (pV) \div (RT)$
$= ((101 \times 10^3) \times (100 \times 10^{-6})) \div (8.31 \times 298)$
$= 0.00407...$ mol
1 mole of H_2 is produced from 1 mole of Ca,
so moles of Ca $= 0.00407...$ mol
Maximum mass of Ca $= 0.00407... \times 40.1 = 0.1635...$ g
$= 0.1635...$ g $\times 1000$
$= 163.54...$ mg $=$ **164 mg (3 s.f.)**
[4 marks for correct answer, otherwise 1 mark for correctly rearranging the ideal gas equation, 1 mark for correct number of moles of H_2, 1 mark for mass of Ca in grams.]

7.4 E.g. some of the gas produced may have been lost from the conical flask before the gas syringe was attached *[1 mark]*.

7.5 Barium would produce the gas in the shortest amount of time *[1 mark]*. This is because the ionisation energy is lower/the outer electron is more easily lost from barium than strontium or calcium, so barium is more reactive *[1 mark]*.

8.1 $1s^2\ 2s^2\ 2p^6\ 3s^2\ 3p^1$ *[1 mark]*

8.2 Aluminium oxidation state: +3
Chlorine oxidation state: −1
[1 mark]

8.3 Aluminium has a giant metallic lattice structure and chlorine is a simple covalent substance *[1 mark]*. In aluminium there are strong electrostatic attractions between the metal ions and the sea of positive electrons *[1 mark]*. In chlorine there are weak intermolecular forces between the molecules *[1 mark]*. Aluminium has a much higher melting point because the forces that need to be overcome in aluminium are much stronger than in chlorine, so more energy is required to break the forces in aluminium *[1 mark]*.

8.4 Moles of Al $= (2.00 \times 1000) \div 27.0 = 74.074...$
From the balanced equation, 2 moles of Al reacts to form 2 moles of $AlCl_3$. So 74.074... moles of Al will react to form 74.074... moles of $AlCl_3$.
Theoretical yield $= 74.074... \times 133.5 = 9888.8...$ g
Percentage yield $= ((7.14 \times 1000) \div 9888.8...) \times 100$
$= 72.202...$
$=$ **72.2 % (3 s.f.)**
[3 marks for correct answer, otherwise 1 mark for moles of Al, 1 mark for theoretical yield.]

8.5 $K_c = \dfrac{[Al_2Cl_6]}{[AlCl_3]^2}$ *[1 mark]*

8.6 109.5° *[1 mark]*

8.7

[2 marks — 1 mark for showing the correct structure, 1 mark for showing 3D bonds.]

Pages 147-150: Mixed Questions — 2

1.1 Two compounds which have the same molecular formula but different structural formulas *[1 mark]*.

1.2

[1 mark]

1.3 $C_6H_{12} + 9O_2 \rightarrow 6CO_2 + 6H_2O$ *[1 mark]*

1.4 How to grade your answer:
Level 0: There is no relevant information. *[No marks]*
Level 1: One stage is covered well OR two stages are covered but they are incomplete and not always accurate. The answer is not in a logical order. *[1 to 2 marks]*
Level 2: Two stages are covered well OR all 3 stages are covered but they are incomplete and not always accurate. The answer is mostly in a logical order. *[3 to 4 marks]*
Level 3: All 3 stages are covered and are complete and accurate. The answer is coherent and is in a logical order. *[5 to 6 marks]*
Indicative content:
Stage 1: Shapes and polarities
Carbon dioxide contains 2 polar C=O bonds.
The molecule is symmetrical/linear, so the charges are evenly spread across the molecule.
This leads to the charges cancelling each other out so a molecule of carbon dioxide has no permanent dipole.
Water contains 2 polar O–H bonds.
The molecule is asymmetrical/bent, so the charges are unevenly spread across the molecule.
This leads to a permanent dipole.
Stage 2: Intermolecular forces
Carbon dioxide is non-polar, so the only intermolecular forces acting between molecules are van der Waals/induced dipole-dipole forces.
Water also has van der Waals/induced dipole-dipole forces acting between molecules.
There are also permanent dipole-dipole forces between water molecules.
These are weak electrostatic forces of attraction between the δ+ and δ− charges on neighbouring molecules.
Water can also undergo hydrogen bonding, as it contains two O–H bonds.
Stage 3: Physical states
The van der Waals/induced dipole-dipole forces between carbon dioxide molecules are very weak.
So, not a lot of energy is required to break them and at room temperature carbon dioxide is a gas.
Water molecules have stronger intermolecular forces than carbon dioxide molecules.
Permanent dipole-dipole forces and hydrogen bonds require a lot more energy to break than van der Waals/induced dipole-dipole forces.
So water is a liquid at room temperature.

1.5 $6C_{(s)} + 6H_{2(g)} \rightarrow H_2C{=}CH(CH_2)_3CH_{3(l)}$
$\Delta_f H = \Sigma\ \Delta_c H$ reactants $- \Sigma\ \Delta_c H$ products
$= ((6 \times -393.5) + (6 \times -285.8)) - (-4003.0)$
$= -4075.8 + 4003.0 =$ **−72.8 kJ mol⁻¹**
[3 marks for correct answer, otherwise 1 mark for stating the formula and 1 mark for correctly substituting in the enthalpies of combustion.]
You'd get the mark if you drew a Hess's law diagram here, instead of stating the formula.

1.6

Reagents and conditions: steam and an acid catalyst.

[5 marks — 1 mark for arrow from C=C to H^+, 1 mark for arrow from O lone pair to C^+, 1 mark for arrow from O–H bond to O^+, 1 mark for correct structure of product, 1 mark for correct reagents and conditions.]

1.7 Hexan-2-ol contains an –OH group, so can undergo hydrogen bonding *[1 mark]*. So, more energy is required to break the intermolecular forces in hexan-2-ol than in hex-1-ene *[1 mark]*.

2.1 Shape: trigonal planar *[1 mark]*
Bond angle: 120° *[1 mark]*

2.2 One of the double-bond carbons has two identical groups attached to it *[1 mark]*.

2.3
[1 mark]

2.4 Use: e.g. drainpipes/window frames *[1 mark]*
Property: e.g. PVC is rigid/hard *[1 mark]*.

2.5 Plasticisers make PVC much more flexible *[1 mark]*.

2.6 $Cl· + C_2H_3Cl → C_2H_3Cl_2·$ *[1 mark]*
$C_2H_3Cl_2· + C_2H_3Cl → C_4H_6Cl_3·$ *[1 mark]*

2.7 E.g. the more chlorine there is in the mixture, the shorter the polymer chains will be *[1 mark]*. This is because there will be more radicals in the mixture, so termination steps are more likely to occur *[1 mark]*.

3.1 2,2-dimethylpropan-1-ol *[1 mark]*

3.2 High energy electrons are fired at the sample *[1 mark]*. This knocks off/removes one electron from each molecule, forming +1 ions *[1 mark]*.

3.3
[1 mark]

3.4 The greater the number of alkyl groups attached to a carbocation, the more stable it is *[1 mark]*. The carbocation/fragment that is responsible for the peak at 57 m/z is a tertiary carbocation/has three alkyl groups attached, so will be relatively stable *[1 mark]*.

Pages 151-154: Mixed Questions — 3

1 B *[1 mark]*
2 D *[1 mark]*

3 C *[1 mark]*
Moles of H_3PO_4 = 1.2 × (30 ÷ 1000) = 0.036 moles
The balanced equation for the reaction is
$2H_3PO_4 + 3Ca(OH)_2 → Ca_3(PO_4)_2 + 6H_2O$, so the number of moles of $Ca(OH)_2$ required to neutralise 0.036 moles of H_3PO_4 is
3 × (0.036 ÷ 2) = 0.054 moles.
M_r of $Ca(OH)_2$ = 40.1 + (2 × (16.0 + 1.0)) = 74.1
Mass of $Ca(OH)_2$ = 74.1 × 0.054 = 4.0014 g = 4.0 g (2 s.f.)

4 B *[1 mark]*

5.1 +7 *[1 mark]*

5.2 $2MnO_4^- + 16H^+ + 10Cl^- → 2Mn^{2+} + 8H_2O + 5Cl_2$ *[1 mark]*

5.3 EMF = $E^⦵_{reduced} - E^⦵_{oxidised}$
= +1.51 – (+1.36)
= **+0.15 V** *[1 mark]*

5.4 The EMF value for the reaction is positive / The reduction of MnO_4^- has a more positive $E^⦵$ than the reduction of Cl_2 *[1 mark]*.

5.5 Moles of MnO_4^- = 0.230 × (18.7 ÷ 1000)
= 4.301 × 10^{-3} moles
From the balanced equation, 2 moles of MnO_4^- react with 10 moles of Cl^-, therefore 4.301 × 10^{-3} moles of MnO_4^- will react with 4.301 × 10^{-3} × (10 ÷ 2) = 0.021505 moles of Cl^-.
Number of Cl^- ions in 35 cm^3 = 0.021505 × 6.02 × 10^{23}
= 1.294601 × 10^{22}
Number of Cl^- ions in 150 cm^3 = 1.294601 × 10^{22} × (150 ÷ 35)
= 5.54829 × 10^{22}
= **5.55 × 10^{22} ions (3 s.f.)**
[4 marks for correct answer, otherwise 1 mark for moles of MnO_4^-, 1 mark for moles of Cl^- in 35 cm^3, 1 mark for number of ions of Cl^- in 35 cm^3 or moles of Cl^- in 150 cm^3.]

5.6 E.g. both the rate and EMF would increase *[1 mark]*, because I^- is a stronger reducing agent/less oxidising than Cl^- *[1 mark]*.

6.1 E.g. one of the products of the breakdown of urea catalysed by urease is ammonia *[1 mark]*, which is basic *[1 mark]*.

6.2 $k = Ae^{\frac{-E_a}{RT}}$
$\ln k = \ln A - \frac{E_a}{RT}$
$\frac{E_a}{RT} = \ln A - \ln k$
$E_a = RT × (\ln A - \ln k)$
E_a = 8.31 × 298 × (ln(7.089 × 10^3) – ln(1.46 × 10^{-7}))
= 60936.84... J mol^{-1}
= 60.93684... kJ mol^{-1}
= **60.9 kJ mol^{-1} (3 s.f.)**
[2 marks for correct answer, otherwise 1 mark for rearranging equation to find E_a.]

6.3 E.g. the $-P=O(NH_2)_2$ group has a similar structure to that of urea *[1 mark]*, so can bind to the active site of urease and prevent urea molecules from binding and being broken down *[1 mark]*.

6.4 8 atoms *[1 mark]*
Each of the oxygen and nitrogen atoms can form hydrogen bonds, as well as the four hydrogen atoms in the two amine groups.

6.5 O–P bond *[1 mark]*
The products of the reaction are an alcohol (phenol) and an acid (diamidophosphoric acid).

6.6
[1 mark]

6.7
[1 mark]

6.8 E.g. lysine would be more soluble, as it has an amine group attached to its side-chain *[1 mark]* which can form hydrogen bonds with water/which makes the side-chain polar *[1 mark]*.

6.9 Any two from: e.g. the students could have used different solvents. / They could have used TLC plates with different compositions. / They could have carried out their experiments at different temperatures. *[2 marks — 1 mark for each correct reason.]*

Pages 155-157: Mixed Questions — 4

1.1

[1 mark]

1.2 +3 *[1 mark]*
Each ethane-1,2-diamine ligand is neutral. As the complex has a 3+ charge, the oxidation state of cobalt must therefore be +3.

1.3 6 *[1 mark]*

1.4 E.g. the entropy would decrease, as three en/ethane-1,2-diamine ligands would be substituted for six H_2O/water ligands *[1 mark]*. A decrease in entropy would cause the Gibbs free-energy to increase (and so the reaction is not thermodynamically feasible) *[1 mark]*.

1.5 A ligand that can form more than one co-ordinate bond to a metal atom/ion *[1 mark]*.

1.6 e.g. chloroethanoic acid/bromoethanoic acid *[1 mark]*
The lone pair on a nitrogen atom in ethane-1,2-diamine would attack the carbon in the carbon-halogen bond present in the reagent. This would keep occurring, until all the H−N bonds in ethane-1,2-diamine had been replaced with C−N bonds.

1.7 E.g. add NaOH *[1 mark]*. This would react with the carboxylic acid groups in EDTA *[1 mark]*, so they would become deprotonated, and therefore charged *[1 mark]*. This would lead to stronger forces of attraction between the EDTA ions and the water molecules and the solubility of EDTA would increase *[1 mark]*.

2.1 $K_a = \dfrac{[H^+][C_6H_5COO^-]}{[C_6H_5COOH]}$

As benzoic acid is a weak acid, it can be assumed that $[H^+] = [C_6H_5COO^-]$.
Therefore it is possible to use the expression:

$K_a = \dfrac{[H^+]^2}{[C_6H_5COOH]}$

$[H^+]^2 = K_a \times [C_6H_5COOH]$

$[H^+] = \sqrt{K_a \times [C_6H_5COOH]}$

$\quad = \sqrt{6.3 \times 10^{-5} \text{ mol dm}^{-3} \times 0.025 \text{ mol dm}^{-3}}$

$\quad = 1.254... \times 10^{-3} \text{ mol dm}^{-3}$

$pH = -\log_{10}[H^+]$

$\quad = -\log_{10}(1.254... \times 10^{-3})$

$\quad = 2.901...$

$\quad = \textbf{2.9 (2 s.f.)}$

[4 marks for correct answer, otherwise 1 mark for a correct expression for K_a, 1 mark for rearranging K_a expression to find $[H^+]$, 1 mark for calculating $[H^+]$.]

2.2 $C_6H_5COOH + OH^- \rightarrow C_6H_5COO^- + H_2O$ /
$H^+ + OH^- \rightarrow H_2O$ *[1 mark]*

2.3 $[H^+]$ at end of reaction $= 10^{-12.2} = 6.309... \times 10^{-13} \text{ mol dm}^{-3}$
$K_w = [H^+][OH^-] = 1.00 \times 10^{-14} \text{ mol dm}^{-3}$
$[OH^-] = K_w \div [H^+] = 1.00 \times 10^{-14} \div 6.309... \times 10^{-13}$
$\quad = 0.0158... \text{ mol dm}^{-3}$
Number of excess moles
$\quad$ of NaOH added $=$ concentration $\times$ volume
$\quad\quad = 0.0158... \times (750 \div 1000)$
$\quad\quad = 0.0118...$ moles
Moles of benzoic acid present
$\quad$ in original solution $=$ concentration $\times$ volume
$\quad\quad = 0.025 \times (750 \div 1000)$
$\quad\quad = 0.01875$ moles
Moles of benzoic acid $=$ moles of NaOH present before excess was added
Therefore the total number of moles of NaOH added to the solution $= 0.0118... + 0.01875$
$\quad\quad = 0.0306...$ moles
Mass of NaOH $=$ moles $\times M_r$
$\quad\quad = 0.0306... \times (23.0 + 16.0 + 1.0)$
$\quad\quad = 1.225...$ g
$\quad\quad = \textbf{1.2 g (2 s.f.)}$

[7 marks for correct answer, otherwise 1 mark for calculating $[H^+]$, 1 mark for rearranging equation for ionic product of water to find $[OH^-]$, 1 mark for calculating $[OH^-]$, 1 mark for calculating the number of moles of NaOH, 1 mark for calculating the number of moles of benzoic acid, 1 mark for finding the number of moles of NaOH added to the solution.]

2.4 Step 1: warm *[1 mark]* with concentrated nitric and sulfuric acids *[1 mark]*.
Step 2: reflux *[1 mark]* with tin metal and hydrochloric acid *[1 mark]*, followed by the addition of e.g. NaOH *[1 mark]*.
You didn't have to write NaOH here. You get the mark for any alkali.

2.5 Number of peaks in ^{1}H NMR spectrum: 4 *[1 mark]*
Number of peaks in ^{13}C NMR spectrum: 5 *[1 mark]*

2.6

[1 mark]

Data Sheet

¹H NMR chemical shift data

Type of proton	δ / ppm
ROH	0.5 - 5.0
RCH₃	0.7 - 1.2
RNH₂	1.0 - 4.5
R₂CH₂	1.2 - 1.4
R₃CH	1.4 - 1.6
R—C(=O)—C—H	2.1 - 2.6
R—O—C—H	3.1 - 3.9
RCH₂Cl or RCH₂Br	3.1 - 4.2
R—C(=O)—O—C—H	3.7 - 4.1
R₂C=CH₂ (C=C)	4.5 - 6.0
R—C(=O)—H	9.0 - 10.0
R—C(=O)—O—H	10.0 - 12.0

¹³C NMR chemical shift data

Type of carbon	δ / ppm
—C—C—	5 - 40
R—C—Cl or R—C—Br	10 - 70
R—C—C(=O)—	20 - 50
R—C—N<	25 - 60
—C—O— (alcohols, ethers or esters)	50 - 90
>C=C<	90 - 150
R—C≡N	110 - 125
⬡ (benzene ring)	110 - 160
R—C(=O)— (esters or acids)	160 - 185
R—C(=O)— (aldehydes or ketones)	190 - 220

Infrared absorption data

Bond	Wavenumber / cm⁻¹
C–C	750 - 1100
C–O	1000 - 1300
C=C	1620 - 1680
C=O	1680 - 1750
C≡N	2220 - 2260
O–H (acids)	2500 - 3000
C–H	2850 - 3300
O–H (alcohols)	3230 - 3550
N–H (amines)	3300 - 3500

Bases

adenine	thymine	guanine	cytosine

Amino acids

alanine	cysteine	serine	aspartic acid

phenylalanine

$H_2N-CH-COOH$
CH_2 (phenyl)

lysine

$H_2N-CH-COOH$
$CH_2-CH_2-CH_2-CH_2-NH_2$

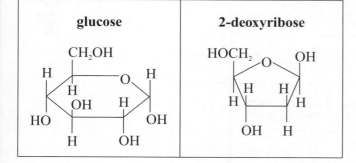

Sugars

glucose	2-deoxyribose

Phosphate

$^-O-P(=O)(OH)(OH)$

Haem B

The Periodic Table

Key:

relative atomic mass		
	1.0	
	H	
	Hydrogen	
	1	

atomic (proton) number

Example shown: 10.8 **B** boron 5 — relative atomic mass / symbol / name / atomic number

Group 1	Group 2		Group 3	Group 4	Group 5	Group 6	Group 7	Group 0
								4.0 **He** helium 2
6.9 **Li** lithium 3	9.0 **Be** beryllium 4		10.8 **B** boron 5	12.0 **C** carbon 6	14.0 **N** nitrogen 7	16.0 **O** oxygen 8	19.0 **F** fluorine 9	20.2 **Ne** neon 10
23.0 **Na** sodium 11	24.3 **Mg** magnesium 12		27.0 **Al** aluminium 13	28.1 **Si** silicon 14	31.0 **P** phosphorus 15	32.1 **S** sulfur 16	35.5 **Cl** chlorine 17	39.9 **Ar** argon 18
39.1 **K** potassium 19	40.1 **Ca** calcium 20	(transition metals)	69.7 **Ga** gallium 31	72.6 **Ge** germanium 32	74.9 **As** arsenic 33	79.0 **Se** selenium 34	79.9 **Br** bromine 35	83.8 **Kr** krypton 36
85.5 **Rb** rubidium 37	87.6 **Sr** strontium 38		114.8 **In** indium 49	118.7 **Sn** tin 50	121.8 **Sb** antimony 51	127.6 **Te** tellurium 52	126.9 **I** iodine 53	131.3 **Xe** xenon 54
132.9 **Cs** caesium 55	137.3 **Ba** barium 56		204.4 **Tl** thallium 81	207.2 **Pb** lead 82	209.0 **Bi** bismuth 83	[209] **Po** polonium 84	[210] **At** astatine 85	[222] **Rn** radon 86
[223] **Fr** francium 87	[226] **Ra** radium 88							

Transition metals (period 4): 45.0 Sc 21, 47.9 Ti 22, 50.9 V 23, 52.0 Cr 24, 54.9 Mn 25, 55.8 Fe 26, 58.9 Co 27, 58.7 Ni 28, 63.5 Cu 29, 65.4 Zn 30

Transition metals (period 5): 88.9 Y 39, 91.2 Zr 40, 92.9 Nb 41, 96.0 Mo 42, [98] Tc 43, 101.1 Ru 44, 102.9 Rh 45, 106.4 Pd 46, 107.9 Ag 47, 112.4 Cd 48

Transition metals (period 6): 138.9 La* 57, 178.5 Hf 72, 180.9 Ta 73, 183.8 W 74, 186.2 Re 75, 190.2 Os 76, 192.2 Ir 77, 195.1 Pt 78, 197.0 Au 79, 200.6 Hg 80

Transition metals (period 7): [227] Ac† 89, [267] Rf 104, [268] Db 105, [271] Sg 106, [272] Bh 107, [270] Hs 108, [276] Mt 109, [281] Ds 110, [280] Rg 111

Elements with atomic numbers 112–116 have been reported but not fully authenticated

* 58 – 71 Lanthanides
140.1 Ce 58, 140.9 Pr 59, 144.2 Nd 60, [145] Pm 61, 150.4 Sm 62, 152.0 Eu 63, 157.3 Gd 64, 158.9 Tb 65, 162.5 Dy 66, 164.9 Ho 67, 167.3 Er 68, 168.9 Tm 69, 173.1 Yb 70, 175.0 Lu 71

† 90 – 103 Actinides
232.0 Th 90, 231.0 Pa 91, 238.0 U 92, [237] Np 93, [244] Pu 94, [243] Am 95, [247] Cm 96, [247] Bk 97, [251] Cf 98, [252] Es 99, [257] Fm 100, [258] Md 101, [259] No 102, [262] Lr 103